Meals
THAT HEAL

Meals
THAT HEAL

OVER 175 SIMPLE
EVERYDAY RECIPES
THAT HELP PREVENT
AND TREAT DISEASE

Anne Egan and Regina Ragone, M.S., R.D.

RODALE

Notice
This book is intended as a reference volume only, not as a medical manual. It is not intended as a substitute for any treatment that may have been prescribed by your doctor. If you suspect that you have a medical problem, we urge you to seek competent medical help. Keep in mind that nutritional needs vary from
person to person, depending upon age, sex, health status, and total diet. The foods discussed and the
recipes given here are designed to help you make informed decisions about your diet and health.

Printed in the United States of America
Rodale Inc. makes every effort to use acid-free ∞, recycled paper ♻.

Cover and Interior Design: Joanna Williams
Cover Photographs: Mitch Mandel/Rodale Images
Interior Photographs: Mitch Mandel/Rodale Images, Kurt Wilson/Rodale Images,
Tad Ware & Co./Rodale Images
Cover Food Stylist: Diane Vezza
Interior Food Stylist: Melissa DeMayo

Library of Congress Cataloging-in-Publication Data

Egan, Anne.
Meals that heal : over 175 simple everyday recipes that help prevent and treat disease / Anne Egan
and Regina Ragone.
    p.   cm.
Includes index.
ISBN 1–57954–419–3   hardcover
1. Cookery for the sick.   2. Functional foods.   I. Ragone, Regina.   II. Title.
RM216 .E19   2001
641.5'631—dc21   2001002168

Distributed to the book trade by St. Martin's Press

2   4   6   8   10   9   7   5   3   1   hardcover

Visit us on the Web at www.rodalestore.com, or call us toll-free at (800) 848-4735.

WE **INSPIRE** AND **ENABLE** PEOPLE TO IMPROVE
THEIR LIVES AND THE WORLD AROUND THEM

contents

acknowledgments

Many thanks to everyone involved in
bringing this book to fruition, especially:

Christine Dreisbach, for her exhaustive research
Kathy Everleth, for her diligent editing
Jennifer Giandomenico, for her talents in layout
Kathleen Hanuschak, for her extensive
nutritional knowledge and analyses
Miriam Rubin, for her development of delicious recipes
Joanna Williams, for her fresh and lively design

how to use this book

A subject as complex as the healing properties of foods can be very difficult to navigate. To further confuse the issue, you've probably heard conflicting information about what to eat and what to avoid. This book has taken all of the guesswork out of this complicated topic. We have hashed through the latest information to give you clear facts in an easy-to-use format.

Often, when you buy a cookbook, you may flip through the pages looking for great-tasting recipes, as you should. You will find plenty of them here. But surrounding the recipe pages are two large chapters of very useful health information directly related to the foods that you will be cooking and eating.

The first chapter, The Healing Power of Food, is a primer of many healing foods and their specific benefits to health as well as the healthiest cooking techniques. This chapter also includes "Putting It All Together," a resource that will help you determine what and how much to eat.

Look to the color pages for descriptions of the top healing foods as well as recipe photos to entice and provide direction if needed when making the recipes. Next, you will find more than 175 recipes divided by dishes. Each recipe includes a list of its top nutrients (up to 10 are listed), rated using our "apple system." Three apples tells you that the recipe contains 20 percent or more of the Daily Value (DV) for that nutrient in a serving, making it an "excellent" source of a nutrient; two apples means that the recipe contains 10 to 20 percent of the DV for that nutrient in a serving, making it a "good" source; and one apple indicates that the recipe has 5 to 10 percent of the DV for the nutrient, making it a small source. Each recipe also lists the top conditions (again, up to 10) that it helps treat or prevent. Keep in mind, though, that all the recipes are very healthful, so in many cases, they'll help with even more than the top 10 conditions listed. And to help you find meals on days when you're particularly rushed, all recipes that are ready in 30 minutes or less are marked with a (quick) symbol.

Last, but certainly not least, is "Eat to Beat: The Healing Food Finder." Here, you can look for a particular condition, whether it be heart disease, cancer, or the flu, and find the best foods to eat to help prevent and/or treat that particular condition. (A few conditions can be treated only with medication and/or by avoiding certain foods. We have included them to help you determine which foods you may want to avoid.) If you prefer to search just for recipes by condition, refer to the Cure Finder for a complete listing.

Our goal was to do all of the hard work for you so that you can get to the fun part easily and effortlessly. What is the fun part? Why, cooking and eating delicious recipes, of course!

the healing power of food

Let food be thy medicine. —Hippocrates

Food has been touted for ages for its healing benefits. And for centuries, food was very healthy, mostly because people ate whole foods from their fields. Today, we have so many food options, many of which are totally manufactured from chemicals, that the quality of much of our food has deteriorated.

We have heard so much conflicting information about what to eat and what to avoid that confusion levels are running high. But we're here to tell you that it's easy to eat the healthiest meals ever.

3

Although certain conditions require specific guidelines, you can improve your health and boost your healing capabilities if you follow the simple recommendations in this book. This is the easiest, most effortless way to cope with stress, lose weight, improve your immunity, prevent aging, tame disease, and more. The idea is very simple, and you've no doubt heard it hundreds of times: The key to a healthy diet is to eat plenty of fruits, vegetables, and whole grains; eat more fish and seafood; include low-fat dairy products and lean meats in your diet; and eat foods that are minimally processed. By using herbs, spices, and healthy condiments, you can pack your food with flavor while maintaining all of the naturally occurring nutrients.

The following information will guide you toward the best food choices, and the recipes throughout the book will ensure you great-tasting meals packed with the most nutritious foods available. Of course, one recipe won't heal you, but incorporating these dishes into your diet can help you become healthier over time.

Healing Foods

There are six top nutrients that our bodies need. Known as macronutrients, these are protein, carbohydrates, fats, vitamins, minerals, and water. The easiest way to fill your meals with these nutrients is to consume whole, minimally processed foods whenever possible. The descriptions that follow will tell you all you need to know about carbs, protein, fats, and water. For a complete guide to vitamins, minerals, and other nutrients, see "Healing Nutrients" on page 59.

Protein

Next to water, protein is the largest component in the body. Essential for growth, protein builds and repairs skin, bones, muscles, organs, and blood while assisting in functions such as blood clotting, water balance, hormone production, and immunity. Protein from animal sources is considered complete since it contains all nine essential amino acids needed by the body. Protein from nuts, seeds, grains, legumes, or vegetables does not contain all nine essential amino acids and is completed by eating protein from animal sources on the same day or by eating a variety of plant foods each day. Protein should make up 20 percent of your daily calorie intake.

Fish and Shellfish

Eat 5 to 6 ounces of fish daily to provide protein, iron, vitamins, and minerals to help prevent disease. Fish is typically low in fat but higher in omega-3 and omega-6 fatty acids than meat and poultry. Try to eat fish at least twice a week.

Finfish. Cold-water fish—Chinook salmon, mackerel, rainbow trout, tuna, fresh whitefish, pickled Atlantic herring, and sardines—virtually swim in polyunsaturated fats, known as omega-3 fatty acids, which are very heart-healthy. They can help lower the risk of heart disease and help prevent certain cancers such as breast cancer. Experiment with the many varieties and broil, grill, or steam with citrus juice and herbs. Avoid dipping or cooking in butter; instead, opt for low-fat yogurt, roasted red-pepper, or citrus sauces.

Shellfish. Shellfish, such as lobster, scallops, shrimp, and oysters, contain a bit of cholesterol and sodium, but they also possess a boatload of other nutrients. Shellfish are a source of omega-3 fatty acids that can help lower blood pressure, cholesterol levels, and the risk of heart disease. They also contain vitamins and minerals, such as vitamin B_{12}, which helps make red blood cells and keep nerves healthy; zinc, which boosts the immune system; iron, which helps prevent anemia; magnesium; potassium; and vitamin C, which helps the body absorb iron. When preparing, cook extra seafood to toss into salads, soups, and sandwiches.

Meat and Poultry

Because it is a good source of protein, iron, vitamins, and minerals, eat 5 to 6 ounces of meat or poultry daily. Be sure to try the latest cuts, designed to make cooking as simple and quick as possible.

Beef. Look for the leanest cuts of beef—those with "loin" in the name. Sirloin and tenderloin as well as round and rib eye are some of the low-fat cuts that'll

Are you getting enough of this essential disease fighter? By eating 25 to 35 grams of fiber every day, you may lower your risk of cancer, heart disease, stroke, obesity, diabetes, diverticulitis, and constipation. Studies have found, however, that the national average of fiber consumed is just 11 to 13 grams a day. Take this test to see if you need to fiber up. Fill in the number of servings of each particular food you eat each day, multiply it by the number of grams of fiber, then add up all your answers.

1.5 g fiber	x ___ servings of fruit	=	___ g
1.5 g fiber	x ___ servings of vegetables	=	___ g
2.5 g fiber	x ___ servings of whole grains *(whole wheat bread and pasta, brown rice)*	=	___ g
1 g fiber	x ___ servings of refined grains *(white bread and pasta, white rice)*	=	___ g
5 g fiber	x ___ servings of dried beans	=	___ g
Fiber in a serving of your breakfast cereal		=	___ g
Total fiber in one day		=	___ g

help you cook up delicious dinners. Because beef contains riboflavin, or vitamin B_2, it supports normal skin and vision health and helps release energy from the nutrients we eat. A great source of iron, beef also can help those with anemia or iron-deficient fatigue.

Chicken. Chicken has an abundance of niacin—a B vitamin, which may help reduce cholesterol levels and cut heart attack risk—and the easily absorbed form of iron (heme iron), which provides us with maximum energy and vitality. Abundant in vitamin B_6, which helps make red blood cells and helps make the feel-good brain chemical serotonin, chicken makes a healthy meal easy.

Lamb. Lamb is a good source of zinc, which can help with wound healing and boosting immunity from infections. Lamb won't blow your fat budget, either. The protein in lamb will boost levels of dopamine and norepinephrine, which help enhance mood and energy levels. And its heme iron levels—more than that in chicken—can help stave off anemia. Lamb also has niacin and a type of fat called conjugated linoleic acid (CLA) that fights cancer. Be sure to serve lamb medium-rare for the most flavorful, tender dishes.

Pork. The other white meat, pork is raised to be a lean protein source. A great source of thiamin, or vitamin B_1, it helps us use food for energy and helps our nerves process information smoothly. And it has more iron than an equal serving of chicken. Pork tenderloin and boneless chops make dinner a quick and easy meal.

Turkey. Typically reserved for Thanksgiving, turkey is now readily available in many quick-cooking cuts. It is a source of niacin, heme iron, vitamin B_6, and zinc. An easy way to add more turkey to your diet is to substitute at least half of the ground beef in recipes with ground turkey.

Dairy Products

Eat two servings of dairy products a day to be sure that you are getting enough calcium. Reach for reduced-fat or fat-free products to keep the fat and calories in check.

Cheeses. When using cheese in place of milk in a recipe, substitute 1 ounce of hard cheese for 1 cup of milk. The harder the cheese, the lower the fat, so keep Parmesan and Romano close at hand.

Milk. Low-fat and fat-free milk—even buttermilk—has a fraction of the artery-clogging saturated fat found in whole or 2 percent milk. Its benefits can go beyond bone building to include helping prevent high blood pressure, stroke, and even cancer. What's more, milk contains substances that can reduce the liver's cholesterol production, which shows up as lowered heart disease risk in the end. Calcium further helps lower cholesterol levels as well as blood pressure.

Yogurt. The live and active cultures mentioned on yogurt labels are actually friendly bacteria that can help strengthen the immune system and help ulcers heal more quickly. These bacteria may also help prevent recurrent yeast infections. Yogurt also has more calcium than a serving of low-fat milk. Be sure that the label reads "live and active cultures," since not all yogurts contain these important bacteria. Go for plain yogurt and add your own fresh fruit for the health-iest version. Use yogurt in salad dressings or as a substitute for sour cream. When cooking with yogurt, never bring it to a boil, as it will curdle. Instead, remove the pan from the heat and gently stir in the yogurt to the slightly cooled mixture.

Legumes

Legumes are seeds harvested from pod-bearing plants, and they're a power-house of protein. They also contain energy-boosting carbohydrates, as well as fiber, shown to be helpful in lowering cholesterol and preventing constipation. Beans, lentils, and peanuts are just a few of the more popular types of legumes. This category also includes foods such as soybeans as well as peas and green beans, but we've listed those foods under the "Soy Foods" and "Vegetables" head-ings, respectively, since that's how they're widely used in cooking.

Beans. Beans are available in a seemingly endless variety—kidney, black, lima, pinto, and chickpeas, to name a few. If you use canned beans, rinse them first to remove excess sodium. If you opt for dried, you'll need to soak them be-fore cooking. (Let them stand overnight in a bowl of cold water, or boil them for 2 minutes, then set aside for 1 hour. Either way, just drain, and you're ready to go.) And if you're looking to lose weight, you can't beat beans; they're extremely filling, so when you eat them, you fill up quickly and may reduce your likelihood of overeating.

Lentils. Frequently used as a meat substitute in main dishes and an essential part of Indian and Middle Eastern cooking, lentils don't require soaking—a real boon to cooks in a hurry. Stores sell them dried; just keep them in an airtight container at room temperature, and they'll keep for up to a year. Stir pureed lentils into soups and stews, or combine them whole with vegetables to liven up ordinary side dishes. In addition to protein, lentils contain bone-friendly calcium as well as vitamins A and B, phosphorus, and iron.

Peanuts. Despite the name, peanuts are not actually nuts at all, but legumes. They're rich in protein, which helps supply energy and repair body tissue, and they also contain monounsaturated and polyunsaturated fat—the "good" fats that help reduce the risk of heart disease and cancer. Sprinkle peanuts onto salads or stir-fries for added crunch, fold them into batter for homemade muffins, or grind them to a powder and stir into soups, sauces, or milkshakes.

Soy Foods

More popular than ever, soy foods contain phytochemicals and soy protein that may help lower cholesterol. Soy may also help reduce the risk of prostate cancer and bone loss. A source of calcium, protein, and iron, soy products do contain some fat, although it is mostly polyunsaturated.

Soybeans. Canned or dried soybeans are a bit firmer to the bite than other legumes, but they can be substituted for other beans. Try edamame or green soybeans, found in the freezer section of supermarkets. Similar to lima beans, these tender bites are delicious steamed and tossed with a bit of soy sauce or added to soups and stews. Roasted dried soybeans, known as soy nuts, are also available. These crunchy treats are great as a snack or sprinkled over salads or side dishes.

Soy milk. Soy milk is made from ground, soaked soybeans and comes in a variety of flavors. Substitute soy milk wherever cow's milk is used. It's especially good in shakes, for baking, and on cereal. Often, a rice/soy milk blend is more enjoyable than straight soy milk, so try various brands until you find the one you like best.

Tempeh. These fermented soybean cakes are more flavorful and dense than tofu. Add to stir-fries, soups, or stews.

Tofu. This tasteless cake of curdled soy milk, sold in several forms, takes on the flavor of whatever it's cooked with—meats, soups, vegetables, pasta, and even desserts. Mash with vegetables and low-fat mayonnaise for a mock tuna salad, cube and stir-fry with vegetables, or slice baked, smoked tofu and layer on a sandwich.

Carbohydrates

The body's main source of energy comes from carbohydrates, which can be simple or complex. Carbohydrates should make up 50 percent of your calorie intake. Simple carbohydrates, also known as sugars, include table sugar, syrups, and candy, and contain no additional nutrients—in other words, they're empty calories. Complex carbohydrates, also known as starches, should be the primary source of carbohydrates in your diet. They break down slowly, which means that they boost your blood sugar levels more gradually, and the boost lasts longer, giving you a steadier supply of energy. Fruits, vegetables, and whole grains are sources of complex carbohydrates, and these foods also supply important vitamins, minerals, and fiber.

Fruits

Three to four servings of fruit daily give the body fiber, vitamins, and minerals to help prevent disease. Fruit is best eaten raw, but don't ignore it if only frozen or canned is available. Either of these choices is best when packed without extra sugar, so opt for canned fruits packed in juice or frozen fruits packed without sugar or syrup. Here are some of the best choices and their healing benefits.

Apples. The old saying "an apple a day keeps the doctor away" was more accurate than we may have once thought. Apples can help lower the risk of heart disease, control diabetes, and prevent cancer and constipation. Loaded with antioxidants and fiber, apples should be eaten with the skin intact to get the most benefit. Cooking apples is fine, too, but again, keep the skin on—that's where the cancer-fighting quercetin is present. And don't think of apples just for dessert. They add a sweetness to savory dishes such as curries and stews.

Apricots. Packed with heart disease–fighting carotenoids, apricots can also help protect the eyes. Delicious eaten out of hand, fresh apricots are lovely grilled or broiled, brushed with a touch of honey or all-fruit spread before cooking, or poached in fruit juice or wine.

Bananas. A bunch of potassium is a great description for this versatile favorite. Bananas can help decrease the risk of stroke, lower high blood pressure, relieve heartburn, prevent ulcers, and aid in abating diarrhea. Pack them in your lunch for a handy snack, and don't forget how useful they are in baking. Always buy a large bunch of bananas and freeze, in the skin, any that you cannot use be-

seven ways to boost your fiber

Research shows that a high-fiber diet can help lower cholesterol, reduce the risk of cancer and heart disease, aid in weight loss, and prevent constipation. Here are some simple trade-offs you can make in your diet to increase your fiber intake.

Eat this . . .	Instead of this . . .	For a fiber boost of (g) . . .
Bagel, oat bran (2 oz)	Bagel, plain (2 oz)	6
Pasta, whole wheat (1 cup)	Pasta, white (1 cup)	4
Popcorn (3½ cups)	Potato chips (10)	3
Potato, with skin	Potato, without skin	3
Cracker, Triscuit (7)	Cracker, Ritz (10)	2
Whole wheat bread (1 slice)	White bread (1 slice)	2
Rice, brown (1 cup)	Rice, white (1 cup)	1

fore they are overripe. Peel and add the frozen bananas to shakes for a quick breakfast. Or, let them defrost, then peel and mash them for muffins and breads.

Berries. These sweet nibbles are brimming with antioxidants and phytonutrients that may help prevent cataracts, cancer, and constipation and reduce the risk of infection. Blueberries pack the most punch, but don't overlook raspberries, blackberries, and strawberries, which are loaded with fiber. Buy fresh berries in season and save extra by placing them on a baking pan in the freezer until just frozen. Then store them in a zip-top freezer bag. Or, purchase bags of frozen unsweetened berries. Toss berries in salads, cereals, or yogurt.

Cantaloupe. Packed with potassium, vitamin C, and beta-carotene, cantaloupe can help lower high blood pressure and high cholesterol levels and help reduce the risk of heart disease, cancer, and cataracts. Ripe cantaloupe is delicious topped with a scoop of yogurt or cottage cheese, but it's also great in fruit or savory salads. For a fruit soup, place chunks in the blender to puree and toss with berries and chopped fruit. Add chopped fresh mint or ginger for some extra zing.

Cherries. Easiest eaten out of hand, cherries contain vitamins C, E, and A along with the antioxidant quercetin. These nutrients may help relieve gout, prevent cancer, and reduce the risk of heart disease and stroke. Try making a delicious fresh cherry pie as a nutritious treat. Look for frozen pitted cherries when you don't have time to pit fresh ones yourself.

Cranberries. These ruby-reds aren't just for Thanksgiving—they're delicious in every season. Cranberries are a great source of flavonoids and antioxidants, which can help prevent and treat urinary tract infections, protect cells from cancerous changes, and reduce the risk of heart attack and stroke. Since they are available fresh in the autumn, buy extra and save some in the freezer. Cranberries make a great relish, but they're also delicious in savory or sweet sauces and baked goods. Commercial cranberry juice contains the same nutrients, except the fiber. Buy juices that contain only fruit juice to avoid getting too much sugar.

Figs. Fresh or dried, figs are a great source of fiber and a good source of potassium, and they also contain some vitamin B_6. Purchase firm figs, either fresh or dried, and use them quickly. Fresh figs make an easy appetizer or dessert when stuffed with a simple cream cheese filling. Or, grill them with a light brushing of honey. Dried figs will last a bit longer than the fresh ones and are great eaten as is, added to fruit or green salads, or tossed into fruit sauces for fish, poultry, or meat.

Grapefruit. The pinker the fruit, the more lycopene is present. All grapefruit, however, contain fiber, vitamin C, and other phytonutrients. These compounds can help relieve cold symptoms, reduce bruising, and help prevent cancer, heart disease, and stroke. Add to fruit salads, top green salads with sections, or broil grapefuit halves sprinkled with brown sugar for a warm and healing dessert.

Grape juice. Like its cousin wine, grape juice contains the healthy flavonoids that can help lower cholesterol and high blood pressure and decrease the risk of heart disease. Since the flavonoids are what gives grapes and grape juice their dark color, opt for purple grape juice over the white variety.

Grapes. An excellent source of vitamin C and a host of phytochemicals, including the powerful resveratrol, grapes are a delicious anti-aging snack. They also can help prevent cancer and heart disease. Most of the goodness in grapes is in the skin, so there's no need to bother with peeling. Add them to tossed salads and chicken salads as well as fruit salads. In hot summer months, freeze a bunch of grapes in a zip-top freezer bag for a cool snack.

Kiwifruit. These jewel-like fruits are jammed with nutrients that can help prevent cancer and heart disease. Two kiwifruit contain 240 percent of the Daily Value for vitamin C and are a good source of fiber, vitamin E, and potassium. Peel the fruit, then slice and eat as is or add to green or fruit salads, tarts, or sandwiches.

Lemons and limes. Though these tart cousins are often thought of as flavorings for drinks, lemons and limes add much to a healthy kitchen. Grate the peel to season fish and poultry dishes, salads, soups, and desserts. Squeeze the juice to prepare salad dressings and marinades or simply add a bit of zing to your dishes. Either way, using these citrus jewels will increase your intake of vitamin C, which can help heal cuts and bruises as well as help prevent cancer and heart disease.

Mangoes. Full of the antioxidants vitamin C and beta-carotene, mangoes can help prevent cancer and heart disease. Eat as a fresh fruit or sprinkle chopped mango on savory curries or spicy meats and fish.

Oranges. Your body will benefit from the cancer-fighting phytonutrients and antioxidants found in oranges. Oranges are also high in vitamin C and fiber, which can help lower the risk of heart disease and stroke and reduce inflammation.

Papayas. Right away, you'll notice the bright color of the cancer-preventing carotenoids present in papayas. Also present is the enzyme papain, which can help ease upset stomach and ulcers. Go for fresh fruit when possible and eat it as soon as it's cut to retain the most nutrients. Pureed papaya makes a nice tenderizing marinade for tougher cuts of meat.

Pears. Fresh pears are packed with fiber that lies close to the skin, so be sure to choose fresh ones over canned whenever possible and be sure to eat the skin. Pears contain lignan, an insoluble fiber, and pectin, a soluble fiber, which can help lower cholesterol, prevent constipation and hemorrhoids, and reduce the risk of colon cancer. They also contain the mineral boron, which appears to play a role in keeping bones strong. Add to salads or savory dishes.

Pineapple. Fresh pineapple is a great source of manganese, which can help build connective tissues like bone, skin, and cartilage. A rich source of vitamin C, pineapple can also help relieve cold symptoms and lower the risk of cancer and heart disease. The bromelain in fresh pineapple can help relieve indigestion. Look for the many varieties of pineapple available these days, the sweetest being the "gold" variety, which also contains the most vitamin C. Cut into chunks and toss with grated fresh ginger and a few star anise for a lovely snack.

Prunes. This famous laxative is getting a name change these days, so look for prunes, or "dried plums," in your market. Either way, you will be getting the same benefit of these high-fiber nuggets. Dried plums can help relieve constipation, lower cholesterol, and reduce the risk of cancer and heart disease. Chop them and toss in salad or add to saucy savory dishes to naturally sweeten them. If cooked for a long time as in a stew, the prunes will mash nicely into the sauce.

Pumpkin. This oversize orange squash is the king of beta-carotene, which may help protect against a variety of cancers as well as heart disease. A mere ½ cup of canned pumpkin has more than 200 percent of the daily amount recommended by experts. Pumpkin also is a source of carotenoids, which may help block the formation of cataracts. If you feel like having fresh pumpkin, try the mini-size Jack Be Littles; they're easier to work with than large pumpkins. Canned pumpkin is almost equal to fresh in nutrients, though, so don't pass it by.

Raisins. These high-energy bits are a good source of potassium, iron, and fiber, making raisins useful in helping improve digestion, lower high blood pressure, and keep the blood healthy. Eating raisins with foods high in vitamin C will help your body absorb the iron, so toss them in citrus salads or add them to tomato sauces.

Rhubarb. Often used for making spring pies, rhubarb is a great source of vitamin C and fiber, which can help prevent cancer, boost immunity, lower cholesterol, and ease digestive problems. Just remember to eat only the rhubarb stalks. Rhubarb leaves contain high levels of oxalates, mineral salts that the body can't metabolize. For people who are sensitive to them, they can be toxic. Try stewing rhubarb with apple juice or orange juice for a sweet dessert or with dried fruits and spices for a savory side dish.

Tangerines. Like their citrus cousins, tangerines are a great source of vitamin C along with beta-cryptoxanthin, which converts to vitamin A in the body. These powerful antioxidants can help prevent heart disease and cancer.

Watermelon. A source of lycopene—the antioxidant that can help prevent prostate cancer and heart disease—watermelon is finding its place in healthy recipes. Add chunks of seeded watermelon to salads or cold soups such as gazpacho. Freeze watermelon slices or chunks for a refreshing snack.

Vegetables

Eat three to five servings of vegetables a day to maintain optimum health. Vegetables are great sources of fiber, phytochemicals, vitamins, and minerals. Choose fresh or frozen vegetables and prepare them using the healthiest methods (see "Healing Cooking Techniques" on page 23). Here is a brief description of the most common, nutritious veggies.

Artichokes. Actually the immature flower of the thistle plant, artichokes can help protect against skin cancer and help prevent heart and liver disease and birth defects. They're a great source of fiber, and these fun-to-eat vegetables are also a good source of vitamin C and folate. When dipping the leaves into a tasty sauce, go for a lower-fat one like salsa or reduced-fat sour cream mixed with herbs to avoid the typically less healthy melted butter.

Asparagus. These healthy spears are filled with folate and other antioxidants and can help prevent birth defects and reduce the risk of heart disease and cancer. Steam or stir-fry asparagus to retain these nutrients. Stir into salads, soups, and stews or serve alongside fish or poultry for an elegant side dish.

Avocados. Once thought to be too high in fat to be nutritious, avocados are now considered a health food. The fat present in avocados is the good monounsaturated kind, and they are great sources of folate and potassium. The tender green flesh can help control cholesterol levels, lower blood pressure, and prevent birth defects. Use avocados to make guacamole for a traditional dish or chop and add to bean salads for a super high-fiber meal.

Beets. Beets are a font of folate and iron, which can be helpful in preventing cancer and birth defects. Although fresh beets can be a chore to prepare, their bright flavor makes them worth the work. The canned varieties work well in a pinch since they maintain most of their nutrients when canned. Top salads with sliced beets or toss with orange marmalade for a sweet side dish.

Bell peppers. Whether green, red, yellow, or orange, sweet and crispy bell peppers contain nutrients that may help battle conditions including cataracts and heart disease. They're full of vitamin C and other antioxidants, and few vegetables contain as much beta-carotene, which plays a key role in keeping the immune system healthy. (As a rule, the redder the peppers, the more beta-carotene they contain.) Cook them lightly to avoid losing fragile vitamin C, and add just a touch of fat, such as olive oil, either before or after cooking to help better absorb the beta-carotene.

Broccoli. This cancer-fighting vegetable contains so many antioxidants and fiber that it can also help boost immunity and protect against heart disease. Steam florets before adding at the last minute to grain dishes, soups, or stews. And don't forget the stems—although not as typical, the stems of broccoli carry all the same nutrients and are delicious tossed into salads or stir-fries.

Brussels sprouts. A member of the healthful cruciferous family, Brussels sprouts pack a punch with plenty of vitamin C, folate, and fiber. These nutrients can help increase immunity, lower cholesterol, prevent constipation, and lower the risk of heart disease and cancer. For a quick side dish, simply steam the sprouts and toss with some all-fruit and spice such as ginger or cinnamon.

Cabbage. Like other members of the cruciferous family, cabbage contains several compounds that can help prevent cancer, heart disease, and cataracts. Folate is most abundant in bok choy and savoy cabbage, helping to prevent birth defects. A simple sauté of cabbage and caraway seeds is a nice use for this vegetable, and so is the traditional coleslaw (go for a reduced-fat dressing).

Carrots. Improve your night vision while helping reduce your risk of cancer and heart disease with these carotene-packed gems. Adding a touch of fat to antioxidant-rich foods helps with the absorption of the nutrients, so cook carrots in a touch of oil or toss into salads topped with reduced-fat dressings.

Cauliflower. The phytonutrients and vitamin C in cauliflower can help boost the immune system, inhibit tumor growth, and prevent cancer. Cauliflower is so often bathed in cheese sauce, but give it a try raw in salads or with a reduced-fat dip. Also try cooking in a curry sauce for a spicy variation.

Celery. Although it contains sodium, celery also contains a compound that can help lower blood pressure and another one that can help inhibit the growth of tumors. Be sure to eat the leaves along with the ribs, as they contain the most potassium, vitamin C, and calcium. For something exciting and different, sauté sliced celery in a touch of olive oil and top with a sprinkling of hot-pepper sauce.

Chile peppers. Capsaicin is the chemical that gives chiles their sting. But along with the antioxidants vitamins A and C, capsaicin can help prevent ulcers, reduce the risk of heart disease and stroke, and clear the sinuses while relieving congestion. The sting is in the raw peppers, so wear plastic gloves when preparing to prevent burning your fingers. Add zing to salsas, stir-fries, and marinades with the addition of hot chile peppers.

Corn. A wonderful source of fiber and thiamin, corn can help lower cholesterol. It is also a source of lutein, a carotenoid associated with a reduced risk of age-related macular degeneration. If getting more fiber is your goal, go for white corn, which contains twice as much fiber as yellow. Yellow carries more lutein, however, so if your goal is to protect your eyes, opt for yellow corn. If fresh is not available, go for frozen corn. Since it has been cooked before freezing, simply thaw the corn and add to cooked dishes during the last few minutes to heat it through.

Greens. Considered by nutritionists to be the most nutrient-dense foods we have available to us, greens give you a boost of vitamins and minerals in every bite, among them calcium, iron, magnesium, folate, vitamins C and B$_6$, and cancer-fighting phytochemicals. Get your green from Swiss chard, kale, escarole, beet greens, mustard greens, chicory greens, dandelion greens, turnip greens, and spinach. Trim the stems and rinse thoroughly to get rid of dirt and grit, then eat them raw in salads (just go easy on the dressing) or sauté with garlic for a lovely side dish or pasta sauce.

Onions. These underground bulbs and their cousins—leeks, shallots, and scallions—are the roots of good health. They contain dozens of compounds that can help provide protection from diseases including cancer, high blood pressure, heart disease, high cholesterol, and asthma. Their healing strength comes from flavonoids, which have potent antioxidant powers, and sulfur compounds, which can help raise levels of beneficial HDL cholesterol, lower levels of dangerous blood fats called triglycerides, and inhibit the allergic, inflammatory response that occurs with asthma.

Parsnips. These strong-tasting, oddly sweet vegetables may not look pretty, but their nutritional profile is quite impressive. A member of the parsley family, parsnips are good sources of folate, fiber, and phenolic acids, and they may help block cancer. You can lose almost half of the water-soluble nutrients by cooking peeled parsnips, so cook them unpeeled. Once they're tender, let them cool, then scrape or peel the skin away.

Peas. The pigment in peas responsible for their bright color—chlorophyllin—is also a cancer-fighting compound that can help prevent carcinogens from being absorbed. The 4 grams of fiber in each ½-cup serving are a great way to lower cholesterol and, with it, the risk for heart disease and other serious conditions. That same serving also packs a punch of cancer-fighting vitamin C, as well as folate, niacin, phosphorus, riboflavin, thiamin, and vitamin A. Not just a side dish, peas can be added to salads, soups, stews, and dips.

Potatoes. A potato's healing abilities start in the peel, which contains an anticarcinogenic compound called chlorogenic acid. Look to potatoes for potassium, which has been shown to help with high blood pressure. They also contain vitamin C, and research indicates that this antioxidant may help people with diabetes. Most of the nutrients are in the skin, so scrub instead of peeling potatoes whether you'll be baking, mashing, steaming, or roasting them.

Squash. Winter squash, such as Hubbard, acorn, and butternut, are loaded with an array of vitamins, minerals, and other compounds that can benefit your health. Two heavy hitters, vitamin C and beta-carotene, may help prevent cancer, heart disease, and age-related conditions such as eye problems. Squash have tough skin, so to make cutting easier, pierce the skin several times with a fork and pop it in the microwave for about 4 minutes to soften it up.

Sweet potatoes. Here's another way to get a heaping helping of beta-carotene and vitamins C and E and help prevent cancer and heart disease at the same time. Feel free to eat up—sweet potatoes are rich in fiber and complex carbohydrates and low in calories (only 117 calories in a 4-ounce serving), so experts recommend them for controlling weight and weight-related conditions like diabetes. Cook or eat them with just a little fat for better beta-carotene absorption.

Tomatoes. These blushing beauties can make cancer see red. Tomatoes are packed with a phytochemical called lycopene (canned tomato products have the most) that appears to act as an antioxidant, helping to prevent breast, lung, endometrial, and prostate cancers as well as heart disease. There's also a healthy dose of vitamin C in tomatoes as well as vitamin A, which has been shown to boost immunity. Add chopped or sliced fresh tomatoes to salads, pasta, and sandwiches, or cut up several tomatoes and drizzle with a little olive oil and some chopped fresh basil for a refreshing side dish.

Watercress. Watercress actually belongs to the family of cruciferous vegetables because its flowers have four petals. The crucifers, including broccoli and cauliflower, are well-known for their cancer-fighting potential. Watercress is also a dark green leafy vegetable, so it's packed with beta-carotene and vitamins C and E, powerful disease-fighting antioxidants. It's best eaten in its natural state—fresh and crisp. When it's cooked, it loses some of its nutritional strength. Try it as a replacement for lettuce in sandwiches and salads.

Grains

Whole grains provide fiber, vitamins, and minerals. Eat five to six servings (½ cup, or one slice of bread) a day. Always opt for grains in their most natural state, such as brown rice over white rice or whole grain bread over white bread.

Barley. Barley is one of the richest sources of tocotrienols, antioxidants that help reduce damage to the body from free radicals. This translates into a lot of heart disease–fighting might. In addition, barley contains lignans, which can provide still more protection by helping prevent blood clots. The soluble fiber in barley can help lower cholesterol and aid in making digestion work more efficiently. Prepare barley in place of rice or pasta in many side dishes.

Buckwheat. Though its popularity waned for a while in this country, this hearty grain is making a comeback. It can help provide protection against cancer, mainly from flavonoids. Buckwheat contains a substance called rutin, which plays an important part in any heart-protection plan by preventing platelets from clumping together and helping shrink particles of dangerous LDL cholesterol. Use light buckwheat flour to make nutritious breads, muffins, and pancakes.

Bulgur. This whole grain healer is simply wheat in its whole form, and it's one of the healthiest foods you can eat. It's extremely high in fiber, helping prevent and treat a variety of digestive problems, including constipation and diverticular disease, as well as helping to lower your cholesterol and your risk for heart disease, cancer, and diabetes. Use the coarse grind of bulgur for pilafs or rice dishes, use medium grind for making breakfast cereals, and use the fine grind for making tabbouleh.

Flaxseed. While many plant foods contain lignans, flaxseed has the absolute most—you'd have to eat about 60 cups of fresh broccoli or 100 slices of whole wheat bread to get the same amount of lignans found in ¼ cup of flaxseed. This powerful antioxidant can help block the damaging effects of harmful free radicals, which are believed to cause changes in the body that lead to cancer. Flaxseed is also high in fiber and contains omega-3 fatty acids, additional cancer fighters. For the best absorption, use ground seeds, available in supermarkets and health food stores, or grind your own in a clean coffee grinder or mortar and pestle prior to using. Stir ground seeds into meat loaf, muffins, breads, and cereals.

Millet. The magnesium present in millet can help ease premenstrual discomfort and keep bones strong. Protein is also present, and this is important for your body's muscles, connective fibers, and other tissues. For a flavor twist, cook it in apple juice or broth instead of water or substitute for pasta in soups.

Oats. Unlike other grains, processed oats retain the bran and germ layers, which is where most of the nutrients reside. In addition, oats contain a variety of compounds that have been shown to help fight heart disease and cancer, lower blood sugar and cholesterol, and improve insulin sensitivity. Try cooking oats in milk instead of water for a creamy porridge.

Quinoa. All grains are good for health, but quinoa stands head and shoulders above the rest. It contains more protein than any other grain, making it a great choice for those who need to limit meat in their diets. And it's such a rich and balanced source of essential nutrients that food experts have called it the super-grain. It's a source of iron, magnesium, and riboflavin, which helps with boosting energy and making blood work more efficiently. Always wash quinoa under cold running water until the water runs clear. This important step removes the saponin, a naturally occurring coating on the grain that has a bitter flavor.

Rice. Go for brown rice, the most nutritious kind, which contains an abundance of fiber—great for helping prevent cancer—complex carbohydrates, and essential B vitamins. Plus, it contains a powerful compound that helps reduce the amount of cholesterol produced by the body, helping prevent heart disease. Many varieties of brown rice are available, since "brown" simply means that the rice still has the nutritious outer layer of the grain intact. All varieties of rice—long-grain, medium-grain, and short-grain—are available in a brown version, so experiment with several different types.

Wheat. For Americans, wheat is by far the number one grain. We eat more than 100 pounds per person per year in our pastas, breads, bagels, and cereals. But what makes wheat truly special is that it contains one thing that many foods do not: vitamin E, which can help lower cholesterol levels and reduce the risk of heart disease. Be sure you are eating whole grain products, and not those made with refined wheat flour, which is stripped of nutrients.

Fats

Yes, fat. Coming off more than a decade of hearing that fat is a no-no, we Americans have realized that depriving ourselves of it has made us fatter and less healthy. Although fat must be kept in check, avoiding it completely is not a healthy practice. Fat is an essential part of anyone's diet, and it can even aid in weight loss. Fats provide energy, insulate against extreme temperatures, protect our organs, are a precursor to vitamin D and sex hormones, and keep our skin healthy. Up to 30 percent of your daily calories should come from fat. The key to a good diet is to eat the best fats for health.

Monounsaturated and polyunsaturated fats. These fats not only help lower heart disease risk but they also may reduce breast cancer risk. Rich in vitamin E, which can stop the cellular damage that can lead to cancer, both these "un-fats" are found in vegetable and seed oils—think olive and sesame—and in nuts and seeds.

Omega-3 fatty acids. A kind of polyunsaturated fatty acid found in fish and flaxseed, omega-3 has been shown to reduce clotting and inflammation in arteries, which can help lower heart disease and stroke risk. They also may be able to help control psoriasis, prevent gallstones, and ease arthritis and asthma symptoms.

Omega-6 fatty acids. Because we eat so much of these polyunsaturated fatty acids—found in everyday vegetable oils such as cotton, soy, and safflower—we actually get too much of it in our diets, especially from processed foods. Also found in meats, these fatty acids are essential, but need to be eaten in the right amounts. It's important that you aim for no more than four times as much omega-6 as you get of omega-3, or 6 grams daily. Experts say that the typical American diet provides 10 to 20 times more omega-6 than we need.

Saturated fats. These are the fats found in meats, dairy products, and eggs—notorious for raising levels of artery-clogging LDL cholesterol. Because they are naturally occurring, as compared with manmade hydrogenated fats, these fats are best eaten only in very small amounts.

Hydrogenated fats. Touted as alternatives to butter, these trans-fatty acids found in vegetable shortening and margarine can clog arteries and raise cholesterol as much as saturated fats. Avoid hydrogenated oils completely.

Water

Present in every cell of the body, water is as essential a nutrient as all the others. Water carries nutrients to the cells while removing toxins and waste products and helps stabilize body temperature and maintain blood volume. The average person loses about 2 percent of his body weight (about 1½ quarts of water) in urine, perspiration, exhalation, and other body fluids every day. To replace these fluids, drink at least eight glasses of water a day. Although juice, milk, and some other liquids do contain some water, try to supplement these liquids with an additional eight glasses of water a day as suggested before. Drinking this much can help reduce the risk of kidney stones, help prevent constipation, restore energy, and aid in weight loss.

Healing Cooking Techniques

Even the healthiest foods are less nutritious when cooked in a less than healthy fashion. Take, for example, the potato, a good source of vitamin C and fiber when eaten with the skin. Baked, steamed, or roasted, a potato enhances any healthy meal. However, peel, sliver, and throw a potato into a vat of boiling oil, and its health benefits will plummet. Whenever possible, prepare foods using the following methods.

Steaming. By steaming, you can cook chicken and fish without added fat. Steam vegetables to lock in the vital nutrients lost during boiling. Steamed foods are most flavorful when prepared with herbs or spices or drizzled with citrus juice.

Baking or roasting. These two methods are great for meats, poultry, fish, and some vegetables, such as squash and potatoes. Cover the food for part of the cooking time to keep it moist. Use a rack for meats and poultry so that they don't soak up pan drippings. Cook chicken with the skin on when possible to keep it moist. Remove the skin before eating, and you'll throw away 10½ grams of fat and 95 calories per 4-ounce serving.

Oven-frying. Cooking in this way lets you mimic the texture of fried foods without getting the unhealthy excess fat and calories that frying would impart. All you need to do is dip the food, such as skinless chicken breasts or fish fillets, into beaten egg whites and then roll it in fine bread crumbs before baking.

Broiling or grilling. These are excellent alternatives to traditional frying. You cook the food directly under or over a heat source and on a rack to allow the fat to drain away.

Braising. Also known as stewing, braising refers to cooking food in liquid. It's one of the best methods for tenderizing lean cuts of meat and poultry. An advantage to braising is that the fat seeps into the cooking liquid so that you can easily skim it off.

Poaching. Generally used with quick-cooking foods like fish or boned poultry, poaching cooks foods in either simmering water or broth. Poaching in broth allows some of the flavor from the broth to seep into the food. Unlike braising, where the cooking liquid is used as a gravy or stew, poaching liquid is often discarded.

Sautéing or stir-frying. These cooking methods help keep the fat content of dishes to a minimum when done in a nonstick skillet or wok. Using nonstick cooking spray or 1 to 2 tablespoons of oil per full recipe allows foods to brown without too much added fat.

Putting It All Together

Now that you know what to eat and why, you also need to know how. Let's start by determining how much food you should eat in a day. Take this quick quiz to see where you stand in reference to your activity level, weight goals, and calorie needs.

Step 1: Find your activity level.

Sedentary: You have a job or lifestyle that involves a lot of sitting, standing, or light walking. At most, you exercise occasionally.

Active: Your job requires more activity than just light walking (such as full-time housecleaning or construction work), or you get 45 to 60 minutes of aerobic exercise three times weekly.

Very active: You get aerobic exercise for at least 45 to 60 minutes four or more times every week.

Step 2: Find your activity factor.

If you are a . . .	Your activity factor is . . .
Sedentary woman	12
Sedentary man	14
Active woman	15
Active man	17
Very active woman	18
Very active man	20

Step 3: Determine your calorie needs.

Multiply your activity factor (from step 2) by your weight in pounds. That is, *activity factor × weight in pounds = calorie needs*. (If you're trying to lose weight, substitute your goal weight for your weight in pounds.)

Step 4: Determine your fat and carbohydrate needs.

Locate your calorie needs (from step 3) on the chart below and read across for your personal daily nutrient totals. Basically, your total fat intake should be 30 percent of calories, saturated fat should be 10 percent of calories, carbohydrates should be 50 percent of calories, and protein should be 20 percent of calories. Use these guidelines when tallying up your daily food intake and when reading nutrition labels on foods at the grocery store.

Calories	Total Fat (g)	Saturated Fat (g)	Carbohydrate (g)	Protein (g)
1,400	38	10	225	35
1,600	44	12	260	40
1,800	50	14	290	45
2,000	56	15	325	50
2,200	61	17	355	55
2,500	69	19	405	62
2,800	77	21	455	70
3,200	88	24	520	80

What to Eat

In the following chart, choose the daily calorie level that is closest to the one you have chosen to reach your weight goals. Then scan the food groups to see how many servings of each food to eat in a day. Of course, these numbers are meant only as a guide. Some days, you may end up eating more or less in any given food category. As always, check with your doctor before beginning any new diet or eating plan.

	Servings per Day for . . .			
Food Group	1,500 Calories	1,800 Calories	2,000 Calories	2,500 Calories
Grains	6	8	9	10
Vegetable	5	5	4	5
Fruit	3	5	5	6
Milk	2	2	2	4
Meat	6	6	8	10
Fat	4	5	5	6

Serving Sizes

Don't look to a restaurant or fast-food joint to determine a correct serving size. Many of them have "super-sized" their meals to the point that you'd end up eating a day's worth of calories in one meal. Here's an easy guide to help you recognize healthy serving sizes.

Fruits. ½ cup chopped, 1 medium piece of fruit, ¾ cup of juice, or ¾ ounce dried fruit

Vegetables. 1 cup raw green leaves, ½ cup cooked or raw vegetables, or ¾ cup of vegetable juice

Grains. 1 slice whole wheat bread; ½ cup cooked brown rice, bulgur, or other whole grain; or ½ cup whole wheat pasta

Fish, meat or poultry, or legumes. 1 ounce cooked fish or shellfish, beef, pork, chicken, or turkey, or ½ cup legumes

Fat. 1 teaspoon butter or oil, 1 tablespoon regular salad dressing, 1 tablespoon peanut butter, 2 tablespoons half-and-half, 3 tablespoons reduced-fat sour cream, or ½ ounce nuts

Dairy products. 1 cup fat-free or 1 percent milk, 1 cup fat-free or low-fat yogurt, or 1 ounce reduced-fat cheese

Curried Sweet Potato and Apple Soup
page 100

Apple Skillet Cake
page 81

Apple Crumble with Toasted-Oat Topping
page 298

apples

can help . . .

- lower risk of heart disease
- prevent constipation and diverticulosis
- stabilize blood sugar and help control diabetes
- prevent cancer
- foster weight control

27

Fresh Berry Shortcakes
page 308

28

berries

can help . . .

- prevent cataracts
- ward off cancer
- boost immunity
- prevent constipation
- delay the signs of aging

Tabbouleh with Fruit
page 228

Cornmeal Flapjacks
page 82

*Multigrain
Blueberry
Waffles
page 86*

29

Beef and Vegetable Stew
page 168

carrots

can help . . .

- improve night vision
- protect against cataracts and macular degeneration
- reduce risk of heart disease and cancer
- boost immunity

Moroccan Carrot Salad with Toasted Cumin
page 135

Carrot Cake with Cream Cheese Frosting
page 304

citrus

can help . . .

- boost immunity
- reduce risk of cancer, heart disease, and stroke
- relieve cold symptoms
- prevent effects of stress, fatigue, and depression
- stabilize blood sugar and control diabetes

Grilled Swordfish with Blueberry Salsa
page 219

Roasted Beet Salad
page 137

Citrus Fruit Bowl
page 70

33

Curried Cauliflower and Carrots with Beans
page 276

cruciferous vegetables

can help . . .

- reduce risk of cancers such as breast cancer
- ward off heart disease
- prevent constipation and diverticulosis
- battle stress and fatigue

*Asian Slaw
page 128*

*Orange Beef and Broccoli
page 183*

dairy

can help . . .

- prevent osteoporosis
- lower blood pressure and cholesterol
- reduce risk of heart disease and stroke
- promote dental health

Grilled Tomato and Cheese Sandwiches page 151

Berry Berry Smoothie page 72

Banana-Ginger Smoothie page 91

Lemon Cheesecake
page 302

*Creamy White Bean Soup
with Cabbage and Salmon
page 420*

fish

can help . . .

- protect against heart disease and stroke
- lower cholesterol and reduce risk of gallstones
- reduce risk of cancer
- fight depression
- ease PMS symptoms

Linguine with Clams page 226

Baked Scallops Newburg page 224

Penne with Salmon and Roasted Vegetables page 213

garlic

can help . . .

- lower cholesterol and triglycerides
- protect against cancer
- prevent heart disease and stroke
- reduce high blood pressure
- boost immunity
- slow effects of aging

Roasted Garlic
page 280

BBQ Butterflied
Leg of Lamb
page 179

Five-Alarm Shrimp
page 221

grains

can help . . .

- reduce cholesterol
- aid digestion
- reduce risk of heart disease, cancer, and diabetes
- keep blood sugar steady

Quinoa with Peppers and Beans
page 248

Strawberry Tart with Oat-Cinnamon Crust
page 294

Mushroom-Barley Soup
page 112

41

Barley with Spring Greens
page 243

greens

can help . . .

- control blood pressure
- reduce risk of
  heart disease and cancer
- protect against vision loss
- prevent constipation
- battle stress and fatigue

*California Chicken
page 190*

*Roasted Sweet-Potato Salad
page 139*

*Minted Lamb Chops
with White Beans
page 180*

44

legumes

can help . . .

- lower cholesterol
- stabilize blood sugar and control diabetes
- reduce risk of cancer and heart disease
- foster weight control
- prevent constipation
- battle stress and fatigue

Baked Stuffed Potatoes with Spinach and Cannellini Beans page 261

Mediterranean Chickpea Salad page 129

45

nuts

can help . . .

- lower cholesterol
- reduce risk of heart disease
- provide antioxidant compounds that may help protect against cancer
- improve memory
- slow effects of aging

Fruit and Nut Cereal
page 75

Fruited Turkey Salad
page 130

*Almond and Chocolate
Flourless Cake
page 306*

47

Kamut, Orange, and Fennel Salad
page 232

48

olive oil and olives

can help . . .

- lower cholesterol
- reduce risk of heart disease
- reduce risk of certain cancers such as breast cancer

*Fish Stew
with
Couscous
page 220*

*Olive Oil–Cornmeal Cake with Blueberry and Red Wine Sauce
page 300*

onions

can help . . .

- raise "good" HDL cholesterol and triglycerides
- lower blood pressure
- reduce risk of cancer
- ease congestion with colds
- reduce inflammation with asthma

Potato Salad with Warm Onion Dressing page 138

Root Vegetable Mash page 262

50

Stuffed Vidalia Onions
page 264

51

Pork and Pepper Stir-Fry
page 172

red peppers

can help . . .

- prevent cataracts
- reduce risk of heart disease
- boost immunity
- maintain vision

Florentine Omelette
page 90

Cauliflower with Red Pepper and Garlic
page 275

53

*Rich 'n' Creamy
Brown Rice Pudding
page 290*

soy

can help . . .

- lower cholesterol
- slow bone loss and reduce risk of osteoporosis
- reduce risk of prostate cancer

*Stir-Fried Broccoli
and Mushrooms with Tofu
page 278*

*Gingery Vegetable Broth with Tofu and Noodles
page 104*

tomatoes

can help . . .

- reduce risk of cancer and heart disease
- prevent cataracts
- boost immunity
- prevent prostate problems

Balsamic Tomato and Roasted Pepper Salad page 136

Orange Roughy Veracruz page 214

Pasta e Fagiole
page 106

Mexican Pork Stew
page 167

Ginger Pumpkin Pie
page 296

Spaghetti Squash Casserole
page 282

winter squash

can help . . .

- protect against cataracts and macular degeneration
- reduce risk of cancer and heart disease
- boost immunity

58

healing nutrients

Whole foods contain an amazing assortment of healing nutrients and compounds. The following chart details what these nutrients do for you as well as some foods that contain them.

The first section consists of the essential nutrients. Each of the essential vitamins and minerals has an established Daily Value (DV), which indicates the amount of nutrients that almost all healthy adults need to maintain adequate nutrition. The DV appears on food labels so that you can compare how different foods supply different amounts of nutrients to your diet. It's based on a 2,000-calorie-a-day diet, so if you eat more or less than 2,000 calories a day, the amount of nutrients you need will be slightly different from the DV.

The second section of the chart, beginning on page 64, details components found in foods that are still being studied for their beneficial contributions to our health, so they do not have established Daily Values.

Essential Nutrients

Nutrient	Daily Value (DV)	Some Food Sources	Healing Benefits
Vitamin A	5,000 IU (1,000 mcg RE)	Liver, fortified reduced-fat milk, eggs	Vital for vision, healthy skin, mucous membranes, reproduction, growth of bones and teeth; enhances immunity
Vitamin B_6	2 mg	Avocado, potatoes, bananas, chickpeas, meats, poultry	Lowers estrogen and raises progesterone levels; helps manufacture serotonin; enhances immunity; helps lower blood levels of homocysteine (a by-product of protein breakdown linked to heart disease); converts amino acids into mood-lifting neurotransmitters; helps metabolic pathways in the brain; important for making red blood cells and DNA
Vitamin B_{12}	6 mcg	Any animal product, such as lean meat, poultry, seafood, milk, cheese, eggs	Helps makes new cells; protects and maintains the protective sheath around nerve fibers; helps metabolic pathways in the brain; helps lower blood levels of homocysteine (a by-product of protein breakdown linked to heart disease); helps metabolize some fatty acids and amino acids; helps make DNA and RNA; helps activate folate

(continued)

healing nutrients (cont.)

Nutrient	Daily Value (DV)	Some Food Sources	Healing Benefits
Biotin	300 mcg	Soybeans, liver, fish, egg yolks, whole grains	Necessary for energy metabolism; makes fatty acids; breaks down amino acids; a deficiency can lead to dry skin, hair loss, and brittle nails
Vitamin C	60 mg	Citrus fruits and juices, vegetables, dark green leafy vegetables	Lowers levels of histamines; strengthens white blood cells, increasing resistance to infection; helps form collagen; increases absorption of chromium; helps form hormones that regulate metabolic rate during illness or stress; used by the body during physical stresses such as infections, injury healing, and exposure to cold weather
Calcium	1,000 mg (1,200 mg over age 50)	Dairy products, sardines and salmon with bones, dark green leafy vegetables	Essential in bone formation and maintenance; important for muscle contraction and relaxation, blood pressure regulation, immunity, nerve health, blood clotting
Carbohydrates	300g	All fruits, vegetables, dark green leafy vegetables, legumes, buckwheat, whole grain foods, brown rice	Provides the body with a steady supply of energy
Chromium	120 mcg	Broccoli, grapefruit, fortified breakfast cereals	Helps the body regulate blood sugar or glucose, thus affecting insulin levels
Copper	2 mg	Meat, seafood, legumes, whole grains	Needed for several enzymes that use oxygen to act in the body, wound healing, and energy production

Nutrient	Daily Value (DV)	Some Food Sources	Healing Benefits
Vitamin D	400 IU or 10 mcg (600 IU or 15 mcg over age 70)	Egg yolks, fatty fish, fortified milk	Increases bone mineralization by raising calcium and phosphorus levels in the blood
Vitamin E	30 IU (20 mg alpha-TE)	Oils, seeds, nuts	An antioxidant; protects the components of cells and their membranes from being destroyed; works with selenium to make both of these nutrients more effective in protecting cell membranes; easily destroyed by heat, as in deep-fat frying
Fiber	25 g	Legumes, whole grains, fresh and dried fruits, vegetables, brown rice	Lowers estrogen levels and may decrease breast cancer risk; helps prevent glucose from being absorbed too quickly; reduces cholesterol levels and prevents constipation; escorts potential cancer-causing compounds out of the body more rapidly
Folate	400 mcg	Leafy green vegetables, legumes, seeds	Helps metabolic processes in the body; decreases the level of the amino acid homocysteine (a by-product of protein breakdown linked to heart disease); helps form DNA in new cells; very important for preventing life-threatening birth defects of the brain and spine; helps reduce risk of polyps in the colon
Folic acid	400 mcg	Fortified foods and supplements	Has the same effects as folate but is the form found in fortified foods and supplements and is easier for your body to absorb than food folate

(continued)

healing nutrients (cont.)

Nutrient	Daily Value (DV)	Some Food Sources	Healing Benefit
Iodine	150 mcg	Shellfish, spinach, kelp	Important for the function of the thyroid gland; helps control the rate at which energy is released during digestion and absorption; regulates growth and development
Iron	18 mg	Meat, fish, eggs, beans, dried fruit	Helps carry oxygen in the bloodstream for circulation and in the muscles for contraction; needed so that energy can be used in reactions in all cells
Vitamin K	80 mcg	Eggs, broccoli, Brussels sprouts, dark green leafy vegetables, liver	Synthesizes proteins involved in blood clotting and other proteins in plasma, bones, and kidneys; supports calcium and vitamin D metabolism; may help nerve growth
Magnesium	400 mg	Whole grains, root vegetables, dark green leafy vegetables	Important in building bone and protein, enzyme action, normal muscle contraction, nerve impulse transmission, good dental health, and the operation of the immune system
Manganese	2 mg	Whole grains, chickpeas, spinach, nuts	Partners with enzymes that help numerous metabolic processes in the body
Molybdenum	75 mcg	Legumes, whole grains, dark green leafy vegetables	Acts as part of enzymes; works in many cell functions
Niacin	20 mg	Poultry, fish, meat, legumes, nuts, whole grains	Helps in the release of energy from foods; important for the health of skin and the nervous and digestive systems
Pantothenic acid	10 mg	Meats, whole grain cereals, legumes, mushrooms, avocados	Helps metabolize food; helps produce cholesterol, red blood cells, and neurotransmitters

Nutrient	Daily Value (DV)	Some Food Sources	Healing Benefits
Potassium	3,500 mg	Fruits, vegetables, legumes, lean meats, seafood, milk	Helps transmit nerve impulses, contract muscles, and maintain normal blood pressure; a potassium-rich diet tends to raise good HDL and lower bad LDL cholesterol
Protein	50g	Lean meats, poultry, fish, legumes, whole grains	Builds and repairs skin, bone, muscles, organs, and blood; assists in blood clotting, water balance, hormone production, and immunity
Riboflavin	1.7 mg	Milk, milk products, dark green leafy vegetables, lean meats, chicken, whole grain breads	Helps convert food into energy, regulate hormones and red blood cells, and keep skin healthy and vision normal; deficiency may cause mood swings from depression to hysteria to lethargy; is easily destroyed by ultraviolet light and irradiation, so look for milk that is packaged in opaque containers
Selenium	70 mcg	Fish, lean meats, chicken, whole grains, Brazil nuts, broccoli	Works with vitamin E to protect body compounds from oxidation; converts amino acids into mood-lifting neurotransmitters; works closely with the enzyme that converts thyroid hormone to its active form
Sodium	2,400 mg or less	Table salt, processed foods, soy sauce	Regulates normal fluid balance in the body; helps maintain the body's acid-base balance; helps in nerve impulse transmission and muscle contraction (2,400 mg of sodium is what's in just over 1 teaspoon of salt)
Thiamin	1.5 mg	Corn, lean pork, liver, legumes, nuts	Helps turn carbohydrates, proteins, and fats into energy; essential for growth and nerve impulses; supports normal appetite and nerve function

(continued)

healing nutrients (cont.)

Nutrient	Daily Value (DV)	Some Food Sources	Healing Benefits
Zinc	15 mg	Lean meats, liver, seafood, poultry, lentils, whole grains, buckwheat, Brazil nuts	Necessary for growth, immune function, blood clotting, wound healing, and sperm production

Other Beneficial Nutrients

Nutrient	Daily Value (DV)	Some Food Sources	Healing Benefits
Allicin	—	Garlic, onions	Discourages cholesterol from lining arteries; discourages red blood cells from sticking together and blocking arteries
Allyl sulfides	—	Garlic	Help destroy cancer-causing substances, lower triglyceride levels, boost enzymes that limit tumor growth, and raise levels of HDL, the "good" cholesterol
Anethole	—	Fennel	Helps stimulate appetite and digestion
Anthocyanins	—	Blueberries, strawberries, cherries, grapes	Help fight cancer and heart disease and may improve age-related memory deficiencies
Antioxidants	—	Broccoli, Brussels sprouts, butternut squash, sweet potatoes, bell peppers	Can neutralize free radicals by stabilizing them with electrons, preventing cell damage. The more antioxidants in the diet, the more the body has the ability to produce natural killer cells.

Nutrient	Daily Value (DV)	Some Food Sources	Healing Benefits
Apiol	—	Parsley	Increases the flow of urine to help ease urinary tract infections
Beta-carotene	—	Sweet potatoes, butternut squash, carrots	Acts as either an antioxidant or converts to vitamin A in the body; helps stimulate the release of natural killer cells
Boron	—	Pears, raisins, peanut butter, peanuts, parsley	Helps the body retain calcium, thereby helping lessen the risk of osteoporosis
Bromelain	—	Fresh pineapple, fresh pineapple juice	Aids digestion
Carnosol	—	Rosemary	Antioxidant and anti-carcinogenic properties
Carotenoids	—	Cantaloupe, carrots, kale, leafy greens, sweet potatoes, winter squash, oranges	Help prevent heart disease and some cancers; some of the carotenoids can be converted into vitamin A by the body as needed
Choline	—	Milk, liver, cauliflower, peanuts	Necessary for the body to make lecithin, which acts as an emulsifier (an emulsifier is both water-soluble and fat-soluble so oils and fats can be mixed in the body); also needed to make a neurotransmitter called acetylcholine
Conjugated linoleic acid (CLA)	—	Milk (not fat-free) and other dairy products	Shown to inhibit chemically induced cancers of the skin, stomach, breast, and colon
Daidzein	—	Soy foods	May help decrease cholesterol levels

(continued)

healing nutrients (cont.)

Nutrient	Daily Value (DV)	Some Food Sources	Healing Benefit
Flavonoids	—	Grapes, grape juice, blueberries, oranges, apples, soybeans, barley, onions, parsley, flaxseed	May help with controlling cholesterol, preventing heart disease and stroke, and fighting infections
Genistein	—	Soy foods	May help decrease cholesterol levels
Glutamine	—	Meat, fish, poultry, dairy products	Increases bloodflow to the stomach and helps strengthen the stomach's protective lining
Glutathione	—	Fruits, vegetables	Found in every living cell; stimulates the immune system to release lots of macrophages (specialized cells that engulf and destroy foreign material)
Hesperidin	—	Pith and peel of oranges	Raised healthy HDL cholesterol levels in studies
Indoles	—	Cabbage, broccoli, Brussels sprouts	Reduce levels of estrogen; stimulate enzymes that help prevent cancer
Isoflavones	—	Fruits, vegetables, soy products	Helps prevent prostate cancer
Isothiocyanates	—	Broccoli, cauliflower, Brussels sprouts	Helps prevent some cancers and lower the level of estrogen
Lactobacillus Acidophilus	—	Yogurt with live active cultures	Can help control yeast in intestines and vagina
Lignans	—	Flaxseed, flaxseed oil	Help lower levels of estrogen; may help prevent some cancers; may prevent clots from forming in the bloodstream; has been found to be helpful for people with lupus whose kidneys have been damaged by the disease

Nutrient	Daily Value (DV)	Some Food Sources	Healing Benefits
Limonene	—	Citrus fruits	May help stall lung and breast cancers and may help cancer cells self-destruct
Lutein	—	Broccoli, dark green leafy vegetables, corn, green peas, parsley	Protects the eyes
Lycopene	—	Tomatoes, tomato products, guavas	May help prevent heart disease and cancer, especially prostate, lung, and stomach cancers
Monoterpenes	—	Citrus peel, cherries, sage	May help prevent cancer
Monounsaturated fats	—	Olives, olive oil, canola oil, avocados, nuts	Helps lower cholesterol levels; may help reduce the risk of breast cancer and high blood pressure
Myristicin	—	Parsley	Helps increase the flow of urine, helping to treat urinary tract infections
Oleic acid	—	Olive oil, olives, nuts, avocados	Helps lower cholesterol levels; may reduce the risk of breast cancer and high blood pressure
Omega-3 fatty acids	—	Salmon, tuna, canola oil, flaxseed	Help relieve menstrual cramps; help control high blood pressure; may help lower the risk of cancer, depression, rheumatoid arthritis, and fatal heart attacks
Omega-6 fatty acids	—	Corn oil, safflower oil, soybean oil	Essential to limit to a small intake; helps lower bad LDL cholesterol but also lowers good HDL cholesterol
Pectin	—	Apples, citrus fruits	Lowers cholesterol; may help prevent atherosclerosis, diabetes, and cancer
Phytochemicals	—	Fruits, vegetables, whole grains, beans	Nonnutrients found in plants that have biological action in the body; may have strong antioxidant action or other health-promoting qualities

(continued)

healing nutrients (cont.)

Nutrient	Daily Value (DV)	Some Food Sources	Healing Benefits
Phytoestrogens	—	Flaxseed, soy products	May help reduce the risk of prostate cancer and osteoporosis; may help control cholesterol
Polyunsaturated fats	—	Processed foods, corn oil, safflower oil, salmon, mackerel, canola oil	A healthier fat than saturated or trans fatty acids, but not as beneficial as monounsaturated
Proantho-cyanidins	—	Cranberries, grape seed, blueberries, cocoa, barley	Prevent bacteria from attaching to the urinary tract; help in vascular relaxation
Quercetin	—	Cranberries, onions, kale, buckwheat	Helps control cholesterol, prevent stroke and heart disease, and fight infections
Resveratrol	—	Concord grape juice, red wine, peanuts	Helps prevent stroke and heart attack
Rutin	—	Buckwheat	Helps prevent heart disease
Sulfur compounds	—	Onions, garlic, chives, shallots, leeks	Help fight infections including yeast; help prevent heart attacks, stroke, and cancer
Tryptophan	—	Turkey, milk, cheese	Helps prevent insomnia, depression, and headaches
Zeaxanthin	—	Broccoli, dark green leafy vegetables, parsley	Helps maintain healthy vision

breakfasts

The most important meal of the day, breakfast jump-starts your energy level and keeps your blood sugar stable, which helps prevent overeating later in the day. To make rushed mornings easier, prepare breakfasts earlier in the week. If you make waffles or pancakes on the weekend, prepare extra and freeze them for a quick reheat. Any fruit sauces will keep in the refrigerator for up to 5 days. If eating on the run is more your style, opt for a breakfast shake or a hearty muffin.

Photograph on page 33

Stroke

Heart Disease

Cancer

Dental Problems

General Vision
Problems

Breast Cancer

Diabetes

Infections

Immunity
Problems

Wrinkles

the
healing
factor

 Vitamin C

 Fiber

 Vitamin A

 Folate

citrus fruit bowl   quick

4	medium navel oranges
3	large pink grapefruit
1/3	cup dried sweetened cranberries
	Fresh mint leaves (optional)

Cut off the peel and pith from the oranges and grapefruit. Working over a large bowl, cut out the sections of fruit from between the membranes, letting the sections fall into the bowl. Squeeze the juice from the membranes over the fruit; discard the membranes.

Add the cranberries and stir to combine. Garnish with the mint, if using.

Makes 6 servings
Per serving: 100 calories, 1 g protein, 25 g carbohydrates, 0 g fat, 0 g saturated fat, 0 mg cholesterol, 4 g fiber, 0 mg sodium

honeyed summer fruit bowl

¼	cup honey
1	tablespoon lemon juice or lime juice
	Pinch of ground cinnamon
1½	pints strawberries, quartered
½	large cantaloupe, cut into chunks or balls
2	medium nectarines, cut into thin wedges
2	medium peaches, cut into thin wedges
2	large or 3 small plums, cut into thin wedges
1	cup blueberries

In a large bowl, combine the honey, lemon juice or lime juice, and cinnamon. Add the strawberries, cantaloupe, nectarines, peaches, plums, and blueberries. Toss just until the fruit is well-mixed and coated with the honey mixture.

Let stand for 30 minutes before serving to allow the flavors to blend.

Makes 8 servings
Per serving: 112 calories, 1 g protein, 28 g carbohydrates, 1 g fat, 0 g saturated fat, 0 mg cholesterol, 3 g dietary fiber, 5 mg sodium

treat ↗ helps prevent

Stroke
Dental Problems
Aging
Cancer
High Blood Pressure
Heart Disease
Immunity Problems
Infections
Stress/Fatigue
Leg Cramps

the healing factor

 Vitamin C

 Vitamin A

 Fiber

 Manganese

Potassium

Heart Disease

Stroke

High Cholesterol

Dental Problems

Diabetes

Cataracts

Immunity Problems

Overweight

Osteoporosis

the
healing factor

🫐🫐🫐 Vitamin C

🫐🫐 Thiamin

🫐🫐 Omega-3 fatty acids

🫐 Manganese

🫐🫐 Fiber

berry berry smoothie (quick)

Photograph on page 36

½	cup frozen unsweetened raspberries
½	cup frozen unsweetened strawberries
¾	cup unsweetened pineapple juice
1	cup soy milk or 1% milk

In a blender, combine the raspberries, strawberries, and pineapple juice. Add the milk and blend until smooth.

Makes 2 servings
Per serving: 102 calories, 4 g protein, 19 g carbohydrates, 3 g fat, 0 g saturated fat, 0 mg cholesterol, 3 g dietary fiber, 16 mg sodium

multigrain cereal

2	cups rolled oats
2	cups wheat flakes
2	cups malted barley flakes
2	cups rye flakes
1	box (1 pound) dark or golden raisins
1½	cups flaxseeds, ground
¾	cup sesame seeds

In an airtight container, combine the oats, wheat flakes, barley flakes, rye flakes, raisins, flaxseeds, and sesame seeds. Store in the freezer until ready to use.

To cook: For 1 serving, bring 1 cup water to a boil in a small saucepan. Add a pinch of salt. Add ⅓ cup of the cereal, cover, and cook, stirring occasionally, for 25 minutes, or until thickened and creamy.

For 4 servings, use 3 cups water, ¼ teaspoon salt, and 1½ cups cereal. Cook for 25 to 30 minutes.

Makes thirty-six ⅓-cup servings
Per serving: 16 calories, 5 g protein, 29 g carbohydrates, 4 g fat, 0 g saturated fat, 0 mg cholesterol, 5 g dietary fiber, 8 mg sodium

treat ♪ helps prevent

Depression
Insomnia
Memory Problems
Cancer
High Cholesterol
Heart Disease
Stroke
Diabetes
PMS
Lupus

the healing factor

- Omega-3 fatty acids
- Manganese
- Fiber
- Folate
- Copper
- Magnesium
- Iron

Aging
Cancer
Heart Disease
Diabetes
Immunity
Problems
Insomnia
Wrinkles
Prostate Problems

toasted oat muesli

6	cups old-fashioned oats, preferably thick-cut
1 1/4	cups sliced natural almonds
1	package (7 ounces) dried fruit bits
1	cup toasted wheat germ
1/2	cup unsalted raw pumpkin seeds
1/2	cup unsalted raw sunflower seeds

the 🌿
healing
factor

🐞🐞🐞 Manganese
🐞🐞🐞 Phosphorus
🐞🐞🐞 Magnesium
🐞🐞🐞 Thiamin
🐞🐞🐞 Fiber
🐞🐞🐞 Copper
🐞🐞🐞 Vitamin E
🐞🐞🐞 Selenium
🐞🐞🐞 Zinc
🐞🐞🐞 Iron

Preheat the oven to 325°F.

Spread the oats out on a jelly-roll pan. Spread the almonds in a small baking pan. Place the oats and almonds in the oven and bake, stirring often, until the oats are lightly browned and the almonds are toasted. The oats will take 30 to 35 minutes; the almonds will toast in 20 to 25 minutes.

Place the oats and almonds in a large bowl and cool completely.

Add the fruit bits, wheat germ, pumpkin seeds, and sunflower seeds. Toss to combine. Store in an airtight container.

To serve, place 1/2 cup of the cereal mixture in a bowl. Top with soy milk, fat-free milk, or yogurt.

Makes twenty-two 1/2-cup servings
Per serving: 300 calories, 12 g protein, 40 g carbohydrates, 11 g fat, 1 g saturated fat, 0 mg cholesterol, 7 g dietary fiber, 2 mg sodium

fruit and nut cereal

Photograph on page 46

2	cups rolled oats
1	cup wheat flakes
2	tablespoons sunflower seeds
1½	tablespoons sesame seeds
¼	cup frozen apple juice concentrate, thawed
¼	cup packed brown sugar
2	tablespoons canola oil
½	teaspoon ground cinnamon
¼	cup chopped dried figs
¼	cup chopped dried apple rings
¼	cup chopped dried apricots
¼	cup slivered toasted almonds

Preheat the oven to 250°F. Coat a jelly-roll pan with cooking spray.

In a medium bowl, combine the oats, wheat flakes, sunflower seeds, sesame seeds, apple juice concentrate, brown sugar, oil, and cinnamon.

Spread the oat mixture in the prepared pan. Bake, stirring occasionally, for 45 to 60 minutes, or until golden brown. Cool completely.

Place the cereal, figs, apples, apricots, and almonds in an airtight container.

To serve, place ⅔ cup of the cereal mixture in a bowl. Top with soy milk, fat-free milk, or yogurt.

Makes about nine ⅔-cup servings
Per serving: 241 calories, 5 g protein, 40 g carbohydrates, 8 g fat, 1 g saturated fat, 0 mg cholesterol, 4 g dietary fiber, 8 mg sodium

treat ᔕ

helps prevent

Aging
Cancer
Heart Disease
Stroke
Diabetes
Depression
Insomnia
Memory Problems
High Cholesterol
Wrinkles

the healing factor

- Omega-3 fatty acids
- Phosphorus
- Fiber
- Iron
- Vitamin E
- Selenium
- Copper
- Thiamin

fiesta cornmeal pudding

Cancer
Osteoporosis
Cataracts
Aging
Diabetes
Memory Problems
General Vision
Problems
Macular
Degeneration
Menopausal
Problems/Hot
Flashes

the 🌿
healing
factor

🍒🍒🍒 Vitamin A
🍒🍒🍒 Vitamin C
🍒🍒🍒 Manganese
🍒🍒🍒 Vitamin K
🍒🍒 Folate
🍒🍒 Calcium
🍒🍒 Magnesium
🍒🍒 Fiber
🍒🍒 Riboflavin
🍒🍒 Phosphorus

2¼	cups water
½	teaspoon salt
¾	cup yellow cornmeal
1	tablespoon extra-virgin olive oil
1	large red bell pepper, chopped
4	scallions, thinly sliced
2	large cloves garlic, minced
1	package (10 ounces) frozen chopped spinach, thawed and squeezed dry
2	egg whites
¼	teaspoon hot-pepper sauce
½	cup (2 ounces) shredded sharp Cheddar cheese

Preheat oven to 350°F. Coat a 9" baking dish with cooking spray.

Bring the water to a boil in a large saucepan over high heat. Add the salt. Reduce the heat to medium-low. Add the cornmeal in a slow, steady stream, whisking constantly. Reduce the heat to low, cover, and cook, stirring frequently, for 10 minutes, or until very thick. Remove from the heat.

Meanwhile, heat the oil in a medium nonstick skillet over medium heat. Add the bell pepper; cook, stirring, for 4 minutes. Add the scallions and garlic; cook, stirring, for 2 minutes, or until the vegetables are tender. Add the bell pepper mixture, spinach, egg whites, and hot-pepper sauce to the cornmeal. Stir well. Place in the baking dish. Sprinkle with the cheese. Bake for 30 minutes, or until firm, puffed, and golden.

Makes 6 servings
Per serving: 145 calories, 7 g protein, 17 g carbohydrates, 6 g fat, 2 g saturated fat, 10 mg cholesterol, 3 g dietary fiber, 323 mg sodium

nutty fruit muffins (quick)

1¾	cups whole grain pastry flour
1½	teaspoons baking powder
1½	teaspoons ground cinnamon
½	teaspoon baking soda
¼	teaspoon salt
1	cup (8 ounces) fat-free vanilla yogurt
½	cup packed brown sugar
1	egg
2	tablespoons canola oil
1	teaspoon vanilla extract
½	cup drained crushed pineapple in juice
⅓	cup currants or raisins
¼	cup finely shredded carrots
¼	cup chopped walnuts, toasted

Preheat the oven to 400°F. Coat a 12-cup muffin pan with cooking spray.

In a large bowl, combine the flour, baking powder, cinnamon, baking soda, and salt.

In a medium bowl, combine the yogurt, brown sugar, egg, oil, and vanilla extract. Stir into the flour mixture just until blended. Stir in the pineapple, currants or raisins, carrots, and walnuts. Divide the batter evenly among the muffin cups. Bake for 20 minutes, or until a wooden pick inserted in the center of a muffin comes out clean.

Cool on a rack for 5 minutes. Remove to the rack to cool completely.

Makes 12 muffins
Per muffin: 174 calories, 5 g protein, 30 g carbohydrates, 4 g fat, 0 g saturated fat, 18 mg cholesterol, 2 g dietary fiber, 178 mg sodium

treat ⌇ helps prevent

Dental Problems
Cancer
Osteoporosis
Overweight

the ℅
healing factor

 Omega-3 fatty acids
 Vitamin A
 Calcium
 Fiber

COOKING TIP
For a more hearty muffin, replace ¼ cup of the whole grain pastry flour with ¼ cup oat bran or wheat bran. You can also try adding ¼ cup chopped dried apricots and ¼ cup semisweet chocolate chips.

Memory Problems
Stress/Fatigue
Aging
Heart Disease
Stroke
PMS
Diabetes
Constipation
Diverticulosis

the
healing
factor

🍊🍊🍊 Manganese

🍊🍊🍊 Omega-3
fatty acids

🍊🍊🍊 Vitamin C

🍊🍊🍊 Fiber

🍊🍊 Phosphorus

🍊🍊 Magnesium

🍊🍊 Thiamin

🍊🍊 Riboflavin

🍊🍊 Iron

🍊🍊 Vitamin B$_6$

orange-bran muffins (quick)

2	cups shredded all-bran cereal
¾	cup hot water
¼	cup canola oil
1	orange
¾	cup buttermilk
2	tablespoons light molasses
2	tablespoons honey
1	egg
1¼	cups whole grain pastry flour
⅓	cup + 2 teaspoons rolled oats
2	teaspoons baking soda
½	teaspoon salt
1	cup raisins
¼	cup chopped toasted walnuts (optional)
¼	cup sugar
¼	cup orange juice

Preheat the oven to 400°F. Coat a 12-cup muffin pan with cooking spray.

In a medium bowl, combine the cereal, water, and oil. Stir until the cereal is softened.

Grate 1 tablespoon of the peel from the orange into another medium bowl; cut the orange in half and squeeze ¼ cup juice into the bowl. Stir in the buttermilk, molasses, honey, and egg until well-blended. Stir into the cereal mixture.

In a large bowl, combine the flour, ⅓ cup of the oats, baking soda, and salt. Add the cereal mixture and stir just until blended. Stir in the raisins and walnuts, if using.

Divide the batter evenly among the prepared muffin cups. Sprinkle with the remaining 2 teaspoons oats. Bake for 15 minutes, or until a wooden pick inserted in the center of a muffin comes out clean. Place the pan on a rack.

Meanwhile, combine the sugar and orange juice in a small saucepan. Bring to a boil over medium heat and stir until the sugar dissolves. Using a wooden pick, poke holes in the muffin tops. Brush with the orange syrup.

Cool on the rack for 5 minutes. Remove to the rack to cool completely.

Makes 12 muffins
Per muffin: 220 calories, 5 g protein, 42 g carbohydrates, 6 g fat, 1 g saturated fat, 18 mg cholesterol, 6 g dietary fiber, 353 mg sodium

the power of
FIBER

Getting the recommended 25 to 35 grams of fiber every day is an easy task with the help of these top 10 fiber-packed cereals. Some give you more than half of your daily fiber in one serving. All are low in fat and added sugar.

Cereal and Serving Size	Fiber (g)	Calories
Kellogg's All-Bran Bran Buds (⅓ cup)	13	80
Kashi Go Lean (¾ cup)	10	120
Kellogg's Original All-Bran (½ cup)	10	80
Kashi Good Friends (¾ cup)	8	90
Post 100% Bran (⅓ cup)	8	80
Kashi Seven Whole Grains and Sesame (¾ cup)	8	90
Post Raisin Bran (1 cup)	8	190
Post Shredded Wheat 'N Bran (1¼ cups)	8	200
Kellogg's Raisin Bran (1 cup)	8	200
General Mills Multi-Bran Chex (1 cup)	7	200

High Cholesterol
Depression
Overweight
General Vision
Problems
Diabetes

southwestern (quick) double-corn muffins

1	cup yellow cornmeal
1	cup whole grain pastry flour
¼	cup soy flour (sifted if lumpy)
2	teaspoons baking powder
¼	teaspoon ground cinnamon
⅛	teaspoon salt
1	egg
1	egg white
¾	cup milk
¼	cup canola oil
1½	cups frozen corn kernels
½	cup golden raisins

Preheat the oven to 400°F. Coat a 12-cup muffin pan with cooking spray.

In a large bowl, combine the cornmeal, pastry flour, soy flour, baking powder, cinnamon, and salt.

In a small bowl, combine the egg, egg white, milk, oil, corn, and raisins. Add to the flour mixture and stir just until blended. Divide evenly among the prepared muffin cups.

Bake for 18 minutes, or until the muffins are firm to the touch and lightly browned at the edges. Cool on a rack for 5 minutes. Remove to the rack to cool completely.

Makes 12 muffins
Per muffin: 178 calories, 5 g protein, 26 g carbohydrates, 7 g fat, 1 g saturated fat, 20 mg cholesterol, 3 g dietary fiber, 121 mg sodium

the
healing factor

🌶🌶🌶 Omega-3 fatty acids

🌶🌶 Fiber

🌶🌶 Folate

COOKING TIPS
Store any leftover muffins in the freezer for a breakfast on the go.

Most recipes for 12 muffins baked in a 12-cup muffin pan can also be baked in an 8" × 4" loaf pan. Bake at the specified temperature, but add 10 to 12 minutes to the baking time.

apple skillet cake

Photograph on page 27

1	tablespoon butter
4	apples, peeled and sliced
2	tablespoons packed brown sugar
½	teaspoon ground cinnamon
½	cup raisins
¾	cup whole grain pastry flour
⅓	cup sugar
⅛	teaspoon salt
1½	cups 1% milk
2	eggs
1	egg white
2	teaspoons vanilla extract

Preheat the oven to 375°F.

Melt the butter in a medium ovenproof skillet over medium-high heat. Add the apples and cook for 2 minutes. Add the brown sugar, cinnamon, and raisins. Cook, stirring, for 5 minutes, or until the apples are tender. Remove from the heat and spread the apples evenly over the bottom of the skillet.

Meanwhile, in a large bowl, combine the flour, sugar, and salt.

In a medium bowl, combine the milk, eggs, egg white, and vanilla extract. Add to the flour mixture and stir just until blended. Pour over the apple mixture in the skillet.

Bake for 40 minutes, or until golden brown and puffed. Remove to a rack to cool for 5 minutes. To serve, cut into wedges.

Makes 6 servings
Per serving: 279 calories, 7 g protein, 54 g carbohydrates, 5 g fat, 2 g saturated fat, 79 mg cholesterol, 5 g dietary fiber, 147 mg sodium

treat

helps
prevent

Aging
Cancer
Stroke
Heart Disease
Depression
Stress/Fatigue
Constipation
Hemorrhoids
Menopausal
Problems/Hot
Flashes
Leg Cramps

the
healing
factor

Fiber
Riboflavin
Calcium
Phosphorus
Selenium
Chromium
Potassium
Vitamin C

Aging
Depression
Cancer
Heart Disease
Memory Problems
Stress/Fatigue

the
**healing
factor**

🌑🌑🌑 Manganese

🌑🌑🌑 Fiber

🌑🌑 Vitamin C

🌑🌑 Riboflavin

🌑🌑 Thiamin

🌑🌑 Phosphorus

🌑🌑 Magnesium

🌑🌑 Selenium

cornmeal flapjacks (quick)

Photograph on page 29

1	cup cornmeal
¾	cup whole grain pastry flour
1	teaspoon baking soda
½	teaspoon salt
1¼	cups buttermilk
1	egg
1	tablespoon vegetable oil
2	tablespoons maple syrup
2	cups berries such as blueberries, raspberries, and blackberries (see note)

Preheat the oven to 200°F. Coat a baking sheet with cooking spray.

In a large bowl, combine the cornmeal, flour, baking soda, and salt.

In a medium bowl, combine the buttermilk, egg, oil, and maple syrup. Add to the flour mixture and stir just until blended.

Coat a large nonstick skillet with cooking spray and warm over medium heat. Pour the batter by scant ¼ cupfuls into the skillet. Cook for 2 minutes, or until tiny bubbles appear on the surface and the edges begin to look dry. Flip and cook for 2 minutes, or until golden. Place the flapjacks on the prepared baking sheet and place in the oven to keep warm.

Coat the skillet with cooking spray. Repeat with the remaining batter to make a total of 18 flapjacks.

Serve the flapjacks with the berries.

Makes 6 servings
Per serving: 240 calories, 7 g protein, 44 g carbohydrates, 5 g fat,
1 g saturated fat, 37 mg cholesterol, 5 g dietary fiber, 477 mg sodium

HEALTH NOTE
People with depression who take monoamine oxidase inhibitors
(MAO inhibitors) should not use the raspberries in this recipe.
Substitute additional blueberries for the raspberries.

Berry-Good Smoothie (quick)

If you experience urinary tract infections, turn to blueberries and cranberries to speed your recovery, and even help prevent future infections.
These tangy berries contain a substance that makes harmful bacteria
slip away and out of your body more easily. Try this creamy smoothie to
help send your infection packing.

    1   cup fresh or thawed frozen blueberries
    1   cup (8 ounces) vanilla yogurt
    ½   cup cran-blueberry juice

In a blender, combine the blueberries, yogurt, and cran-blueberry juice.
Blend until smooth.

Makes 2 servings
Per serving: 184 calories, 5 g protein, 38 g carbohydrates, 2 g fat, 1 g saturated fat,
6 mg cholesterol, 2 g dietary fiber, 78 mg sodium

Remedy Recipe for Urinary Tract Infections

Dental Problems
Depression
Stress/Fatigue
Heart Disease
Cancer
Memory Problems
Osteoporosis
Diabetes
Constipation
Menopausal
Problems/Hot
Flashes

the
**healing
factor**

🍐🍐🍐 Manganese
🍐🍐🍐 Vitamin C
🍐🍐🍐 Calcium
🍐🍐🍐 Fiber
🍐🍐🍐 Riboflavin
🍐🍐🍐 Phosphorus
🍐🍐🍐 Thiamin
🍐🍐🍐 Selenium
🍐🍐🍐 Magnesium
🍐🍐 Potassium

oat-berry pancakes with vanilla-ricotta cream

Sauce

2	teaspoons cornstarch
1	cup orange juice
1	tablespoon lime juice
1	tablespoon honey

Ricotta Cream

2/3	cup fat-free ricotta cheese
2	tablespoons fat-free cream cheese
1	tablespoon honey
	Grated peel of 1 lime
1	teaspoon vanilla extract

Pancakes

1	cup oat bran
1	cup whole grain pastry flour
1½	teaspoons baking powder
½	teaspoon baking soda
3	egg whites
2	cups buttermilk
2	cups mixed berries

To make the sauce: Place the cornstarch in a cup. Add 2 table-spoons of the orange juice and stir until smooth.

Place the remaining orange juice in a small saucepan. Add the lime juice and honey and cook, stirring constantly, over medium heat for 1 minute, or until the honey is dissolved. Add the cornstarch mixture. Cook, stirring constantly, for 1 minute, or until thickened. Remove from the heat and set aside to cool. Cover and refrigerate for at least 3 hours before serving.

To make the ricotta cream: In a food processor or blender, process the ricotta until smooth. Add the cream cheese, honey, lime peel, and vanilla extract. Process until smooth. Refrigerate until ready to use.

To make the pancakes: Preheat the oven to 200°F. Coat a baking sheet with cooking spray.

In a large bowl, combine the oat bran, flour, baking powder, and baking soda.

In a medium bowl, combine the egg whites and buttermilk. Add to the flour mixture and stir just until blended.

Heat a large nonstick skillet coated with cooking spray over medium heat. For each pancake, spoon about 3 tablespoons batter into the skillet and spread to form a 3" pancake. Cook for 2 minutes, or until tiny bubbles appear on the surface and the edges begin to look dry. Flip and cook for 2 minutes, or until golden. Place the pancakes on the prepared baking sheet and place in the oven to keep warm. Repeat with the remaining batter to make a total of 8 pancakes.

For each serving, spread a pancake with the ricotta cream and top with a second pancake. Drizzle with the sauce.

Makes 4 servings
Per serving: 370 calories, 22 g protein, 72 g carbohydrates, 4 g fat, 1 g saturated fat, 9 mg cholesterol, 10 g dietary fiber, 602 mg sodium

helps
prevent

treat

Aging
Cancer
Dental Problems
Overweight
Stress/Fatigue
High Cholesterol
Constipation
Hemorrhoids
Menopausal
Problems/Hot
Flashes

the
healing
factor

🍒🍒🍒 Manganese
🍒🍒🍒 Vitamin C
🍒🍒 Fiber
🍒🍒 Riboflavin
🍒🍒 Calcium

multigrain blueberry waffles

Photograph on page 29

1 ½	cups whole grain pastry flour
½	cup rolled oats
½	teaspoon baking powder
½	teaspoon baking soda
½	teaspoon salt
1 ⅔	cups fat-free milk
2	egg whites
3	tablespoons packed brown sugar
1	tablespoon vegetable oil
2	cups blueberries
1 ½	cups sliced strawberries
½	cup maple syrup

Preheat the oven to 200°F. Coat a baking sheet with cooking spray.

In a large bowl, combine the flour, oats, baking powder, baking soda, and salt.

In a medium bowl, combine the milk, egg whites, brown sugar, and oil. Add to the flour mixture and stir just until blended. Fold in 1 cup of the blueberries.

Coat a nonstick waffle iron with cooking spray. Preheat the iron.

Pour ½ cup of the batter onto the center of the iron. Cook for 5 minutes, or until steam no longer escapes from under the waffle-iron lid and the waffle is golden. Place the waffles on the prepared baking sheet and place in the oven to keep warm.

Repeat with the remaining batter to make a total of 8 waffles.

Meanwhile, in a small saucepan over medium heat, combine the remaining 1 cup blueberries, the strawberries, and maple syrup. Cook for 5 minutes, or until the berries are softened and the mixture is hot. Serve with the waffles.

Makes 8 waffles

Per waffle: 239 calories, 7 g protein, 49 g carbohydrates, 3 g fat, 0 g saturated fat, 1 mg cholesterol, 4 g dietary fiber, 217 mg sodium

COOKING TIP

This batter also makes excellent pancakes. To create your own nutritious convenience mix, double or triple the recipe for the dry ingredients and store in an airtight container in a cool cupboard. To make pancakes, measure 2 cups of the dry mix into a bowl and then add the liquid ingredients from the recipe.

Aging
Diabetes
Cancer
Heart Disease
Insomnia
Constipation
Hemorrhoids

the
**healing
factor**

🐞🐞🐞 Manganese

🐞🐞🐞 Chromium

🐞🐞🐞 Selenium

🐞🐞🐞 Vitamin A

🐞🐞🐞 Fiber

🐞🐞🐞 Riboflavin

🐞🐞🐞 Phosphorus

🐞🐞 Copper

🐞🐞 Iron

🐞🐞 Potassium

whole grain french toast with nutmeg-scented fruit

Fruit

½	cup apricot all-fruit spread
¼	cup water
2	teaspoons lemon juice
½	teaspoon freshly ground nutmeg
3	pears (about 1¼ pounds), unpeeled, cored, and cut into 1" slices
⅓	cup dried apricot halves, halved

French Toast

2	eggs
2	egg whites
1	teaspoon vanilla extract
¼	teaspoon freshly ground nutmeg
¼	cup fat-free milk
8	slices whole wheat or multigrain bread, cut diagonally in half

To make the fruit: In a large skillet over medium heat, combine the all-fruit spread, water, lemon juice, and nutmeg. Bring to a boil.

Add the pears and apricots. Reduce the heat to low, cover, and simmer, stirring occasionally, for 10 minutes, or until the pears are tender. Cover to keep warm.

To make the French toast: Preheat the oven to 425°F. Coat a large baking sheet with cooking spray.

In a shallow bowl, beat the eggs, egg whites, vanilla extract, and nutmeg with a fork. Beat in the milk.

Dip the bread slices, one at a time, into the egg mixture, letting the slices soak briefly. Arrange the soaked slices on the prepared baking sheet, fitting them together tightly if necessary. Spoon any remaining egg mixture over the bread.

Bake, without turning, for 20 to 25 minutes, or just until the outside slices are lightly golden.

Serve with the fruit.

Makes 4 servings
Per serving: 395 calories, 11 g protein, 80 g carbohydrates, 5 g fat, 1 g saturated fat, 107 mg cholesterol, 7 g dietary fiber, 332 mg sodium

florentine omelette

Photograph on page 53

Photograph on page 53

2	eggs
2	egg whites
3	tablespoons water
1	teaspoon dried Italian seasoning, crushed
¼	teaspoon salt
8	ounces mushrooms, sliced
1	onion, chopped
1	red bell pepper, chopped
1	clove garlic, minced
4	ounces (2 packed cups) spinach leaves, chopped
¾	cup (3 ounces) shredded low-fat mozzarella cheese

Preheat the oven to 200°F. Coat a baking sheet with cooking spray.

In a medium bowl, whisk together the eggs, egg whites, water, Italian seasoning, and salt.

Coat a large nonstick skillet with cooking spray and place over medium-high heat. Add the mushrooms, onion, pepper, and garlic and cook, stirring often, for 4 minutes, or until the pepper starts to soften. Add the spinach and cook for 1 minute, or until the spinach is wilted. Place in a small bowl and cover.

Wipe the skillet with a paper towel. Coat with cooking spray and place over medium heat. Pour in half of the egg mixture. Cook for 2 minutes, or until the bottom begins to set. Using a spatula, lift the edges to allow the uncooked mixture to flow to the bottom of the pan. Cook for 2 minutes longer, or until set. Sprinkle with half of the reserved vegetable mixture and half of the cheese. Cover and cook for 2 minutes, or until the cheese

helps prevent / treat

Aging
Memory Problems
Stress/Fatigue
Dental Problems
Osteoporosis
General Vision Problems
Menopausal Problems/Hot Flashes

the
healing factor

🍓🍓🍓 Vitamin C
🍓🍓🍓 Vitamin K
🍓🍓🍓 Vitamin A
🍓🍓🍓 Riboflavin
🍓🍓🍓 Phosphorus
🍓🍓 Calcium
🍓🍓 Selenium
🍓🍓 Copper
🍓🍓 Potassium
🍓🍓 Niacin

melts. Using a spatula, fold the egg mixture in half. Place on the prepared baking sheet and place in the oven to keep warm.

Coat the skillet with cooking spray. Repeat with the remaining egg mixture, vegetable mixture, and cheese to cook another omelette. To serve, cut each omelette in half.

Makes 4 servings
Per serving: 128 calories, 13 g protein, 7 g carbohydrates, 7 g fat, 3 g saturated fat, 115 mg cholesterol, 3 g dietary fiber, 346 mg sodium

Banana-Ginger Smoothie
Photograph on page 36

Ginger has long been touted as a remedy for all manner of the "queezies," including heartburn, as well as nausea and motion sickness. Here, ginger teams up with a banana, which acts as a natural antacid. So before you reach for an over-the-counter product for relief, whip up one of these soothing smoothies—it just may do the trick.

1   banana, sliced
¾   cup (6 ounces) vanilla yogurt
1   tablespoon honey
½   teaspoon freshly grated ginger

In a blender, combine the banana, yogurt, honey, and ginger. Blend until smooth.

Makes 2 servings
Per serving: 142 calories, 3 g protein, 36 g carbohydrates, 2 g fat, 1 g saturated fat, 0 mg cholesterol, 2 g dietary fiber, 16 mg sodium

Remedy Recipe for Heartburn

frittata with red-pepper sauce

Aging
Memory Problems
Stress/Fatigue
Cancer
Dental Problems
Diabetes
Osteoporosis
General Vision Problems
Menopausal Problems/Hot Flashes

the
healing factor

🍒🍒🍒 Vitamin C
🍒🍒🍒 Vitamin K
🍒🍒🍒 Vitamin A
🍒🍒 Selenium
🍒🍒 Riboflavin
🍒🍒 Chromium
🍒🍒 Phosphorus
🍒🍒 Calcium
🍒🍒 Potassium
🍒🍒 Vitamin B₆

Sauce

1	large red bell pepper, cut into chunks
1/2	cup water
1	tablespoon tomato paste
1	clove garlic, sliced
1/4	teaspoon sugar
1/8	teaspoon salt
2	tablespoons chopped fresh basil

Frittata

2	large red potatoes, halved
1	tablespoon extra-virgin olive oil
1/2	teaspoon salt
1/2	teaspoon freshly ground black pepper
6	scallions, thinly sliced
4	eggs
2	egg whites
2	tablespoons chopped fresh basil
1/2	cup (2 ounces) shredded reduced-fat Jarlsberg cheese

To make the sauce: In a medium saucepan, combine the pepper, water, tomato paste, garlic, sugar, and salt. Bring to a boil over high heat. Reduce the heat to low, cover, and simmer, stirring occasionally, for 18 minutes, or until the pepper is very tender. Place in a food processor or blender and process until very smooth. Return to the saucepan. Stir in the basil and cover to keep warm.

To make the frittata: Place a steamer basket in a large saucepan with ½" of water. Place the potatoes in the steamer. Bring to a boil over high heat. Reduce the heat to medium, cover, and cook for 20 minutes, or until the potatoes are very tender. Cool briefly under cold running water and drain. Cool completely. Cut the potatoes into ¼"-thick slices.

Heat the oil in a large nonstick skillet over medium heat. Add the potatoes. Sprinkle with ¼ teaspoon each of the salt and pepper and toss to coat well. Cook, turning often, for 8 minutes, or until golden and crisp. Add the scallions and cook, tossing gently, for 3 minutes.

Meanwhile, in a medium bowl, whisk together the eggs, egg whites, basil, cheese, and the remaining ¼ teaspoon each of the salt and pepper. Pour into the skillet over the potato mixture and reduce the heat to low. Cover and cook, without stirring, for 3 minutes, or until the eggs start to set at the edges. Using a spatula, lift the edges and tilt the skillet to allow the uncooked mixture to flow to the bottom of the pan. Cover and cook for 4 minutes longer, occasionally loosening the frittata at the bottom and shaking the pan until the eggs are set and firm.

Slide the frittata onto a plate. Cut into wedges and serve with the sauce.

Makes 6 servings
Per serving: 148 calories, 10 g protein, 13 g carbohydrates, 6 g fat, 2 g saturated fat, 145 mg cholesterol, 2 g dietary fiber, 347 mg sodium

asparagus and leek frittata

 quick

the *healing factor*

🐝🐝🐝 Vitamin K
🐝🐝🐝 Riboflavin
🐝🐝🐝 Selenium
🐝🐝 Vitamin A
🐝🐝 Vitamin C
🐝🐝 Phosphorus
🐝🐝 Vitamin B$_6$
🐝🐝 Vitamin B$_{12}$

1	tablespoon extra-virgin olive oil
1	medium leek, white and some green parts, halved lengthwise, rinsed, and thinly sliced
¾	pound thin asparagus, tips left whole and stems sliced ¼" thick
2	tablespoons chicken broth
¼	teaspoon salt
¼	teaspoon freshly ground black pepper
2	tablespoons chopped flat-leaf parsley
1	tablespoon snipped fresh chives
6	eggs
2	egg whites
3	tablespoons crumbled feta cheese

Preheat the broiler.

Heat the oil in a medium nonstick skillet with an ovenproof handle over medium-high heat. Add the leek and cook, stirring often, for 3 minutes, or until soft.

Add the asparagus, broth, ⅛ teaspoon each of the salt and pepper, parsley, and chives. Cook, stirring often, for 3 minutes, or until the asparagus is tender-crisp and the broth has evaporated. Spread the asparagus mixture evenly in the bottom of the skillet.

Meanwhile, in a medium bowl, whisk together the eggs, egg whites, cheese, and the remaining ⅛ teaspoon each of the salt and pepper. Pour into the skillet with the asparagus. Shake the skillet to evenly distribute the egg mixture. Reduce the heat to low, cover, and cook, without stirring, for 3 minutes, or until the eggs begin to set at the edges.

With a spatula, lift up an edge of the frittata and tilt the skillet to allow the uncooked mixture to flow to the bottom of the pan.

Place under the broiler. Broil for 1 to 3 minutes, or until the eggs are set on the top and the frittata is lightly puffed.

Cut into wedges to serve.

Makes 6 servings
Per serving: 131 calories, 10 g protein, 4 g carbohydrates, 9 g fat, 3 g saturated fat, 217 mg cholesterol, 2 g dietary fiber, 248 mg sodium

Banana-Orange Smoothie

Remedy Recipe for Constipation

If you take a fiber supplement to stay regular, you may want to try a "flaxative" instead. Two tablespoons of nutty-tasting flaxseeds offers enough insoluble fiber to keep you regular, plus cholesterol-lowering soluble fiber, breast cancer–fighting lignan precursors, and depression-fighting omega-3 fatty acids.

> 1   cup orange juice
> 1   banana
> 2   tablespoons flaxseeds, ground

In a blender, combine the orange juice, banana, and flaxseed. Blend until smooth and frothy.

Makes 1 serving
Per serving: 338 calories, 8 g protein, 62 g carbohydrates, 9 g fat, 1 g saturated fat, 0 mg cholesterol, 10 g dietary fiber, 114 mg sodium

Memory Problems

Aging

Cancer

Immunity
Problems

Cataracts

General Vision
Problems

the
healing
factor

🍐🍐🍐 Vitamin C

🍐🍐🍐 Fiber

🍐🍐🍐 Vitamin A

🍐🍐🍐 Riboflavin

🍐🍐🍐 Selenium

🍐🍐 Iron

🍐🍐 Thiamin

🍐🍐 Folate

🍐🍐 Vitamin K

🍐🍐 Potassium

breakfast burritos (quick)

4	fat-free honey-wheat tortillas (8" diameter)
1	tablespoon olive oil
1	medium zucchini, halved lengthwise and cut into ¼"-thick slices
1	small red bell pepper, chopped
¼	teaspoon freshly ground black pepper
¾	cup fresh or frozen and thawed corn kernels
3	eggs
3	egg whites
2	tablespoons 1% milk
½	avocado, cut lengthwise into 8 thin slices
1	cup mild or medium-spicy salsa

Preheat the oven to 350°F.

Wrap the tortillas in foil. Place in the oven to heat for 10 minutes. Turn the oven off, leaving the tortillas in the oven to stay warm.

Meanwhile, heat the oil in a large nonstick skillet over medium heat. Add the zucchini, bell pepper, and black pepper. Cook the vegetables, stirring often, for 5 minutes, or until tender. Add the corn and cook, stirring often, for 1 minute.

In a medium bowl, combine the eggs, egg whites, and milk.

Reduce the heat to low. Pour the egg mixture into the skillet and scramble gently until the eggs are cooked but still moist.

Evenly divide the eggs, avocado slices, and salsa among the tortillas. Roll up and serve immediately.

Makes 4 servings
Per serving: 255 calories, 13 g protein, 28 g carbohydrates, 11 g fat, 2 g saturated fat, 160 mg cholesterol, 10 g dietary fiber, 774 mg sodium

soups
and stews

A steaming bowl of soup or stew beckons with warmth and goodness. The blending of vegetables, broth, and often meat or fish can deliver a meal's worth of nutrients in one bowl. Soups and stews allow the cook to create low-fat meals flavored with nutritious garlic, ginger, chile peppers, and other aromatics that are chock-full of phytonutrients without any added fat or sodium. So versatile, feel free to substitute your favorite vegetables, herbs, and spices for those listed in the recipes.

Memory Problems
Heart Disease
Diabetes
Depression
Stress/Fatigue
Prostate Problems
High Cholesterol
*Immunity
Problems*
*General Vision
Problems*
Cancer

the
**healing
factor**

🐞🐞🐞 Vitamin C
🐞🐞🐞 Vitamin A
🐞🐞🐞 Chromium
🐞🐞🐞 Potassium
🐞🐞🐞 Vitamin K
🐞🐞 Manganese
🐞🐞 Fiber
🐞🐞 Vitamin B$_6$
🐞🐞 Folate
🐞🐞 Thiamin

cold tomato and cucumber soup

2	pounds tomatoes, peeled and cut into chunks
1	large clove garlic
1	large cucumber, peeled, halved, seeded, and finely chopped
1	cup tomato juice
½	cup finely chopped fresh basil
1	tablespoon extra-virgin olive oil
1	tablespoon red wine vinegar (see note)
½	teaspoon salt
¼	teaspoon freshly ground black pepper

In 2 batches in a food processor, process the tomatoes and garlic until smooth. Place in a bowl.

Add the cucumber, tomato juice, basil, oil, vinegar, salt, and pepper to the bowl. Cover and chill for at least 3 hours, or until very cold and the flavors have blended.

Makes 4 servings
Per serving: 100 calories, 3 g protein, 16 g carbohydrates, 4 g fat, 1 g saturated fat, 0 mg cholesterol, 3 g dietary fiber, 410 mg sodium

HEALTH NOTE
People with depression who take monoamine oxidase inhibitors (MAO inhibitors) should not use alcohol or other fermented products, such as the vinegar in this recipe. Substitute broth for the vinegar.

cold beet borscht

1½	pounds beets, peeled and quartered
3½	cups vegetable broth
1	cup water
2	tablespoons lemon juice
1	tablespoon red wine vinegar
1	small cucumber, peeled and finely chopped
3	tablespoons reduced-fat sour cream
1	tablespoon snipped fresh dill

In a large saucepan or Dutch oven over high heat, combine the beets, broth, and water. Bring to a boil. Reduce the heat to low, cover, and simmer for 30 minutes, or until the beets are very tender.

With a slotted spoon, place the beets in a large bowl and allow to cool to room temperature. Pour the cooking liquid into another large bowl and refrigerate.

Finely chop the cooled beets and add to the cooking liquid. Cover and refrigerate until cold.

Add the lemon juice and vinegar to the soup. Place half of the soup in a blender or food processor and blend or process until smooth. Add to the soup with the cucumber.

Ladle the soup into bowls. In a cup, combine the sour cream and dill. Dollop onto each serving.

Makes 6 servings
Per serving: 67 calories, 5 g protein, 13 g carbohydrates, 1 g fat, 1 g saturated fat, 3 mg cholesterol, 4 g dietary fiber, 484 mg sodium

treat ⸱ helps prevent

Cancer
High Cholesterol
Heart Disease
Diabetes
Memory Problems
Overweight
Osteoporosis
Anemia

the healing factor

🌰🌰🌰 Folate
🌰🌰🌰 Manganese
🌰🌰🌰 Vitamin C
🌰🌰🌰 Vitamin K
🌰🌰🌰 Fiber
🌰🌰🌰 Potassium
🌰 Magnesium
🌰🌰 Iron
🌰🌰 Phosphorus
🌰🌰 Copper

Stroke
Heart Disease
Dental Problems
Breast Cancer
Immunity
Problems
High Cholesterol
General Vision
Problems
Osteoarthritis
Diabetes
Infections

the
healing factor

🍐🍐🍐 Vitamin A
🍐🍐🍐 Vitamin C
🍐🍐 Manganese
🍐🍐 Fiber
🍐🍐 Vitamin B$_6$

curried sweet potato and apple soup

Photograph on page 27

1	tablespoon olive oil
1	large onion, sliced
2	cloves garlic, sliced
1	tablespoon finely chopped fresh ginger
1	teaspoon curry powder
¾	teaspoon ground cumin
½	teaspoon salt
¼	teaspoon ground cinnamon
4	cups water
1¼	pounds sweet potatoes, peeled and cut into chunks
3	large Granny Smith apples, peeled, cored, and cut into chunks
½	cup chopped fresh cilantro

Heat the oil in a large saucepan or Dutch oven over medium heat. Add the onion and garlic and cook, stirring occasionally, for 5 minutes, or until tender.

Add the ginger, curry powder, cumin, salt, and cinnamon. Cook, stirring constantly, for 1 minute. Add the water, sweet potatoes, and apples and bring to a boil over high heat. Reduce the heat to low, cover, and simmer, stirring often, for 20 minutes, or until the sweet potatoes are very tender.

In a food processor or blender, puree the soup in batches until very smooth, pouring each batch into a bowl. Reheat if necessary. Stir in the cilantro.

Makes 8 servings
Per serving: 134 calories, 2 g protein, 29 g carbohydrates, 2 g fat, 0 g saturated fat, 0 mg cholesterol, 4 g dietary fiber, 162 mg sodium

turnip and carrot (quick) soup with parmesan

1	pound white turnips, peeled and cut into chunks
4	large carrots, cut into chunks
2	large red or white new potatoes, peeled and cut into chunks
1	large onion, cut into chunks
5	cloves garlic, sliced
1½	cups chicken broth
1½	cups water
½	teaspoon dried thyme, crushed
½	teaspoon rubbed sage
¼	teaspoon salt
¼	teaspoon freshly ground black pepper
1	cup 1% milk
½	cup (2 ounces) freshly grated Parmesan cheese

In a large saucepan or Dutch oven, combine the turnips, carrots, potatoes, onion, garlic, broth, water, thyme, sage, salt, and pepper. Bring to a boil over high heat. Reduce the heat to medium, cover, and simmer for 20 minutes, or until the vegetables are very tender.

In a food processor or blender, puree the soup in batches until very smooth, pouring each batch into a bowl. When all the soup has been pureed, return it to the pan. Stir in the milk. Cook over low heat just until heated through (do not boil). Remove from the heat and stir in the cheese.

Makes 8 servings
Per serving: 108 calories, 6 g protein, 17 g carbohydrates, 2 g fat, 1 g saturated fat, 6 mg cholesterol, 3 g dietary fiber, 364 mg sodium

treat 〜 helps prevent

Stroke
Aging
Dental Problems
High Blood Pressure
Heart Disease
Immunity Problems
Kidney Stones
Osteoporosis
Breast Cancer
General Vision Problems

the healing factor

🍒🍒🍒 Vitamin A
🍒🍒🍒 Vitamin C
🍒🍒 Calcium
🍒🍒 Potassium
🍒🍒 Manganese
🍒🍒 Vitamin B₆
🍒🍒 Phosphorus
🍒 Fiber

helps
prevent ~ treat

Diabetes
Memory Problems
Stress/Fatigue
Cancer
High Cholesterol
Heart Disease
Dental Problems
General Vision Problems
Macular Degeneration
Depression

the 🌿
healing factor

🐞🐞🐞 Vitamin K
🐞🐞🐞 Vitamin C
🐞🐞🐞 Vitamin A
🐞🐞🐞 Manganese
🐞🐞 Fiber
🐞🐞 Iron
🐞🐞 Magnesium
🐞🐞 Folate
🐞🐞 Potassium
🐞🐞 Thiamin

minestrone verde

2	teaspoons extra-virgin olive oil
2	small leeks, white and green parts, halved lengthwise, rinsed, and thinly sliced
2	large ribs celery with leaves, thinly sliced
2	cloves garlic, minced + 1 whole clove garlic, peeled
1/4	teaspoon dried oregano, crushed
1/4	teaspoon freshly ground black pepper
1/8	teaspoon salt
2	cups water
1	cup chicken broth
4	cups chopped Swiss chard
2/3	cup frozen baby lima beans
1/4	cup ditalini or other small pasta
1/4	cup chopped Italian parsley
1/2	cup frozen green peas
4	teaspoons shredded Parmesan cheese (see note)

Heat the oil in a large saucepan over medium heat. Add the leeks, celery, minced garlic, oregano, pepper, and salt. Cook, stirring frequently, for 4 minutes, or until the vegetables begin to soften.

Add the water, broth, Swiss chard, lima beans, and pasta. Bring to a boil over high heat. Reduce the heat to medium-low, cover, and simmer for 8 minutes, or until the vegetables are tender and the pasta is al dente.

Meanwhile, coarsely chop the remaining garlic clove, then mince it together with the parsley. Stir the garlic-parsley mixture and the peas into the soup. Cover and cook for 5 minutes, or until the peas are heated through.

Ladle the soup into 4 bowls and top each with 1 teaspoon of the cheese.

Makes 4 servings
Per serving: 145 calories, 6 g protein, 24 g carbohydrates, 3 g fat, 1 g saturated fat, 1 mg cholesterol, 5 g dietary fiber, 413 mg sodium

HEALTH NOTE
People with depression who take monoamine oxidase inhibitors (MAO inhibitors) should not use alcohol or other fermented or aged products, such as the cheese in this recipe.

Memory Problems

Depression

Dental Problems

Diabetes

Osteoporosis

Stress/Fatigue

Immunity
Problems

General Vision
Problems

Heart Disease

the healing factor

🌿🌿🌿 Vitamin A

🌿🌿🌿 Vitamin K

🌿🌿🌿 Manganese

🌿🌿🌿 Omega-3
fatty acids

🌿🌿🌿 Vitamin C

🌿🌿🌿 Fiber

🌿🌿🌿 Thiamin

🌿🌿🌿 Niacin

🌿🌿🌿 Phosphorus

🌿🌿 Magnesium

gingery vegetable broth with tofu and noodles

Photograph on page 55

1	tablespoon canola oil
8	ounces cremini mushrooms, finely chopped
2	large carrots, finely chopped
2	ribs celery, finely chopped
1	medium onion, finely chopped
6	large cloves garlic, minced
2	tablespoons finely chopped fresh ginger
3	tablespoons dry sherry (see note)
4	cups low-sodium vegetable broth
¼	teaspoon salt
1	cup snow peas, cut into julienne strips
4	ounces thin soba noodles, broken in half
8	ounces baked smoked tofu, cut into ¼" cubes
4	scallions, thinly sliced on the diagonal

Heat the oil in a large saucepan or Dutch oven over medium-high heat. Add the mushrooms, carrots, celery, onion, garlic, and ginger and cook, stirring often, for 10 minutes, or until the vegetables are lightly browned.

Add the sherry and cook for 1 minute, stirring to loosen browned bits from the pan. Add the broth and salt and bring to a boil over high heat. Reduce the heat to low, cover, and simmer for 45 minutes, adding the snow peas during the last 3 minutes.

Meanwhile, prepare the soba noodles according to package directions. Drain and set aside.

Stir the tofu, soba noodles, and scallions into the broth and simmer for 3 minutes, or until heated through.

Makes 4 servings
Per serving: 297 calories, 17 g protein, 40 g carbohydrates, 8 g fat, 2 g saturated fat, 5 mg cholesterol, 6 g dietary fiber, 575 mg sodium

HEALTH NOTE
People with depression who take monoamine oxidase inhibitors (MAO inhibitors) should not use alcohol or other fermented products, such as the sherry in this recipe. Substitute broth for the sherry.

Memory Problems
Cancer
Heart Disease
Dental Problems
Depression
Diabetes
Insomnia
Stress/Fatigue
General Vision
Problems

the
healing factor

🍎🍎🍎 Vitamin K
🍎🍎🍎 Vitamin C
🍎🍎🍎 Fiber
🍎🍎 Vitamin A
🍎🍎 Omega-3
     fatty acids
🍎🍎 Iron
🍎🍎 Folate
🍎🍎 Magnesium
🍎🍎 Phosphorus
🍎🍎 Niacin

pasta e fagiole

Photograph on page 57

2	teaspoons olive oil
2	onions, chopped
2	cloves garlic, chopped
4	cups low-sodium chicken broth
1	can (15 ounces) diced tomatoes
2	cans (14–19 ounces each) cannellini or white beans, rinsed and drained
½	cup ditalini or other small pasta
4	cups chopped Swiss chard or spinach

Heat the oil in a large saucepan over medium heat. Add the onions and garlic and cook, stirring occasionally, for 5 minutes, or until the onions are soft.

Add the broth, tomatoes (with juice), beans, and pasta and cook, stirring occasionally, for 15 minutes, or until the pasta is al dente. Add the Swiss chard or spinach and cook, stirring occasionally, for 3 minutes, or until the chard or spinach is wilted.

Makes 6 servings
Per serving: 186 calories, 11 g protein, 30 g carbohydrates, 3 g fat, 1 g saturated fat, 3 mg cholesterol, 5 g dietary fiber, 584 mg sodium

stracciatelle with (quick) escarole and chickpeas

1	tablespoon extra-virgin olive oil
5	cloves garlic, minced
2	large carrots, shredded
1	medium head escarole, shredded
1/8	teaspoon freshly ground black pepper
4	cups low-sodium chicken broth
2¾	cups water
1	bunch broccoli, cut into small florets
1	can (14–19 ounces) chickpeas, rinsed and drained
2	eggs
1/3	cup (1½ ounces) freshly grated Parmesan cheese

Heat the oil in a large saucepan or Dutch oven over medium-high heat. Add the garlic and carrots and cook, stirring constantly, for 3 minutes, or until tender.

Add half of the escarole; cook, stirring, for 2 minutes, or until the escarole is wilted. Add the remaining escarole and the pepper; cook, stirring, for 2 minutes, or until wilted.

Add the broth, 2½ cups of the water, the broccoli, and chickpeas. Bring to a boil over high heat. Reduce the heat to low, cover, and simmer for 8 minutes, or until the broccoli is tender.

In a small bowl, using a fork, stir together the eggs, cheese, and the remaining ¼ cup water. Slowly pour into the soup and stir briskly with the fork to create fine threads.

Makes 4 servings
Per serving: 318 calories, 19 g protein, 37 g carbohydrates, 13 g fat, 4 g saturated fat, 118 mg cholesterol, 11 g dietary fiber, 534 mg sodium

treat ∫ helps prevent

Aging
Cancer
Dental Problems
Memory Problems
Osteoporosis
Cataracts
Stress/Fatigue
General Vision Problems
Menopausal Problems/Hot Flashes

the healing factor

🌶🌶🌶 Vitamin K
🌶🌶🌶 Vitamin A
🌶🌶🌶 Vitamin C
🌶🌶🌶 Folate
🌶🌶🌶 Fiber
🌶🌶🌶 Manganese
🌶🌶🌶 Phosphorus
🌶🌶 Calcium
🌶🌶🌶 Riboflavin
🌶🌶 Iron

Memory Problems
Cancer
Dental Problems
Osteoporosis
Anemia
Diabetes
Constipation
Diverticulosis
Overweight

the
healing factor

🐞🐞🐞 Vitamin A

🐞🐞🐞 Fiber

🐞🐞🐞 Folate

🐞🐞🐞 Manganese

🐞🐞🐞 Iron

🐞🐞🐞 Phosphorus

🐞🐞🐞 Copper

🐞🐞🐞 Vitamin C

🐞🐞🐞 Vitamin K

🐞🐞🐞 Thiamin

greek-style lentil soup

1	pound brown lentils, picked over and rinsed
9	cups water
6	cloves garlic, minced
3	large carrots, cut into ¼" pieces
2	large onions, chopped
1	teaspoon dried thyme, crushed
1	teaspoon freshly ground black pepper
½	teaspoon dried rosemary, crushed
1½	cups tomato puree
1	teaspoon salt
¼	teaspoon ground cinnamon
2	tablespoons extra-virgin olive oil
1	tablespoon red wine vinegar
3	tablespoons coarsely chopped fresh marjoram or oregano (optional)

In a large saucepan or Dutch oven, combine the lentils, water, garlic, carrots, onions, thyme, pepper, and rosemary. Bring to a boil over high heat. Reduce the heat to low, cover, and simmer, stirring occasionally, for 35 minutes, or until the lentils are tender. Stir in the tomato puree, salt, and cinnamon, and simmer for 20 minutes to blend the flavors.

Remove from the heat and stir in the oil, vinegar, and marjoram or oregano, if using.

Makes 6 servings
Per serving: 351 calories, 23 g protein, 55 g carbohydrates, 5 g fat, 1 g saturated fat, 0 mg cholesterol, 26 g dietary fiber, 434 mg sodium

black bean soup (quick)

2	cans (14–19 ounces each) black beans, rinsed and drained
1¾	cups low-sodium chicken broth
1	cup water
1	teaspoon ground cumin
¼	teaspoon dried oregano, crushed
¼	teaspoon freshly ground black pepper
	Large pinch of ground red pepper
1	teaspoon olive oil
½	large red bell pepper, slivered
½	large green bell pepper, slivered
½	teaspoon grated lemon peel

In a large saucepan, combine the beans, broth, water, cumin, oregano, black pepper, and ground red pepper. Bring to a boil over high heat. Reduce the heat to low, cover, and simmer, stirring once or twice, for 15 minutes, or until the flavors are blended.

Meanwhile, heat the oil in a small nonstick skillet over medium heat. Add the bell peppers and cook, stirring frequently, for 4 minutes, or until tender.

Ladle half of the soup into a food processor or blender. Process or blend until pureed. Return the puree to the pan; add the lemon peel.

Ladle the soup into bowls and top each serving with the bell peppers.

Makes 4 servings
Per serving: 188 calories, 13 g protein, 39 g carbohydrates, 2 g fat, 1 g saturated fat, 2 mg cholesterol, 14 g dietary fiber, 616 mg sodium

treat ~ **helps prevent**

Dental Problems
Cancer
Diabetes
Kidney Stones
Breast Cancer
High Cholesterol
Heart Disease
Overweight

the
healing factor

🍐🍐🍐 Vitamin C
🍐🍐🍐 Fiber
🍐🍐🍐 Potassium
🍐🍐🍐 Vitamin A
🍐🍐 Calcium

COOKING TIP
To make this soup with dried beans, place 1 pound of beans in a large pot with cold water to cover and let sit overnight. Drain, cover with fresh water, and simmer for 1¼ hours, or until tender. You'll have enough for this recipe, plus leftovers for other dishes.

seven-bean soup with greens

⅓	cup black beans
⅓	cup red kidney beans
⅓	cup appaloosa or small red beans
⅓	cup cranberry or pinto beans
⅓	cup great Northern or navy beans
⅓	cup Steuben yellow-eye beans or black-eyed peas
3	tablespoons extra-virgin olive oil
10	cloves garlic, minced
2	large onions, coarsely chopped
2	ribs celery, sliced
2	teaspoons dried Italian herb seasoning, crushed
¾	teaspoon freshly ground black pepper
⅓	cup green or yellow split peas
6	cups water
2	cans (28 ounces each) crushed tomatoes in tomato puree
¼	cup tomato paste
2	packages (10 ounces each) frozen chopped greens, such as collard, turnip, or kale
½	teaspoon salt
1½	cups chopped fresh basil

Pick over and rinse all the beans. Place in a large saucepot and cover with 3" of water. Cover and let stand overnight. Drain.

Rinse and dry the pot. Heat the oil in the pot over medium-high heat. Add the garlic, onions, and celery and cook, stirring frequently, for 5 minutes, or until soft. Add the Italian seasoning and pepper and cook, stirring, for 30 seconds.

Add the beans, split peas, and water. Bring to a boil over high heat. Reduce the heat to medium-low, cover, and simmer, stirring occasionally, for 1½ hours, or until the beans are tender. (The black beans will take the longest to cook, so use them as a guide.)

Add the tomatoes, tomato paste, greens, and salt. Bring to a boil over high heat. Reduce the heat to medium-low, cover, and simmer, stirring occasionally, for 30 minutes longer, or until the greens are tender. Stir in the basil.

Makes 8 servings
Per serving: 349 calories, 19 g protein, 56 g carbohydrates, 6 g fat, 1 g saturated fat, 0 mg cholesterol, 18 g dietary fiber, 688 mg sodium

the power of
TOMATOES The press has had a field day with the latest studies on tomatoes and their healing powers, and the news has been great! Tomatoes contain two antioxidants (compounds that fight free radicals—molecules that contribute to the breakdown of healthy cells, leading to everything from wrinkles to heart disease), lycopene and vitamin C, which protect against heart disease and cancers of the prostate and lungs. Lycopene is most available in processed tomato products such as tomato paste and spaghetti sauce. If using fresh, select ripe red tomatoes, not pale ones. To make the lycopene in fresh tomatoes more absorbable, cook them in a little oil.

Depression

Immunity
Problems

Memory Problems

Stress/Fatigue

Asthma

Cancer

Diabetes

Insomnia

Overweight

Irritable Bowel
Syndrome

the healing factor

🍄🍄🍄 Vitamin A

🍄🍄🍄 Fiber

🍄🍄🍄 Manganese

🍄🍄🍄 Selenium

🍄🍄🍄 Copper

🍄🍄 Niacin

🍄🍄 Vitamin B₆

🍄🍄 Pantothenic acid

🍄🍄 Vitamin C

🍄🍄 Phosphorus

mushroom-barley soup

Photograph on page 41

1	ounce dried mushrooms
3	cups boiling water
4	carrots, chopped
2	large onions, chopped
2	ribs celery, chopped
12	ounces cremini or button mushrooms, stems removed, sliced
1½	teaspoons dried oregano, crushed
5	cups chicken broth
1	cup barley
¼	teaspoon salt

Place the dried mushrooms in a small bowl and cover with the water. Let stand for 15 minutes.

Meanwhile, coat a large saucepan or Dutch oven with cooking spray. Add the carrots, onions, and celery. Coat lightly with cooking spray and set over medium heat. Cook, stirring occasionally, for 3 minutes. Add the sliced mushrooms and oregano. Cook, stirring occasionally, for 6 minutes, or until the vegetables are soft. Add the broth, barley, and salt. Cook for 10 minutes.

Line a sieve with a coffee filter or paper towel. Strain the dried mushroom water into the pot. Remove and discard the filter or paper towel. Rinse the dried mushrooms under running water to remove any grit. Chop and add to the pot.

Cook for 20 minutes, or until the barley is tender.

Makes 6 servings
Per serving: 185 calories, 8 g protein, 39 g carbohydrates, 1 g fat, 0 g saturated fat, 0 mg cholesterol, 9 g dietary fiber, 628 mg sodium

tortilla soup with lime

treat

helps
prevent

Heart Disease
Memory Problems
Stress/Fatigue
Aging
Cancer
Dental Problems
Immunity Problems
General Vision Problems

4	corn tortillas (6" diameter), halved and cut into ¼"-wide strips
2¼	cups chicken broth
1¼	cups water
12	ounces thinly sliced turkey breast cutlets, cut into ½"-thick strips
2	large onions, halved and thinly sliced
2	large red bell peppers, cut into thin strips
1	large jalapeño chile pepper, seeded and minced
2	teaspoons ground cumin
¼	teaspoon dried oregano, crushed
½	cup frozen corn kernels
½	cup quartered cherry tomatoes
¼	cup chopped fresh cilantro
2	tablespoons lime juice
½	ripe avocado, diced

the
healing factor

- 🐦🐦🐦 Vitamin C
- 🐦🐦🐦 Vitamin A
- 🐦🐦🐦 Vitamin B$_6$
- 🐦🐦🐦 Niacin
- 🐦🐦🐦 Phosphorus
- 🐦🐦🐦 Fiber
- 🐦🐦🐦 Potassium
- 🐦🐦🐦 Folate
- 🐦🐦 Manganese
- 🐦🐦 Magnesium

Preheat the oven to 400°F. Coat 1 or 2 large baking sheets with cooking spray.

Arrange the tortilla strips on the prepared baking sheets and bake for 2 minutes, or until crisped and lightly browned on the edges.

In a large saucepan, combine the broth, water, turkey, onions, bell peppers, chile pepper, cumin, and oregano. Bring to a boil over high heat. Reduce the heat to medium-low, cover, and simmer for 10 minutes.

Add the corn and simmer for 5 minutes. Stir in the tomatoes, cilantro, and lime juice. Ladle the soup into bowls and top each portion with avocado and tortilla crisps.

Makes 4 servings
Per serving: 258 calories, 25 g protein, 29 g carbohydrates, 6 g fat, 1 g saturated fat, 53 mg cholesterol, 6 g dietary fiber, 419 mg sodium

helps
prevent ↘
treat

Diabetes
Cancer
High Cholesterol
Heart Disease
Dental Problems
Depression
Memory Problems
Stress/Fatigue
General Vision Problems

the
healing factor

🍐🍐🍐 Vitamin A
🍐🍐🍐 Fiber
🍐🍐🍐 Vitamin C
🍐🍐🍐 Manganese
🍐🍐🍐 Folate
🍐🍐🍐 Thiamin
🍐🍐🍐 Potassium
🍐🍐🍐 Copper
🍐🍐🍐 Magnesium
🍐🍐🍐 Phosphorus

split pea soup with ham and winter squash

1	smoked ham hock (12 ounces)
11	cups water
4	cloves garlic, minced
1	teaspoon dried thyme, crushed
½	teaspoon dried sage, crushed
½	teaspoon freshly ground black pepper
1	pound green split peas, picked over and rinsed
1	medium butternut squash (2 pounds), peeled and cut into ½" chunks
1	pound white potatoes, scrubbed and cut into ½" chunks
3	large carrots, cut into ½" chunks
3	ribs celery, sliced
2	large onions, coarsely chopped
¾	teaspoon salt

In a large saucepot or Dutch oven, combine the ham hock, water, garlic, thyme, sage, and pepper. Bring to a boil over high heat. Reduce the heat to low, cover, and simmer, turning the ham hock once, for 1 hour. Cool. Refrigerate for at least 4 hours or overnight.

After the broth has chilled, skim and discard the fat from the surface. Remove the ham hock and cut the meat off the bone; set aside. Discard the bone and any fat.

Add the split peas to the broth and bring to a boil over high heat. Skim off any foam that rises to the surface. Reduce the heat to low, cover, and simmer, stirring occasionally, for 1 hour, or until the peas are soft and tender.

Add the squash, potatoes, carrots, celery, onions, salt, and ham. Return to a boil. Cover and simmer, stirring occasionally, for 20 to 25 minutes, or until the vegetables are tender.

Makes 8 servings
Per serving: 350 calories, 20 g protein, 64 g carbohydrates, 3 g fat, 1 g saturated fat, 7 mg cholesterol, 19 g dietary fiber, 464 mg sodium

Stress/Fatigue
Memory Problems
Depression
Diabetes
Aging
Dental Problems
Osteoporosis

the
**healing
factor**

🌰🌰🌰 Vitamin A
🌰🌰🌰 Vitamin C
🌰🌰🌰 Vitamin K
🌰🌰🌰 Chromium
🌰🌰🌰 Potassium
🌰🌰🌰 Thiamin
🌰🌰🌰 Manganese
🌰🌰🌰 Fiber
🌰🌰🌰 Vitamin B₆
🌰🌰🌰 Niacin

country-style potato and green bean soup with ham

3	cloves garlic, minced
2	very large or 3 medium russet potatoes, quartered lengthwise and sliced ¼" thick
1	large onion, chopped
4	ounces coarsely cubed ham
1½	cups chicken broth
1½	cups water
1	teaspoon dried marjoram, crushed
¼	teaspoon freshly ground black pepper
12	ounces green beans, halved
3	carrots, sliced
½	cup (4 ounces) reduced-fat sour cream

In a large saucepot or Dutch oven, combine the garlic, potatoes, onion, ham, broth, water, marjoram, and pepper. Bring to a boil over high heat. Reduce the heat to low, cover, and simmer, stirring occasionally, for 15 minutes, or until the potatoes are very tender.

Using a potato masher, mash the potatoes slightly, breaking them up to give the soup a chunky (not smooth) texture.

Add the green beans and carrots, cover, and cook, stirring occasionally, for 10 minutes, or until tender. Add the sour cream and bring to a simmer, stirring constantly, until the soup is slightly thickened and creamy.

Makes 4 servings

Per serving: 288 calories, 13 g protein, 41 g carbohydrates, 9 g fat, 4 g saturated fat, 26 mg cholesterol, 8 g dietary fiber, 645 mg sodium

COOKING TIPS

Cut the ham from a well-trimmed ham steak instead of a deli slice. It will be more moist and flavorful, and you can freeze any remainder for another meal.

You can also make this soup without the ham or substitute smoked turkey or chunks of smoked salmon, but add the salmon at the end of the cooking time.

root vegetable soup

Memory Problems
Heart Disease
Stress/Fatigue
Cancer
Dental Problems
Diabetes
General Vision
Problems

the 🌿
**healing
factor**

🍇🍇🍇 Vitamin A
🍇🍇🍇 Vitamin C
🍇🍇🍇 Manganese
🍇🍇🍇 Vitamin B$_{12}$
🍇🍇🍇 Vitamin B$_6$
🍇🍇 Fiber
🍇🍇 Potassium
🍇🍇 Folate
🍇🍇 Phosphorus
🍇🍇 Niacin

1	tablespoon olive oil
6	cloves garlic, minced
2	large onions, chopped
½	teaspoon dried marjoram, crushed
½	teaspoon dried sage, crushed
¼	teaspoon salt
½	teaspoon freshly ground black pepper
1	pound lean, well-trimmed beef round, cut into 1" cubes
3	cups low-sodium beef broth
3	cups water
1	can (28 ounces) whole tomatoes, drained and broken up
4	small turnips, peeled and cut into ½" chunks
3	medium beets, peeled and cut into ½" chunks
3	large carrots, cut into ½" chunks
2	medium parsnips, peeled and cut into ½" chunks

Heat the oil in a large saucepan over medium heat. Add the garlic and onions and cook, stirring, for 5 minutes, or until soft. Add the marjoram, sage, salt, and pepper. Add the beef and cook, stirring, for 5 minutes, or until browned.

Add the broth, water, and tomatoes. Bring to a boil over high heat. Reduce the heat to low, cover, and simmer, stirring occasionally, for 45 minutes, or until the beef is very tender.

Add the turnips, beets, carrots, and parsnips. Return to a simmer. Cover and cook, stirring occasionally, for 25 minutes longer, or until the vegetables are very tender.

Makes 6 servings
Per serving: 311 calories, 24 g protein, 36 g carbohydrates, 7 g fat,
2 g saturated fat, 36 mg cholesterol, 9 g dietary fiber, 583 mg sodium

Not Your Mother's Chicken Soup

The hot water vapor that you inhale when you eat chicken soup does much to help clear your sinuses when you have a cold. The added splash of hot-pepper sauce gives this soup an extra punch of sinus-clearing benefits.

4   whole bone-in chicken legs
4   cups chicken broth
2   cups water
5   cloves garlic, minced
2   tablespoons finely chopped fresh ginger
1/4   teaspoon freshly ground black pepper
3   carrots, sliced
1   large leek, white part and some of the green, rinsed and cut into 1/2" slices
1   large sweet potato (12 ounces), peeled and cut into large chunks
6   cups packed torn spinach
1   large tomato, cut into 1/2" chunks
1/4–1   teaspoon hot-pepper sauce

Divide the chicken legs into thigh and drumstick portions. Remove and discard the skin and any visible fat.

Place the chicken in a large saucepot or Dutch oven. Add the broth, water, garlic, ginger, and pepper. Bring to a boil over high heat. Skim off any foam that rises to the surface. Reduce the heat to low, cover, and simmer for 15 minutes, skimming the surface occasionally.

Stir in the carrots, leek, and sweet potato. Cover and simmer for 20 minutes, or until the vegetables are tender and the chicken is cooked through.

Add the spinach and tomato and cook for 5 minutes, or until the spinach is wilted and the tomato is heated through. Add the hot-pepper sauce to taste.

Makes 4 servings
Per serving: 320 calories, 30 g protein, 39 g carbohydrates, 5 g fat, 1 g saturated fat, 91 mg cholesterol, 11 g dietary fiber, 525 mg sodium

Cancer
Heart Disease
Memory Problems
Depression
Asthma
Diabetes
General Vision
Problems
Breast Cancer
Ulcers

the ❧
healing factor

🍃🍃🍃 Vitamin K

🍃🍃🍃 Fiber

🍃🍃🍃 Folate

🍃🍃🍃 Selenium

🍃🍃🍃 Omega-3
fatty acids

🍃🍃🍃 Manganese

🍃🍃🍃 Phosphorus

🍃🍃🍃 Vitamin C

🍃🍃🍃 Thiamin

🍃🍃🍃 Magnesium

creamy white bean soup with cabbage and salmon

Photograph on page 38

1	cup navy beans, picked over, rinsed, and soaked overnight
2½	cups water
2	cups chicken broth
6	cloves garlic, minced
1	bay leaf
2	tablespoons extra-virgin olive oil
½	head cabbage, coarsely chopped
1	large onion, chopped
½	pound skinned salmon fillet, cut into 1" chunks
2	ounces (2 thick slices) Canadian bacon, coarsely chopped
1	tablespoon chopped fresh thyme

In a large saucepan or Dutch oven, combine the beans, water, broth, garlic, and bay leaf. Bring to a boil over high heat. Reduce the heat to low, cover, and simmer, stirring occasionally, for 50 minutes, or until the beans are very tender. Remove and discard the bay leaf.

In a food processor or blender, puree the soup in batches until smooth. Return the soup to the pot and bring to a boil over medium heat. Cover to keep warm.

Meanwhile, heat 1 tablespoon of the oil in a large nonstick skillet over high heat. Add the cabbage and onion. Cook, stirring frequently, for 6 minutes, or until lightly browned and tender. Add to the soup.

In the same skillet, heat the remaining 1 tablespoon oil over medium heat. Add the salmon and bacon. Sprinkle with the thyme. Cook, stirring gently, for 3 minutes, or until the salmon is lightly browned and just opaque.

Gently stir the salmon mixture into the soup.

Makes 4 servings
Per serving: 340 calories, 27 g protein, 37 g carbohydrates, 10 g fat, 2 g saturated fat, 37 mg cholesterol, 14 g dietary fiber, 536 mg sodium

helps
prevent~

Depression

Aging

*Immunity
Problems*

Memory Problems

*General Vision
Problems*

PMS

treats

the *✿*
healing
factor

🐾🐾 Vitamin D

🐾🐾 Selenium

🐾🐾 Vitamin C

🐾🐾 Omega-3
fatty acids

🐾🐾 Phosphorus

🐾🐾 Potassium

🐾🐾 Vitamin A

🐾🐾 Vitamin B$_{12}$

🐾🐾 Niacin

🐾🐾 Magnesium

neptune's bounty
bouillabaisse

1	teaspoon olive oil
2	cloves garlic, minced
1	medium bulb fennel, white part only, cut into ¼"-thick slices
1	large onion, chopped
12	ounces small red potatoes, cut into ½" cubes
2	cups crushed tomatoes
1	jar (6½ ounces) clam juice
1	cup water
1	cup canned light coconut milk
½	teaspoon crushed saffron threads (optional)
¼	teaspoon salt
¼	teaspoon freshly ground black pepper
8	ounces halibut fillets, cut into 2" cubes
8	ounces sea scallops
8	ounces large shrimp, peeled and deveined
12	mussels, scrubbed and beards removed
½	teaspoon hot-pepper sauce (optional)

Heat the oil in a large saucepot or Dutch oven over medium heat. Add the garlic, fennel, and onion and cook, stirring often, for 7 minutes, or until the fennel is soft and tender. Add the potatoes, tomatoes, clam juice, water, coconut milk, saffron (if using), salt, and pepper. Cook for 15 minutes, or until the potatoes are just tender.

Add the halibut, scallops, shrimp, mussels, and hot-pepper sauce, if using. Reduce the heat to low, cover, and simmer for 5 minutes, or until the mussels have opened and the halibut and shrimp are opaque. (Discard any mussels that remain closed after 5 minutes of cooking time.)

Makes 4 servings
Per serving: 372 calories, 41 g protein, 33 g carbohydrates, 8 g fat,
1 g saturated fat, 6 g dietary fiber, 135 mg cholesterol, 883 mg sodium

COOKING TIPS

Shrimp, scallops, halibut, and mussels provide a healthy dose of omega-3 fatty acids in this elegant yet easy seafood soup. Mussels need to be cleaned thoroughly before cooking. Soak for about an hour in a mixture of salted water and cornmeal to rid them of any excess sand. Throw out any that are open before soaking.

The tomato-based broth is accented with tropical-tasting reduced-fat coconut milk. Canned light coconut milk can be found in the international aisle of most supermarkets and at Asian grocery stores. It's lower in fat than regular coconut milk and coconut cream.

Aging
Heart Disease
Diabetes
Stress/Fatigue
Cancer
Depression
Infections
Immunity
Problems
General Vision
Problems

the
healing
factor

🍒🍒 Vitamin C
🍒🍒 Vitamin A
🍒🍒 Potassium
🍒🍒 Iron
🍒 Fiber
🍒 Vitamin B₆
🍒 Manganese
🍒 Chromium
🍒 Vitamin K
🍒 Folate

manhattan clam chowder

2	teaspoons olive oil
2	ribs celery with leaves, chopped
2	carrots, chopped
1	onion, finely chopped
1	small clove garlic, minced
1	large potato, peeled and diced
1	green bell pepper, chopped
1	red bell pepper, chopped
¾	cup bottled clam juice
2	cans (6½ ounces each) chopped clams, drained with juice reserved
2½	cups reduced-sodium stewed tomatoes
1	teaspoon dried thyme, crushed
¼	teaspoon freshly ground black pepper
2–3	drops hot-pepper sauce

Heat the oil in a large saucepan or Dutch oven over medium heat. Add the celery, carrots, onion, and garlic, and cook, stirring, for 5 minutes, or until the onion is tender.

Add the potato, bell peppers, bottled clam juice, and the reserved clam juice. Bring to a boil. Reduce the heat to low, cover, and simmer, stirring, for 10 minutes, or until the potato is tender.

Add the tomatoes (with juice), thyme, black pepper, hot-pepper sauce, and the reserved clams. Bring to a simmer. Cover and simmer for 8 minutes, or until the flavors are blended.

Makes 4 servings
Per serving: 138 calories, 10 g protein, 20 g carbohydrates, 3 g fat, 1 g saturated fat, 17 mg cholesterol, 4 g dietary fiber, 754 mg sodium

salads and sandwiches

A bowl of leafy greens and crisp vegetables is one of life's finest and simplest pleasures. So are slices of meat, cheese, and vegetables nestled between two slabs of bread. Salads and sandwiches are most often eaten for lunch because they are fast and easy—but don't limit them to just the midday meal. Both can be a powerhouse of nutrients when vegetables are the main focus. Try the many lettuces and greens available and experiment with vegetable combinations. Creativity with ingredients at mealtime keeps healthy eating exciting.

Diabetes
Memory Problems
Cancer
Aging
Dental Problems
Immunity Problems
Stress/Fatigue
General Vision Problems
Prostate Problems
Leg Cramps

the healing factor

🍶🍶🍶 Vitamin C
🍶🍶🍶 Vitamin A
🍶🍶 Folate
🍶🍶 Vitamin K
🍶🍶 Potassium
🍶🍶 Manganese
🍶🍶 Fiber
🍶🍶 Magnesium
🍶🍶 Omega-3 fatty acids
🍶🍶 Vitamin B$_6$

cool greens and tomatoes with creamy dill dressing

quick

2	tablespoons reduced-fat mayonnaise
2	tablespoons buttermilk
2	tablespoons minced fresh dill
2	teaspoons lemon juice
2	teaspoons coarse Dijon mustard
1/8	teaspoon salt
1/8	teaspoon freshly ground black pepper
1	package (5 ounces) mesclun leaves or baby greens
2	cups mixed red and yellow cherry tomatoes, halved
1	medium cucumber, peeled, halved, seeded, and thinly sliced
1/2	ripe avocado, cut into 1/4" chunks
1/2	small red onion, chopped

In a large serving bowl, combine the mayonnaise, buttermilk, dill, lemon juice, mustard, salt, and pepper.

Add the greens, tomatoes, cucumber, avocado, and onion and toss to coat well.

Makes 4 servings
Per serving: 103 calories, 3 g protein, 10 g carbohydrates, 7 g fat, 1 g saturated fat, 0 mg cholesterol, 3 g dietary fiber, 184 mg sodium

strawberry (quick) and red onion salad

3	tablespoons strawberry all-fruit spread
2	teaspoons balsamic vinegar
1	teaspoon olive oil
1	teaspoon flaxseed oil
1/8	teaspoon salt
1/8	teaspoon crushed red-pepper flakes
1	pound fresh strawberries, hulled and sliced
1/4	cantaloupe, cut into 1/4" chunks
1/2	small red bell pepper, finely chopped
1/2	small red onion, finely chopped
1	medium head escarole, torn (about 3 cups)
1/2	ripe avocado, cut into 1/4" chunks
	Freshly ground black pepper

In a medium glass bowl, combine the all-fruit spread, vinegar, olive oil, flaxseed oil, salt, and red-pepper flakes until well-blended. Gently fold in the strawberries, cantaloupe, bell pepper, and onion. Cover and let stand for 15 minutes to allow the flavors to blend.

Place the escarole in a serving bowl. Add the avocado and strawberry mixture and toss to coat well. Season with black pepper to taste.

Makes 4 servings
Per serving: 163 calories, 2 g protein, 27 g carbohydrates, 7 g fat, 1 g saturated fat, 0 mg cholesterol, 6 g dietary fiber, 110 mg sodium

treat ⸽ helps prevent

Memory Problems
Stress/Fatigue
Aging
Cataracts
Cancer
High Cholesterol
Diabetes
Infections
Osteoarthritis

the healing factor

🍐🍐🍐 Vitamin C
🍐🍐🍐 Vitamin K
🍐🍐🍐 Vitamin A
🍐🍐🍐 Manganese
🍐🍐🍐 Folate
🍐🍐🍐 Fiber
🍐🍐 Potassium
🍐🍐 Omega-3 fatty acids
🍐🍐 Vitamin B$_6$
🍐🍐 Riboflavin

Memory Problems
Heart Disease
Aging
Diabetes
Cataracts
High Cholesterol
Cancer
Immunity
Problems
Asthma

asian slaw (quick)

Photograph on page 35

¼	cup rice wine vinegar or white wine vinegar
2	tablespoons soy sauce
1	tablespoon grated fresh ginger
2	teaspoons toasted sesame oil
½	head napa or savoy cabbage, shredded
3	scallions, sliced
2	carrots, shredded
½	red bell pepper, cut into thin strips
2	tablespoons chopped fresh cilantro
2	teaspoons sesame seeds, toasted (optional)

In a large bowl, combine the vinegar, soy sauce, ginger, and oil. Add the cabbage, scallions, carrots, pepper, and cilantro. Toss to coat well. Sprinkle with the sesame seeds, if using. Let stand for at least 15 minutes to allow the flavors to blend.

Makes 4 servings
Per serving: 106 calories, 4 g protein, 14 g carbohydrates, 3 g fat, 0 g saturated fat, 0 mg cholesterol, 5 g dietary fiber, 561 mg sodium

the healing factor

- 🍐🍐🍐 Vitamin A
- 🍐🍐🍐 Vitamin C
- 🍐🍐🍐 Vitamin K
- 🍐🍐🍐 Folate
- 🍐🍐🍐 Fiber
- 🍐🍐 Manganese
- 🍐🍐 Vitamin B$_6$
- 🍐🍐 Potassium
- 🍐🍐 Magnesium
- 🍐🍐 Vitamin E

mediterranean chickpea salad
(quick)

Photograph on page 45

1	can (15 ounces) chickpeas, rinsed and drained
3	plum tomatoes, chopped
2	roasted red peppers, chopped
½	small red onion, quartered and thinly sliced
½	cucumber, peeled, halved, seeded, and chopped
2	tablespoons chopped parsley
2	cloves garlic, chopped
3	tablespoons lemon juice
1½	teaspoons extra-virgin olive oil
1½	teaspoons flaxseed oil
¼	teaspoon salt

In a large bowl, combine the chickpeas, tomatoes, peppers, onion, cucumber, parsley, garlic, lemon juice, olive oil, flaxseed oil, and salt. Toss to coat well. Let stand for at least 15 minutes to allow the flavors to blend.

Makes 8 servings
Per serving: 104 calories, 4 g protein, 18 g carbohydrates, 3 g fat, 0 g saturated fat, 0 mg cholesterol, 4 g dietary fiber, 158 mg sodium

treat ⸗ helps prevent

Cancer
Heart Disease
Dental Problems
Memory Problems
Cataracts
General Vision Problems
Diabetes
High Cholesterol
Overweight

the healing factor

🌱🌱🌱 Vitamin C
🌱🌱🌱 Vitamin A
🌱🌱 Fiber
🌱🌱 Vitamin K
🌱🌱 Folate

helps
prevent

Aging

Stress/Fatigue

Depression

Immunity Problems

Stroke

Memory Problems

Osteoporosis

General Vision Problems

treat

the healing factor

🍒🍒🍒 Selenium

🍒🍒🍒 Niacin

🍒🍒🍒 Vitamin B_6

🍒🍒🍒 Phosphorus

🍒🍒🍒 Manganese

🍒🍒 Potassium

🍒🍒 Vitamin A

🍒🍒 Zinc

🍒🍒 Thiamin

🍒🍒 Iron

fruited turkey salad (quick)

Photograph on page 46

½	cup (4 ounces) fat-free sour cream
¼	cup low-fat mayonnaise
2	teaspoons chopped fresh thyme or 1 teaspoon dried, crushed
2	teaspoons lemon juice
½	teaspoon grated lemon peel
1	pound cooked skinless turkey breasts, cut into ½" cubes
2	ribs celery, chopped
1	apple, cut into ½" cubes
⅓	cup dried apricots, sliced
¼	cup toasted coarsely chopped walnuts

In a large bowl, combine the sour cream, mayonnaise, thyme, lemon juice, and lemon peel. Add the turkey, celery, apple, and apricots. Toss gently to coat. Sprinkle with the walnuts.

Makes 4 servings
Per serving: 322 calories, 38 g protein, 19 g carbohydrates, 10 g fat, 1 g saturated fat, 94 mg cholesterol, 2 g dietary fiber, 201 mg sodium

barley vegetable salad

Bring 1½ cups water to a boil in a medium saucepan over high heat. Add the barley and ¼ teaspoon of the salt. Reduce the heat to low, cover, and simmer for 35 minutes, or until the barley is tender but firm to the bite. Drain off any remaining liquid. Place the barley in a medium bowl, cover, and refrigerate for 30 minutes, or until cooled.

Meanwhile, in a large serving bowl, whisk together the lemon juice, olive oil, flaxseed oil, mint, pepper, and the remaining ¼ teaspoon salt. Add the barley, tomatoes, cucumber, onion, and cilantro; toss to coat well. Let stand for at least 15 minutes to allow the flavors to blend.

Makes 4 servings
Per serving: 160 calories, 3 g protein, 23 g carbohydrates, 7 g fat, 1 g saturated fat, 0 mg cholesterol, 5 g dietary fiber, 306 mg sodium

Memory Problems
Stress/Fatigue
Aging
Cancer
Depression
Dental Problems
Diabetes
Immunity Problems
Osteoporosis

the 🌿
healing factor

🍏🍏🍏 Vitamin A
🍏🍏🍏 Vitamin C
🍏🍏🍏 Vitamin K
🍏🍏🍏 Manganese
🍏🍏🍏 Fiber
🍏🍏 Thiamin
🍏🍏 Vitamin B$_6$
🍏🍏 Folate
🍏🍏 Potassium
🍏🍏 Copper

chopped salad with millet

½	cup millet
1¼	cups water
⅛	teaspoon + ½ teaspoon salt
3	tablespoons white wine vinegar (see note)
1½	tablespoons extra-virgin olive oil
1½	tablespoons flaxseed oil
¼	teaspoon freshly ground black pepper
2	scallions, thinly sliced
1	pound thin asparagus, tips left whole and stems cut into 1" slices
1	small head napa cabbage, chopped
6	radishes, chopped
2	medium carrots, shredded
1	roasted red pepper, blotted dry and finely chopped
¼	cup chopped flat-leaf parsley

In a medium saucepan over medium-high heat, cook the millet, stirring frequently, for 3 to 4 minutes, or until lightly browned and the grains begin to crackle. Add the water and ⅛ teaspoon of the salt. Bring to a boil over high heat. Reduce the heat to low, cover, and simmer for 25 minutes, or until the millet is tender, some grains have burst, and the water has evaporated. Remove from the heat and let stand for 10 minutes.

Fluff the millet with a fork and place in a medium bowl. Cover and refrigerate for 30 minutes, or until cooled.

Meanwhile, in a large serving bowl, whisk together the

vinegar, olive oil, flaxseed oil, black pepper, and the remaining ½ teaspoon salt. Stir in the scallions and let stand for at least 10 minutes to allow the flavors to blend.

Place a steamer basket in a saucepan with ½" of water. Place the asparagus in the steamer. Bring to a boil over high heat. Reduce the heat to medium, cover, and cook for 4 minutes, or until tender-crisp. Rinse briefly under cold running water and drain.

Add the millet, cabbage, radishes, carrots, roasted pepper, parsley, and asparagus to the dressing. Toss to coat well. Let stand for at least 15 minutes to allow the flavors to blend.

Makes 6 servings
Per serving: 160 calories, 5 g protein, 19 g carbohydrates, 8 g fat, 1 g saturated fat, 0 mg cholesterol, 5 g dietary fiber, 275 mg sodium

HEALTH NOTE
People with depression who take monoamine oxidase inhibitors (MAO inhibitors) should not use alcohol or other fermented products, such as the vinegar in this recipe. Substitute orange or apple juice for the vinegar.

Dental Problems
Diabetes
Memory Problems
Osteoporosis
Cancer
General Vision
Problems
High Cholesterol
Stress/Fatigue
Immunity
Problems
Infections

the *healing
factor*

🐞🐞🐞 Chromium
🐞🐞🐞 Vitamin C
🐞🐞🐞 Vitamin K
🐞🐞 Vitamin A
🐞🐞 Fiber
🐞🐞 Thiamin
🐞🐞 Manganese

garden bounty salad

6	ears corn
8	ounces green beans, halved
2	tablespoons lime juice
1	tablespoon extra-virgin olive oil
1	tablespoon flaxseed oil
½	teaspoon ground cumin
½	teaspoon salt
½	teaspoon freshly ground black pepper
2	large tomatoes, cut into ½" chunks
½	small red onion, chopped
3	tablespoons chopped fresh cilantro

Preheat the grill. Rinse the corn to moisten the husks. Pull back the husks, remove the silks, and pull the husks back over the kernels (some kernels will be exposed). Place the corn on the grill rack. Grill the corn, turning, for 15 minutes, or until the kernels are tender and charred in spots.

Meanwhile, place a steamer basket in a saucepan with ½" of water. Place the green beans in the steamer. Bring to a boil over high heat. Reduce the heat to medium, cover, and cook for 6 minutes, or until tender-crisp. Rinse briefly under cold running water and drain.

In a large bowl, combine the lime juice, olive oil, flaxseed oil, cumin, salt, and pepper. Add the tomatoes, onion, cilantro, and green beans. Cut the kernels off the corn cobs and add to the bowl. Toss to coat well.

Makes 8 servings
Per serving: 99 calories, 3 g protein, 16 g carbohydrates, 4 g fat, 0 g saturated fat, 0 mg cholesterol, 3 g dietary fiber, 156 mg sodium

moroccan carrot (quick) salad with toasted cumin

Photograph on page 31

¾	teaspoon ground cumin
¼	teaspoon ground coriander
½	cup (4 ounces) reduced-fat sour cream
4	teaspoons lemon juice
1½	teaspoons extra-virgin olive oil
1½	teaspoons flaxseed oil
¼	teaspoon freshly grated orange peel
¼	teaspoon salt
7	medium carrots, shredded
½	cup currants
2	tablespoons chopped red onion

In a small skillet over medium heat, cook the cumin and coriander, stirring often, for 2 minutes, or until fragrant and slightly darker in color. Place in a medium bowl and let cool. Stir in the sour cream, lemon juice, olive oil, flaxseed oil, orange peel, and salt.

Add the carrots, currants, and onion and toss to coat well. Let stand for 15 minutes to allow the flavors to blend.

Makes 4 servings
Per serving: 185 calories, 3 g protein, 29 g carbohydrates, 7 g fat, 3 g saturated fat, 12 mg cholesterol, 5 g dietary fiber, 201 mg sodium

treat

helps prevent

Depression
Memory Problems
Stress/Fatigue
Dental Problems
Aging
Cancer
Immunity Problems
General Vision Problems
Cataracts
Night Blindness

the healing factor

🥕🥕🥕 Vitamin A
🥕🥕🥕 Folate
🥕🥕🥕 Vitamin C
🥕🥕 Fiber
🥕🥕 Potassium
🥕🥕 Vitamin B₆
🥕🥕 Manganese
🥕🥕 Phosphorus
🥕🥕 Thiamin

Immunity
Problems

Infections

Aging

Colds and Flu

Diabetes

Dental Problems

General Vision
Problems

Breast Cancer

Asthma

the
healing
factor

🌺🌺🌺 Vitamin C

🌺🌺🌺 Vitamin A

🌺🌺 Chromium

🌺🌺 Vitamin B$_6$

🌺🌺 Manganese

balsamic tomato and roasted pepper salad

Photograph on page 56

1 ½	teaspoons balsamic vinegar
1	teaspoon extra-virgin olive oil
1	teaspoon flaxseed oil
1	small clove garlic, minced
¼	teaspoon salt
⅛	teaspoon freshly ground black pepper
2	large red bell peppers, halved and seeded
2	large tomatoes, cut into ½"-thick slices
⅓	cup julienne-cut fresh basil leaves

Preheat the broiler. Coat a broiler-pan rack with cooking spray.

In a cup, whisk together the vinegar, olive oil, flaxseed oil, garlic, salt, and pepper; set aside.

Place the bell peppers, skin side up, on the prepared rack. Broil, without turning, for 8 to 12 minutes, or until the skins are blackened and blistered in spots.

Place the peppers in a bowl and cover with a kitchen towel. Let stand for 10 minutes, or until cool enough to handle. Peel the skin from the peppers and discard. Cut the peppers into ½"-wide strips.

Arrange the tomato slices on a platter. Scatter the pepper strips on top and sprinkle with the basil. Drizzle the dressing over the salad. Let stand for at least 15 minutes to allow the flavors to blend.

Makes 4 servings
Per serving: 53 calories, 1 g protein, 8 g carbohydrates, 3 g fat, 0 g saturated fat, 0 mg cholesterol, 2 g dietary fiber, 153 mg sodium

roasted beet salad

Photograph on page 32

4	medium beets (about 1 pound), stems trimmed to 1"
2	tablespoons apricot all-fruit spread
1	tablespoon white balsamic vinegar
1½	teaspoons olive oil
1½	teaspoons flaxseed oil
2	tablespoons snipped fresh chives or thinly sliced scallion greens
½	teaspoon salt
¼	teaspoon freshly ground black pepper
2	medium navel oranges
4	cups mixed bitter salad greens, such as arugula, watercress, endive, and escarole

Preheat the oven to 400°F. Coat a 9" baking pan with cooking spray.

Place the beets in the prepared baking pan and cover tightly with foil. Roast for 1 hour, or until very tender. Uncover and let the beets stand until cool enough to handle.

Meanwhile, in a large bowl, whisk the all-fruit spread, vinegar, olive oil, flaxseed oil, chives or scallions, salt, and pepper.

Slip the skins off the beets and discard the skins. Chop the beets. Cut off the peel and white pith from the oranges. Section the oranges into the bowl with the dressing. Add the beets and toss to coat well. Let stand for at least 15 minutes to allow the flavors to blend.

Just before serving, arrange the greens on a serving plate. Top with the beet mixture.

Makes 4 servings
Per serving: 144 calories, 3 g protein, 27 g carbohydrates, 4 g fat, 0 g saturated fat, 0 mg cholesterol, 5 g dietary fiber, 390 mg sodium

treat ∫ helps prevent

Diabetes

Cancer

High Cholesterol

Heart Disease

Memory Problems

Osteoporosis

General Vision Problems

Immunity Problems

the healing factor

🌿🌿🌿 Vitamin C
🌿🌿🌿 Vitamin K
🌿🌿🌿 Folate
🌿🌿🌿 Vitamin A
🌿🌿🌿 Manganese
🌿🌿 Fiber
🌿🌿 Potassium
🌿🌿 Magnesium

Stress/Fatigue
Memory Problems
Diabetes
Heart Disease
Aging
Cancer
High Cholesterol
Depression
High Blood Pressure
Kidney Stones

the **healing factor**

🍒🍒🍒 Vitamin C
🍒🍒🍒 Chromium
🍒🍒🍒 Potassium
🍒🍒🍒 Vitamin K
🍒🍒🍒 Omega-3 fatty acids
🍒🍒 Vitamin B$_6$
🍒🍒 Manganese
🍒🍒 Fiber
🍒🍒 Thiamin

HEALTH NOTE
People with depression who take monoamine oxidase inhibitors (MAO inhibitors) should not use fermented products, such as the vinegar in this recipe. Substitute juice for the vinegar.

potato salad with warm onion dressing

Photograph on page 50

2	pounds red potatoes, cut into large chunks
1	tablespoon canola oil
1	large red onion, chopped
1	clove garlic, chopped
3	tablespoons cider vinegar (see note)
3	tablespoons apple juice
1	tablespoon stone-ground mustard
¼	cup chopped parsley
⅛	teaspoon salt

Place a steamer basket in a saucepan with ½" of water. Place the potatoes in the steamer. Bring to a boil over high heat. Reduce the heat to medium, cover, and cook for 20 minutes, or until tender. Rinse briefly under cold running water and drain. Place in a large serving bowl.

Meanwhile, heat the oil in a medium nonstick skillet over medium heat. Add the onion and garlic and cook, stirring, for 8 minutes, or until the onion is very soft.

Add the vinegar, apple juice, mustard, parsley, and salt. Cook for 2 minutes, or until heated through. Pour over the potatoes. Toss to coat well. Let stand for at least 15 minutes to allow the flavors to blend.

Makes 6 servings
Per serving: 145 calories, 4 g protein, 27 g carbohydrates, 3 g fat, 0 g saturated fat, 0 mg cholesterol, 3 g dietary fiber, 103 mg sodium

roasted sweet-potato salad

Photograph on page 43

2	tablespoons olive oil
¼	teaspoon salt
¼	teaspoon freshly ground black pepper
2	pounds sweet potatoes, scrubbed and cut into 1" chunks
2	large red bell peppers, cut into 1" pieces
2	tablespoons white balsamic or white wine vinegar (see note)
1	pound spinach or arugula, torn into bite-size pieces

Preheat the oven to 425°F.

In a large roasting pan, combine the oil, salt, and black pepper. Add the sweet potatoes and bell peppers and toss to coat well. Roast, stirring occasionally, for 40 minutes, or until the potatoes are tender. Remove from the oven and stir in the vinegar.

Place the spinach or arugula in a large serving bowl. Add the potato mixture and toss to coat well. Serve immediately.

Makes 4 servings
Per serving: 336 calories, 7 g protein, 61 g carbohydrates, 8 g fat, 1 g saturated fat, 0 mg cholesterol, 18 g dietary fiber, 312 mg sodium

HEALTH NOTE
People with depression who take monoamine oxidase inhibitors (MAO inhibitors) should not use alcohol or other fermented products, such as the vinegar in this recipe. Substitute apple juice for the vinegar.

Aging

Heart Disease

Dental Problems

Depression

Diabetes

Immunity Problems

Insomnia

Headaches

Osteoporosis

General Vision Problems

the
healing factor

🐛🐛🐛 Vitamin A

🐛🐛🐛 Vitamin K

🐛🐛🐛 Vitamin C

🐛🐛🐛 Manganese

🐛🐛🐛 Fiber

🐛🐛 Iron

🐛🐛🐛 Vitamin B₆

🐛🐛🐛 Riboflavin

🐛🐛🐛 Magnesium

🐛🐛🐛 Copper

Breast Cancer

Aging

Asthma

Cancer

Diabetes

Immunity Problems

Infections

Memory Problems

Insomnia

smoked turkey salad

the 🌿
healing factor

🐦🐦🐦 Vitamin K
🐦🐦🐦 Vitamin A
🐦🐦🐦 Fiber
🐦🐦🐦 Vitamin C
🐦🐦🐦 Iron
🐦🐦🐦 Magnesium
🐦🐦🐦 Vitamin E
🐦🐦🐦 Selenium
🐦🐦🐦 Riboflavin
🐦🐦 Phosphorus

2	eggs
2	tablespoons frozen apple juice concentrate
2	teaspoons olive oil
2	teaspoons flaxseed oil
2	teaspoons red wine vinegar
¼	teaspoon salt
¼	teaspoon freshly ground black pepper
	Pinch of ground cinnamon
6	cups loosely packed fresh spinach
2	large nectarines, cut into thin wedges
3	ounces smoked turkey, cut into small pieces
½	small red onion, thinly sliced
⅓	cup sliced natural almonds, toasted

Place the eggs in their shells in a small saucepan and cover with cold water. Bring to a boil over high heat. Boil for 1 minute. Remove from the heat, cover, and let stand for 10 minutes. Drain and run cold water into the pan. Let the eggs cool, then shell and slice.

In a large serving bowl, whisk together the apple juice concentrate, olive oil, flaxseed oil, vinegar, salt, pepper, and cinnamon. Add the spinach, nectarines, turkey, and onion and toss to coat well. Top with the eggs and almonds.

Makes 4 servings
Per serving: 230 calories, 14 g protein, 15 g carbohydrates, 13 g fat, 2 g saturated fat, 121 mg cholesterol, 7 g dietary fiber, 250 mg sodium

asian noodle salad

1	pound sea scallops or peeled and deveined large shrimp, either halved crosswise
1/4	teaspoon ground red pepper
8	ounces whole wheat spaghetti
2	medium carrots, cut into julienne strips
1	teaspoon toasted sesame oil
1/4	cup smooth natural peanut butter
2	tablespoons low-sodium soy sauce
2	tablespoons grated fresh ginger
1	clove garlic, minced
2	cucumbers, peeled, halved, seeded, and cut into strips

Preheat the broiler. Coat a baking sheet with cooking spray.

Place the scallops or shrimp on the prepared sheet and coat with the pepper. Let stand for 5 minutes.

Prepare the spaghetti according to package directions, adding the carrots during the last 2 minutes of cooking. Reserve 1/2 cup of the cooking liquid. Drain the spaghetti and carrots. Rinse briefly under cold running water and toss with the oil.

Meanwhile, broil the scallops or shrimp, turning often, for 4 minutes, or until the scallops or shrimp are opaque.

In a large bowl, combine the peanut butter, soy sauce, ginger, garlic, and 2 to 3 tablespoons of the pasta cooking liquid. Add the scallops or shrimp, spaghetti mixture, and cucumbers. Toss to coat well.

Makes 4 servings
Per serving: 466 calories, 33 g protein, 58 g carbohydrates, 14 g fat, 2 g saturated fat, 36 mg cholesterol, 8 g dietary fiber, 812 mg sodium

treat 〜 helps prevent

Memory Problems
Osteoporosis
Stress/Fatigue
Diabetes

the healing factor

🌰🌰🌰 Vitamin A
🌰🌰🌰 Manganese
🌰🌰🌰 Phosphorus
🌰🌰🌰 Chromium
🌰🌰🌰 Magnesium
🌰🌰🌰 Fiber
🌰🌰🌰 Niacin
🌰🌰🌰 Potassium
🌰🌰🌰 Thiamin

COOKING TIP
The dressing for this salad should be smooth, creamy, and fairly thick. Add more pasta cooking liquid to the salad if the dressing is too thick.

Memory Problems
Stress/Fatigue
Aging
Heart Disease
Dental Problems
Depression
Diabetes
Immunity Problems
Osteoporosis
Insomnia

thai rice and turkey salad

the **healing factor**

🐜🐜🐜 Vitamin K
🐜🐜🐜 Vitamin C
🐜🐜🐜 Vitamin A
🐜🐜🐜 Vitamin B$_6$
🐜🐜🐜 Niacin
🐜🐜🐜 Chromium
🐜🐜🐜 Phosphorus
🐜🐜🐜 Fiber
🐜🐜🐜 Manganese
🐜🐜🐜 Iron

1	cup brown basmati rice
½	cup water
½	cup chicken broth
1	tablespoon grated fresh ginger
2	cloves garlic, minced
12	ounces boneless, skinless turkey breast, cut crosswise into strips
3	tablespoons smooth natural peanut butter
3	tablespoons lime juice
1	teaspoon honey
¼	teaspoon salt
2	cups shredded napa cabbage
1	large red bell pepper, finely chopped
1	small red onion, finely chopped
3	tablespoons coarsely chopped fresh mint
3	cups small tender spinach or kale leaves
2	tablespoons coarsely chopped roasted unsalted peanuts

Prepare the rice according to package directions. Spread the rice in a shallow baking pan and place it in the freezer for 10 minutes to chill slightly.

Meanwhile, place the water, broth, ginger, and garlic in a medium skillet. Bring to a boil over high heat. Reduce the heat to low, cover, and simmer for 5 minutes. Add the turkey, cover, and cook, stirring frequently, for 4 minutes, or until the turkey is no longer pink. Using a slotted spoon, remove the turkey to a plate; cover loosely with waxed paper to keep it moist.

Increase the heat to high and return the broth to a boil. Boil for 6 minutes, or until the broth is thickened and reduced to about ¼ cup.

In a large bowl, whisk together the peanut butter, lime juice, honey, and salt. Whisk in the reduced broth and continue whisking until smooth (add a few drops of hot water if the mixture becomes too thick). Add the rice, turkey and any accumulated juices, cabbage, pepper, onion, and mint. Toss to coat well.

Arrange the spinach or kale on a platter. Mound the salad in the center and sprinkle with the peanuts.

Makes 4 servings
Per serving: 408 calories, 30 g protein, 49 g carbohydrates, 9 g fat, 2 g saturated fat, 53 mg cholesterol, 7 g dietary fiber, 295 mg sodium

good-for-you salad dressing

Rich, creamy, and loaded with calories is how we often think of salad dressings. No more. These tasty dressings have just enough good oil to make them healthy, and plenty of great flavor to make them delicious. Each has less than 20 calories and 2 grams of fat per tablespoon. Always shake the dressings well before using.

Tomato Vinaigrette. In a small jar, combine ½ cup low-sodium tomato-vegetable juice; ¼ cup white balsamic vinegar; 2 tablespoons extra-virgin olive oil; 2 tablespoons chopped fresh herbs, such as basil, oregano, cilantro, or thyme; 1 small clove garlic, minced; and ⅛ teaspoon black pepper.

Orange Vinaigrette. In a small jar, combine ⅔ cup orange juice; 3 tablespoons white balsamic vinegar; 2 tablespoons extra-virgin olive oil; 2 tablespoons chopped fresh herbs, such as tarragon, basil, cilantro, or thyme; 1 small shallot, minced; 1 teaspoon sugar; ⅛ teaspoon salt; and ⅛ teaspoon black pepper.

Mustard Vinaigrette. In a small jar, combine ⅓ cup lemon juice; 3 tablespoons water; 2 tablespoons extra-virgin olive oil; 1 tablespoon Dijon mustard; 2 tablespoons chopped fresh herbs, such as tarragon, basil, cilantro, or thyme; 1 tablespoon minced chives; 1 teaspoon sugar; and ⅛ teaspoon black pepper.

Stress/Fatigue

Aging

Stroke

Depression

*Immunity
Problems*

Memory Problems

Anemia

Heart Disease

Diabetes

the **healing factor**

🐞🐞🐞 Vitamin B$_{12}$
🐞🐞🐞 Vitamin B$_{6}$
🐞🐞🐞 Vitamin C
🐞🐞🐞 Selenium
🐞🐞🐞 Potassium
🐞🐞🐞 Zinc
🐞🐞🐞 Niacin
🐞🐞🐞 Phosphorus
🐞🐞🐞 Iron
🐞🐞 Chromium

grilled steak and potato salad

Steak and Vegetables

1	pound well-trimmed boneless beef top sirloin or top round steak, about 1" thick
4	cloves garlic, minced
½	teaspoon coarsely ground black pepper
¼	teaspoon salt
1	large red onion, cut into ½"-thick slices, rings separated
1	teaspoon extra-virgin olive oil
1	teaspoon red wine vinegar (see note)
8	small red or white new potatoes, scrubbed and halved

Salad

2½	teaspoons red wine vinegar (see note)
2	teaspoons extra-virgin olive oil
2	teaspoons flaxseed oil
1½	teaspoons coarse Dijon mustard
1	teaspoon water
1	small clove garlic, minced
¼	teaspoon freshly ground black pepper
⅛	teaspoon salt
1	package (5 ounces) mesclun leaves or baby greens

To make the steak and vegetables: Coat a grill rack or broiler-pan rack with cooking spray. Preheat the grill or broiler.

Rub the steak on both sides with the garlic, pepper, and salt, pressing them into the surface. Place on one side of the prepared rack. On a plate, toss the onion with the oil and vinegar and place on the other side of the rack. Let stand for 5 minutes.

Meanwhile, place a steamer basket in a saucepan with ½" of water. Place the potatoes in the steamer. Bring to a boil over high heat. Reduce the heat to medium, cover, and cook for 7 minutes, or until fork-tender.

Grill or broil the steak and onion for 6 minutes, turning once, or until a thermometer inserted in the center of the steak registers 145°F for medium-rare. Place on a plate. Let stand for 10 minutes, then slice. Grill or broil the onion rings, turning frequently, for 10 minutes, or until tender and lightly charred.

To make the salad: In a large bowl, whisk together the vinegar, olive oil, flaxseed oil, mustard, water, garlic, pepper, and salt until well-blended. Add the greens, potatoes, onion, steak, and any accumulated meat juices; toss to coat well.

Makes 4 servings
Per serving: 273 calories, 30 g protein, 18 g carbohydrates, 9 g fat, 2 g saturated fat, 49 mg cholesterol, 3 g dietary fiber, 326 mg sodium

HEALTH NOTE
People with depression who take monoamine oxidase inhibitors (MAO inhibitors) should not use alcohol or other fermented products, such as the vinegar in this recipe. Substitute apple juice for the vinegar.

tropical pork salad

Memory Problems
Depression
Stress/Fatigue
Aging
Immunity
Problems
Heart Disease
Osteoporosis
General Vision
Problems
Cataracts

the healing factor

🌰🌰🌰 Vitamin C
🌰🌰🌰 Vitamin K
🌰🌰🌰 Vitamin A
🌰🌰🌰 Manganese
🌰🌰🌰 Thiamin
🌰🌰🌰 Selenium
🌰🌰🌰 Vitamin B₆
🌰🌰🌰 Phosphorus
🌰🌰🌰 Riboflavin
🌰🌰🌰 Niacin

2	tablespoons sliced natural almonds
2	teaspoons ground cumin
1	cup chicken broth
12	ounces pork tenderloin, cut into 1" strips
1	tablespoon cornstarch
1	tablespoon cold water
1/4	cup apricot nectar
2	tablespoons chopped fresh cilantro
1	tablespoon lime juice
1	tablespoon honey
1/4	teaspoon freshly ground black pepper
1/8	teaspoon crushed red-pepper flakes
2	cups fresh pineapple chunks or juice-packed canned pineapple, drained
1/2	ripe papaya, peeled, seeded, and cut into chunks
1	ripe mango, peeled, seeded, and cut into chunks
4	cups (about 1 large bunch) torn watercress or spinach

In a medium nonstick skillet over medium-high heat, toast the almonds, tossing frequently, for 4 minutes, or until lightly browned. Place on a plate; set aside.

Reduce the heat to medium. Add the cumin to the skillet and cook, stirring frequently, for 4 minutes, or until the cumin is toasted and fragrant. Place half of the cumin in a large bowl. Pour the broth into the skillet and bring to a boil over high heat.

Add the pork to the skillet. Reduce the heat to medium, cover, and cook, stirring frequently, for 4 minutes, or until the pork is no longer pink. With a slotted spoon, remove the pork to the bowl with the cumin; toss to coat well.

Increase the heat to high and bring the cooking liquid to a boil. Boil for 3 minutes, or until the liquid is reduced to about ¼ cup.

In a cup, combine the cornstarch and water. Stir into the skillet and return to a boil, whisking constantly (the mixture will be extremely thick). Remove from the heat.

Place the thickened liquid in another bowl and whisk in the apricot nectar, cilantro, lime juice, honey, black pepper, and red-pepper flakes; continue whisking until smooth.

Add to the bowl with the pork, along with the pineapple, papaya, and mango. Toss to coat well.

Place the watercress or spinach on a large platter. Top with the pork salad and sprinkle with the toasted almonds.

Makes 4 servings
Per serving: 262 calories, 21 g protein, 33 g carbohydrates, 6 g fat, 1 g saturated fat, 55 mg cholesterol, 4 g dietary fiber, 207 mg sodium

Memory Problems

Depression

Immunity
Problems

Heart Disease

Cancer

General Vision
Problems

Cataracts

Anemia

Insomnia

Prostate Problems

the
healing
factor

🐞🐞🐞 Vitamin C

🐞🐞🐞 Vitamin A

🐞🐞🐞 Vitamin K

🐞🐞🐞 Selenium

🐞🐞🐞 Thiamin

🐞🐞 Niacin

🐞🐞 Iron

🐞🐞 Phosphorus

🐞🐞 Riboflavin

pasta salad with shrimp and broccoli

8	ounces small pasta shells
1½	cups broccoli florets
1	medium carrot, sliced
1	red bell pepper, sliced
1	tablespoon olive oil
2	cloves garlic, minced
1	scallion, minced
12	ounces shrimp, peeled, deveined, and sliced lengthwise in half
1	large tomato, chopped
½	cup buttermilk
2	tablespoons red wine vinegar (see note)
1	tablespoon flaxseed oil
1	tablespoon Dijon mustard
1	teaspoon freshly ground black pepper
½	teaspoon salt

Prepare the pasta according to package directions, adding the broccoli, carrot, and bell pepper during the last 5 minutes of cooking.

Meanwhile, heat the olive oil in a large skillet over medium heat. Add the garlic and scallion and cook for 1 minute. Add the shrimp and cook, stirring frequently, for 3 minutes, or until the shrimp are opaque. Add the tomato and cook for 1 minute. Remove from the heat.

Meanwhile, in a large bowl, combine the buttermilk, vinegar, flaxseed oil, mustard, black pepper, and salt. Add the shrimp mixture and pasta mixture and toss to coat well.

Makes 8 servings
Per serving: 205 calories, 14 g protein, 26 g carbohydrates, 5 g fat, 1 g saturated fat, 65 mg cholesterol, 2 g dietary fiber, 244 mg sodium

HEALTH NOTE
People with depression who take monoamine oxidase inhibitors (MAO inhibitors) should not use alcohol or other fermented products, such as the vinegar in this recipe. Substitute apple juice for the vinegar.

the power of
BROCCOLI

Broccoli contains two powerful cancer-fighting compounds, as well as fiber and beta-carotene, which ward off heart disease, certain cancers, and cataracts.

When purchasing, look for dark—almost purple—heads, which contain the most beta-carotene. Lightly steam broccoli to help release its healing compounds.

herbed chicken sandwiches
(quick)

Lemon-Dill Mayonnaise

½	cup low-fat mayonnaise
1	teaspoon lemon juice
2	teaspoons chopped fresh basil or ½ teaspoon dried, crushed
2	teaspoons chopped fresh dill or ½ teaspoon dried, crushed

Sandwiches

12	thin slices multigrain bread, toasted
½	pound cooked skinless chicken breast, sliced
⅓	English cucumber, thinly sliced
1	large tomato, cut into 8 slices
1	cup mesclun or spring mix salad greens

To make the lemon-dill mayonnaise: In a small bowl, combine the mayonnaise, lemon juice, basil, and dill.

To make the sandwiches: Place 4 of the bread slices on a work surface. Spread 2 teaspoons of the lemon-dill mayonnaise on each slice. Top with layers of chicken and cucumber.

Spread 4 of the remaining bread slices each with 2 teaspoons of the lemon-dill mayonnaise. Place the bread, mayonnaise side up, on the 4 sandwiches. Top with layers of tomato and greens.

Spread the remaining 4 bread slices with the remaining lemon-dill mayonnaise. Place, mayonnaise side down, on top of the sandwiches. Cut in half diagonally and secure with wooden picks.

Makes 4 servings
Per serving: 375 calories, 26 g protein, 44 g carbohydrates, 11 g fat, 2 g saturated fat, 56 mg cholesterol, 5 g dietary fiber, 587 mg sodium

grilled tomato and cheese sandwiches

 quick

Photograph on page 36

8	slices multigrain bread
8	slices low-fat Jarlsberg or Cheddar cheese
1	large tomato, cut into 8 slices
2	roasted red peppers, halved
12	large leaves fresh basil

Coat both sides of the bread with olive oil–flavored cooking spray. In a large nonstick skillet over medium heat, cook the bread on 1 side for 2 minutes, or until lightly toasted. Do this in batches, if necessary. Remove from the pan.

Arrange 4 of the slices, toasted side up, on a work surface. Top with the cheese, tomato, peppers, and basil. Top with the remaining bread slices, toasted sided down.

Carefully place the sandwiches in the skillet. Cook for 2 minutes per side, or until toasted and the cheese melts.

Makes 4 servings
Per serving: 264 calories, 22 g protein, 33 g carbohydrates, 6 g fat, 2 g saturated fat, 20 mg cholesterol, 6 g dietary fiber, 451 mg sodium

treat ⸮ helps **prevent**

Aging
Osteoporosis
Dental Problems
General Vision Problems
PMS
Menopausal Problems/Hot Flashes

the
healing factor

🍐🍐🍐 Vitamin C
🍐🍐🍐 Vitamin A
🍐🍐🍐 Manganese
🍐🍐🍐 Calcium
🍐🍐🍐 Selenium
🍐🍐🍐 Phosphorus
🍐🍐🍐 Zinc
🍐🍐🍐 Fiber
🍐🍐🍐 Riboflavin
🍐🍐🍐 Magnesium

Memory Problems

Aging

Stress/Fatigue

General Vision Problems

Dental Problems

Osteoporosis

Macular Degeneration

Menopausal Problems/Hot Flashes

the
healing
factor

🍒🍒🍒 Vitamin C

🍒🍒🍒 Calcium

🍒🍒🍒 Phosphorus

🍒🍒🍒 Manganese

🍒🍒🍒 Folate

🍒🍒🍒 Thiamin

🍒🍒🍒 Selenium

🍒🍒🍒 Vitamin A

🍒🍒🍒 Riboflavin

🍒🍒🍒 Niacin

grilled vegetable melts

Basil Spread

1	cup packed fresh basil leaves
2	tablespoons grated Parmesan cheese
1	tablespoon toasted walnuts
1	clove garlic
¼	cup (2 ounces) fat-free cream cheese or sour cream

Sandwiches

2	zucchini, cut lengthwise into ¼"-thick slices
2	yellow and/or red bell peppers, quartered
1	red onion, cut crosswise into ¼"-thick slices
¼	teaspoon salt
1½	tablespoons balsamic vinegar (see note)
8	slices Italian bread, lightly toasted
4	slices low-fat Jarlsberg cheese

To make the basil spread: In a food processor, combine the basil, Parmesan, walnuts, and garlic. Process to puree. Add the cream cheese or sour cream. Process to mix. Set aside.

To make the sandwiches: Preheat the grill or broiler. Coat a grill rack or broiler-pan rack with cooking spray.

Arrange the zucchini, peppers, and onion in a single layer on the prepared rack. Coat lightly with cooking spray. Sprinkle with the salt. Grill or broil for 10 minutes, turning once, or until lightly browned. Place on a plate and drizzle with the vinegar.

Arrange 4 of the bread slices on the rack. Spread with the basil mixture. Top with layers of zucchini, bell pepper, onion, and cheese. Grill or broil for 1 minute, or until the cheese melts. Top with the remaining bread slices.

Makes 4 servings
Per serving: 311 calories, 20 g protein, 46 g carbohydrates, 6 g fat, 2 g saturated fat, 13 mg cholesterol, 5 g dietary fiber, 705 mg sodium

HEALTH NOTE
People with depression who take monoamine oxidase inhibitors (MAO inhibitors) should not use alcohol or other fermented products, such as the vinegar in this recipe. Omit the vinegar from this recipe.

helps
prevent ～ treat

Aging
Memory Problems
Stress/Fatigue
General Vision
Problems
Cataracts
Diabetes

mediterranean muffuletta

the
healing factor

🐞🐞🐞 Vitamin C
🐞🐞🐞 Vitamin A
🐞🐞🐞 Manganese
🐞🐞🐞 Fiber
🐞🐞🐞 Thiamin
🐞🐞🐞 Folate
🐞🐞🐞 Phosphorus
🐞🐞🐞 Selenium
🐞🐞🐞 Riboflavin
🐞🐞🐞 Potassium

2	tablespoons chopped dry-packed sun-dried tomatoes
1	large eggplant (1 pound), cut lengthwise into ¼"-thick slices
1	large yellow squash, cut lengthwise into ¼"-thick slices
1	red onion, sliced crosswise
2	red bell peppers, cut into strips
2	ounces fat-free cream cheese, at room temperature
2	ounces goat cheese, crumbled
2	tablespoons fat-free sour cream
2	teaspoons chopped fresh thyme
1	tablespoon chopped pistachios (optional)
1	loaf crusty multigrain French bread, halved lengthwise through the side

Coat a grill rack with cooking spray. Preheat the grill.

Place the tomatoes in a small bowl. Cover with boiling water and let soak for 10 minutes, or until soft. Drain and discard the liquid.

Meanwhile, place the eggplant, squash, onion, and peppers on the prepared grill rack and cook for 6 minutes, turning once, or until lightly browned and softened; remove from the grill and set aside.

In another small bowl, combine the cream cheese, goat cheese, sour cream, thyme, pistachios (if using), and tomatoes.

Remove the soft insides from the crust of each half of the bread. Reserve for another use. Spread the tomato mixture over both halves of the bread. Layer the grilled vegetables on the bottom half, then cover with the top half of the bread. Cut into 4 sandwiches.

Makes 4 servings
Per serving: 290 calories, 13 g protein, 47 g carbohydrates, 7 g fat, 4 g saturated fat, 13 mg cholesterol, 8 g dietary fiber, 508 mg sodium

the power of
NUTS
Take nuts off your taboo list! People who eat nuts four or five times a week have far less incidence of heart disease than people who don't, several large studies reveal. Just a few nuts deliver a jolt of heart-healthy monounsaturated or omega-3 fats, vitamin E, magnesium, and copper.

But here's a nutty problem: How do you eat "just a few"? Nuts are high in calories and fat, so you need to stay in control. One ounce is the perfect serving (about ¼ cup whole) and can be easily added to many dishes. Here are some suggestions.

- Toss on salads, soups, and stews.
- Use as a topping for casseroles.
- Add finely chopped nuts into bread coating for fish or chicken.
- Add to batter for baked goods such as scones, muffins, and quick breads.
- Sprinkle on cereal, yogurt, or canned fruit.
- Grind and add to sauces to thicken.

To help you avoid getting too many calories from nuts, check the list below to find the calorie counts for a 1-ounce serving of some of the most common nuts.

Nuts	Calories	Nuts	Calories
3½ chestnuts	70	12 hazelnuts	180
18 cashews	160	14 walnut halves	180
20 peanuts	160	8 Brazil nuts	190
47 pistachios	160	15 pecan halves	190
24 almonds	170	12 macadamia nuts	200

Cancer

Heart Disease

Depression

Memory Problems

Stress/Fatigue

Insomnia

Headaches

*Immunity
Problems*

Asthma

the ✤
healing
factor

🍒🍒🍒 Vitamin K

🍒🍒🍒 Selenium

🍒🍒🍒 Manganese

🍒🍒🍒 Vitamin C

🍒🍒🍒 Fiber

🍒🍒🍒 Niacin

🍒🍒🍒 Phosphorus

🍒🍒🍒 Magnesium

🍒🍒 Iron

🍒🍒 Vitamin B$_6$

niçoise salad pockets

Dressing

½	cup balsamic or cider vinegar (see note)
1	tablespoon extra-virgin olive oil
1	tablespoon flaxseed oil
1	teaspoon Dijon mustard
1	teaspoon dried Italian seasoning, crushed
1	clove garlic, minced

Sandwiches

¾	pound red potatoes, cut into ¼"-thick slices
¼	pound small green beans
1	can (6 ounces) water-packed white tuna, drained and flaked
¼	red onion, thinly sliced
2	hard-cooked egg whites, coarsely chopped
¼	cup coarsely chopped niçoise olives
2	cups baby spinach leaves
4	whole wheat pitas, halved crosswise

To make the dressing: In a large bowl, combine the vinegar, olive oil, flaxseed oil, mustard, Italian seasoning, and garlic.

To make the sandwiches: Place a steamer basket in a saucepan with ½" of water. Place the potatoes and beans in the steamer. Bring to a boil over high heat. Reduce the heat to medium, cover, and cook for 7 minutes, or until tender-crisp. Rinse briefly under cold running water and drain.

To the bowl with the dressing, add the potatoes, beans, tuna, onion, egg whites, olives, and spinach. Toss to coat well.

Spoon the tuna mixture into each pita pocket. Drizzle lightly with any dressing left in the bowl.

Makes 4 servings
Per serving: 406 calories, 21 g protein, 56 g carbohydrates, 12 g fat, 1 g saturated fat, 18 mg cholesterol, 9 g dietary fiber, 633 mg sodium

HEALTH NOTE
People with depression who take monoamine oxidase inhibitors (MAO inhibitors) should not use alcohol or other fermented products, such as the vinegar in this recipe. Substitute apple juice for the vinegar.

the power of
FLAX

For centuries, flaxseed (and the plant from which it comes) was used for just about everything except food. Flax is one of the oldest sources of textile fiber, used in making linen. Its seed, also known as linseed, is used for making paint. Through the 20th century, the seed has been used for livestock feed but not human "feed." Until recently. Flaxseed is one of the best sources of plant-provided omega-3 fatty acids, contains the antioxidant lignans, and is very high in fiber, helping prevent heart attack, lower cholesterol levels, fight depression, and battle breast and other cancers. It also helps alleviate the pain associated with rheumatoid arthritis. Since it is so new to the kitchen, here are some simple tips when using flaxseed products.

- Flaxseed oil loses its power when cooked, so it must be eaten raw. Typically, it has little flavor, so substitute half of the olive oil in recipes with flaxseed oil.

- Always purchase organic flaxseed oil in dark bottles and store in the refrigerator.

- Grind whole flaxseeds in a clean coffee grinder. Always grind only as much as you plan to use because it turns rancid faster when ground.

- Store flaxseeds in the freezer to keep them fresh longer.

- Sprinkle ground flaxseeds on cereal, yogurt, or salads. Start with 1 teaspoon and see how your intestines react. Since they are a great source of fiber, too much can cause gas.

- Add 2 tablespoons of ground flaxseeds to muffin and quick bread batter or cookie dough.

Aging
Memory Problems
Stress/Fatigue
Immunity Problems
Anemia
General Vision Problems
Cataracts

roast beef (quick) and charred vegetable sandwiches

¼	cup buttermilk or fat-free plain yogurt
2	tablespoons low-fat mayonnaise
¼	cup (1 ounce) crumbled blue cheese
2	tablespoons chopped fresh chives or scallion greens
4	plum tomatoes, halved lengthwise
1	small red onion, cut into 4 slices
¾	pound thinly sliced cooked lean roast beef
4	leaves lettuce
4	onion sandwich buns, toasted

In a small bowl, combine the buttermilk or yogurt, mayonnaise, cheese, and chives or scallion greens.

Heat a large nonstick skillet coated with cooking spray over medium-high heat. Add the tomatoes and onion and cook for 3 minutes per side, or until lightly charred.

Layer the roast beef, onion, tomatoes, and lettuce on the bottoms of the buns. Drizzle with the blue cheese dressing. Cover with the bun tops.

Makes 4 servings
Per serving: 428 calories, 35 g protein, 40 g carbohydrates, 14 g fat, 4 g saturated fat, 69 mg cholesterol, 3 g dietary fiber, 544 mg sodium

the
healing factor

- Selenium
- Vitamin B$_{12}$
- Vitamin C
- Zinc
- Phosphorus
- Niacin
- Riboflavin
- Thiamin
- Iron
- Folate

beef, pork, and lamb

Although meat has gotten a lot of bad press, you don't have to give it up entirely in order to be a healthy cook. Meats are wonderful sources of vitamins, minerals, and protein. They also deliver satisfying tastes and textures, whether you're preparing a burger, grilled steak, or lamb stew. Choosing the leanest cuts and the healthiest cooking methods allows meat to be a perfect part of a healthy eating plan.

mile-high burgers

treat

Aging
Depression
Immunity Problems
Memory Problems
Stress/Fatigue
General Vision Problems
Anemia

the healing factor

🌰🌰🌰 Vitamin C
🌰🌰🌰 Selenium
🌰🌰🌰 Niacin
🌰🌰🌰 Vitamin B$_{12}$
🌰🌰🌰 Zinc
🌰🌰 Vitamin A
🌰🌰 Riboflavin
🌰🌰 Iron
🌰🌰 Phosphorus
🌰🌰 Manganese

HEALTH NOTE
People with depression who take monoamine oxidase inhibitors (MAO inhibitors) should not use alcohol or other fermented or aged products, such as the cheese in this recipe.

1½	ounces dry-packed sun-dried tomatoes
2	tablespoons low-fat mayonnaise
⅓	cup packed fresh basil leaves
1	clove garlic
1¼	pounds extra-lean ground beef
1	roasted red pepper, quartered
2	slices (2 ounces) low-fat mozzarella cheese, halved (see note)
4	large leaves lettuce
4	Italian-style sandwich buns

Coat a grill rack or broiler-pan rack with cooking spray. Preheat the grill or broiler.

Place the sun-dried tomatoes in a medium bowl. Cover with boiling water and soak for 10 minutes, or until very soft. Drain and discard the liquid. In a food processor, combine the tomatoes, mayonnaise, basil, and garlic. Process until smooth.

Combine the beef and tomato mixture in the same bowl. Mix just until blended. Shape into 4 burgers.

Place the burgers on the prepared rack. Cook 4" from the heat for 4 minutes per side, or until a thermometer inserted in the center registers 160°F and the meat is no longer pink. Top each burger with a slice of pepper and cheese. Cook for 30 seconds longer, or until the cheese melts.

Divide the lettuce among the buns. Top each with a burger.

Makes 4 servings
Per serving: 591 calories, 64 g protein, 45 g carbohydrates, 16 g fat, 8 g saturated fat, 135 mg cholesterol, 3 g dietary fiber, 840 mg sodium

beef stroganoff

12	ounces medium no-yolk egg noodles
1	teaspoon vegetable oil
3/4	pound beef tenderloin or top round, cut into thin strips
1/4	teaspoon salt
1	onion, cut into thin wedges
8	ounces shiitake mushrooms, stems removed and caps sliced
1 1/2	tablespoons whole wheat flour
2	cups vegetable or beef broth
1	teaspoon Worcestershire sauce
1/4	cup (2 ounces) reduced-fat sour cream
2	tablespoons chopped parsley

Prepare the noodles according to package directions. Drain and place in a serving bowl.

Meanwhile, heat the oil in a large nonstick skillet over medium-high heat. Sprinkle the beef with the salt. Place in the skillet and cook, turning occasionally, for 3 minutes, or until browned. Remove to a plate and keep warm.

Coat the skillet with cooking spray and reduce the heat to medium. Add the onion and cook, stirring occasionally, for 3 minutes. Add the mushrooms and cook, stirring occasionally, for 3 minutes, or until they begin to release liquid. Sprinkle with the flour and cook, stirring constantly, for 1 minute. Add the broth and Worcestershire sauce and cook, stirring, for 3 minutes, or until slightly thickened. Remove from the heat. Stir in the beef, sour cream, and parsley. Serve over the noodles.

Makes 6 servings
Per serving: 427 calories, 23 g protein, 54 g carbohydrates, 14 g fat, 5 g saturated fat, 41 mg cholesterol, 5 g dietary fiber, 406 mg sodium

treat ʃ helps prevent

Depression
Aging
Memory Problems
Stress/Fatigue
Immunity Problems

the healing factor

- Copper
- Vitamin B$_{12}$
- Pantothenic acid
- Selenium
- Zinc
- Vitamin B$_6$
- Omega-3 fatty acids
- Niacin
- Riboflavin
- Phosphorus

italian chili

Aging
Depression
Memory Problems
Stress/Fatigue
Anemia
General Vision
Problems

the 🌿
healing
factor

🐞🐞🐞 Vitamin C
🐞🐞🐞 Vitamin A
🐞🐞🐞 Potassium
🐞🐞🐞 Fiber
🐞🐞🐞 Niacin
🐞🐞🐞 Iron
🐞🐞 Vitamin B$_6$
🐞🐞 Vitamin B$_{12}$
🐞🐞 Phosphorus
🐞🐞 Folate

³⁄₄	pound lean ground beef
1	tablespoon extra-virgin olive oil
2	large onions, chopped
2	large red bell peppers, chopped
1	large green bell pepper, chopped
5	cloves garlic, minced
2	tablespoons chili powder
1	teaspoon dried Italian herb seasoning, crushed
1	teaspoon salt
¼	cup dry red wine (see note)
3	small zucchini, chopped
1	can (14½ ounces) diced tomatoes with mild green chile peppers
1	can (14½ ounces) crushed tomatoes
2	tablespoons tomato paste
1	can (14–19 ounces) cannellini beans, rinsed and drained

In a large saucepot or Dutch oven over high heat, cook the beef, stirring occasionally, for 5 minutes, or until no longer pink. Drain and set aside. Wipe the pot with a paper towel.

Heat the oil in the same pot over medium-high heat. Add the onions, bell peppers, and garlic and cook, stirring frequently, for 5 minutes, or until soft.

Add the chili powder, Italian seasoning, and salt and cook, stirring constantly, for 1 minute. Add the wine and bring to a boil.

Add the zucchini, diced tomatoes (with juice), crushed tomatoes, tomato paste, and beef. Bring to a boil. Reduce the heat to low, cover, and simmer, stirring occasionally, for 30 minutes.

Add the beans and return to a simmer. Cover and cook, stirring occasionally, for 15 minutes, or until the zucchini is tender.

Makes 8 servings
Per serving: 257 calories, 15 g protein, 25 g carbohydrates, 11 g fat, 4 g saturated fat, 32 mg cholesterol, 7 g dietary fiber, 670 mg sodium

HEALTH NOTE
People with depression who take monoamine oxidase inhibitors (MAO inhibitors) should not use alcohol and other fermented products, such as the wine in this recipe. Substitute broth for the wine.

the power of
ONIONS
Many recipes begin by cooking onions prior to adding other ingredients in the dish. Not only does this flavor the dish beautifully but it also offers a great health benefit. Onions, both raw and cooked, contain compounds that help lower cholesterol, thin the blood, and prevent hardening of the arteries (all helping to stave off heart disease). These compounds may also help ward off cancers, especially those of the gastrointestinal tract. Choose red and yellow onions, which have the highest flavonoid content; white onions have the least.

helps
prevent

Aging
Memory Problems
Stress/Fatigue
Depression
Immunity Problems
Anemia

treat

the healing factor

🍐🍐🍐 Vitamin B$_{12}$

🍐🍐🍐 Zinc

🍐🍐🍐 Selenium

🍐🍐🍐 Vitamin C

🍐🍐🍐 Niacin

🍐🍐🍐 Vitamin B$_6$

🍐🍐🍐 Vitamin K

🍐🍐🍐 Phosphorus

🍐🍐🍐 Potassium

🍐🍐 Iron

grilled flank steak with chile-tomato salsa

 quick

2	tablespoons ground cumin
3	cloves garlic, minced
3	tablespoons lime juice
1	teaspoon coarsely ground black pepper
¾	teaspoon salt
1	beef flank steak or top round steak (1¼ pounds), trimmed of all visible fat
1	large tomato, finely chopped
1	can (4½ ounces) chopped mild green chiles, drained
3	scallions, thinly sliced

Lightly oil a grill rack or broiler-pan rack. Preheat the grill or broiler.

Place the cumin in a small skillet over medium heat and cook, stirring, for 3 minutes, or until fragrant and darker in color. Place in a small bowl and let cool.

Remove 1 teaspoon toasted cumin and place in a medium bowl. To the small bowl, add the garlic, 2 tablespoons of the lime juice, the black pepper, and ½ teaspoon of the salt and mix well. Place the steak on the prepared rack and rub the cumin mixture over both sides of the steak. Let stand at room temperature.

Meanwhile, in the medium bowl with the reserved cumin, combine the tomato, chiles, scallions, the remaining 1 tablespoon lime juice, and the remaining ¼ teaspoon salt. Let stand at room temperature.

Grill or broil the steak for 4 minutes per side, or until a thermometer inserted in the center registers 145°F for medium-rare.

Place the steak on a cutting board and let stand for 5 minutes. Cut the steak into thin slices and serve with the salsa.

Makes 4 servings
Per serving: 269 calories, 33 g protein, 7 g carbohydrates, 11 g fat, 5 g saturated fat, 58 mg cholesterol, 2 g dietary fiber, 605 mg sodium

COOKING TIP
The steak may be rubbed with the spice mixture and refrigerated up to 1 day ahead.

pot roast with dried fruit and red wine

Aging

Depression

Immunity
Problems

Stress/Fatigue

Memory Problems

General Vision
Problems

Constipation

the ✿ healing factor

🥄🥄🥄 Vitamin A

🥄🥄🥄 Vitamin B₁₂

🥄🥄🥄 Chromium

🥄🥄🥄 Potassium

🥄🥄🥄 Vitamin B₆

🥄🥄🥄 Selenium

🥄🥄🥄 Niacin

🥄🥄 Zinc

🥄🥄 Iron

🥄🥄 Phosphorus

1	well-trimmed boneless beef rump roast (2 pounds), tied
3/4	teaspoon salt
1/2	teaspoon freshly ground black pepper
1	cup beef broth
1	cup dry red wine (see note)
1/2	cup orange juice
1/2	teaspoon ground allspice
2	large red onions, cut into wedges
2	cups pitted prunes
2	cups dried apricot halves

Preheat the oven to 325°F. Rub the roast with the salt and pepper.

In an ovenproof Dutch oven, bring the broth, wine, orange juice, and allspice to a boil over high heat. Place the roast in the pot and return to a boil.

Cover the pot and place in the oven. Bake, turning the roast several times, for 2 hours. Add the onions, prunes, and apricots and cook for 1 hour, or until the roast is very tender. Place on a cutting board, cover, and let stand for 15 minutes.

Remove the strings from the roast and cut into thin slices. Arrange the meat on a platter and spoon the pan juices and fruit over top.

Makes 6 servings
Per serving: 570 calories, 37 g protein, 73 g carbohydrates, 14 g fat, 5 g saturated fat, 84 mg cholesterol, 9 g dietary fiber, 531 mg sodium

HEALTH NOTE
People with depression who take monoamine oxidase inhibitors (MAOs) should not use alcohol or other fermented products, such as the wine in this recipe. Substitute broth for the wine.

mexican pork stew

Photograph on page 58

2	tablespoons olive oil
1	pound pork tenderloin, cut into 1½" cubes
1	large onion, chopped
2	cloves garlic, minced
½	teaspoon ground cumin
¼	teaspoon ground cinnamon
2	cups low-sodium vegetable broth
1	can (15 ounces) diced tomatoes
1	can (4½ ounces) chopped green chiles, drained
¼	teaspoon freshly ground black pepper
1	small butternut squash or pumpkin (2 pounds), peeled, halved, seeded, and cut into ¾" chunks
1	medium zucchini, halved lengthwise and cut into ½"-thick slices
1	large red bell pepper, cut into thin strips
¼	cup whole blanched almonds, ground

Heat the oil in a large saucepot or Dutch oven over high heat. Add the pork, onion, garlic, cumin, and cinnamon. Cook, stirring, for 5 minutes, or until the pork is lightly browned.

Add the broth, tomatoes (with juice), chiles, and black pepper and bring to a boil. Reduce the heat to low, cover, and simmer, stirring occasionally, for 25 minutes.

Stir in the butternut squash or pumpkin, zucchini, and bell pepper. Cover and simmer, stirring occasionally, for 1 hour, or until the pork and squash are tender. Stir in the almonds. Cover and simmer for 5 minutes longer, or until slightly thickened.

Makes 4 servings
Per serving: 244 calories, 24 g protein, 18 g carbohydrates, 10 g fat, 2 g saturated fat, 45 mg cholesterol, 4 g dietary fiber, 594 mg sodium

treat ∫ helps prevent

Stress/Fatigue
Aging
Depression
Memory Problems
Immunity Problems
Anemia
General Vision Problems

the 🌿 healing factor

🐛🐛🐛 Vitamin C
🐛🐛🐛 Vitamin A
🐛🐛🐛 Thiamin
🐛🐛🐛 Selenium
🐛🐛🐛 Vitamin B$_6$
🐛🐛🐛 Phosphorus
🐛🐛🐛 Riboflavin
🐛🐛🐛 Niacin
🐛🐛🐛 Potassium
🐛🐛 Iron

Aging
Heart Disease
Depression
Immunity
Problems
Memory Problems
Stress/Fatigue
Anemia
Infections

beef and vegetable stew

Photograph on page 30

¾	teaspoon dried thyme, crushed
½	teaspoon dried sage, crushed
½	teaspoon salt
½	teaspoon freshly ground black pepper
1¼	pounds top round steak or sirloin steak, trimmed of all visible fat and cut into 2" cubes
1	tablespoon canola oil
4	cloves garlic, minced
2	tablespoons minced fresh ginger
1¾	cups fat-free beef broth
1	cup water
2	medium tomatoes, chopped, or 1 can (14½ ounces) diced tomatoes, drained
2	large sweet potatoes, peeled and cut into ¾" chunks
8	ounces small cremini or white button mushrooms, quartered
4	small onions, quartered
3	large carrots, cut into 1" pieces
¾	pound spinach, mustard greens, or kale, chopped

In a large bowl, combine the thyme, sage, salt, and pepper. Add the beef and toss to coat well.

Heat the oil in a large saucepot or Dutch oven over high heat. Add half of the beef and cook, stirring, for 4 minutes, or until browned. Place the browned beef in a bowl. Repeat with the remaining beef.

Return all the browned beef to the pot. Add the garlic and ginger and cook, stirring, for 1 minute. Stir in the broth and

🔔🔔🔔 Vitamin A
🔔🔔🔔 Vitamin K
🔔🔔🔔 Vitamin C
🔔🔔🔔 Vitamin B₆
🔔🔔🔔 Manganese
🔔🔔🔔 Vitamin B₁₂
🔔🔔🔔 Fiber
🔔🔔🔔 Iron
🔔🔔🔔 Potassium
🔔🔔🔔 Omega-3 fatty acids

water and bring to a boil. Reduce the heat to low, cover, and simmer, stirring occasionally, for 1½ hours, or until the beef is tender.

Add the tomatoes, sweet potatoes, mushrooms, onions, and carrots. Bring to a boil over high heat. Reduce the heat to low, cover, and simmer, stirring occasionally, for 40 minutes, or until the vegetables are tender. Add the spinach, mustard greens, or kale, cover, and cook for 2 minutes, or until wilted.

Makes 6 servings
Per serving: 310 calories, 28 g protein, 27 g carbohydrates, 10 g fat, 3 g saturated fat, 57 mg cholesterol, 11 g dietary fiber, 404 mg sodium

Depression
Stress/Fatigue
Aging
Memory Problems
Diabetes
Immunity Problems
Anemia
Cancer
Constipation

the
healing
factor

🍠🍠🍠 Thiamin

🍠🍠🍠 Selenium

🍠🍠🍠 Vitamin B$_6$

🍠🍠🍠 Niacin

🍠🍠🍠 Phosphorus

🍠🍠🍠 Vitamin A

🍠🍠🍠 Potassium

🍠🍠🍠 Riboflavin

🍠🍠🍠 Chromium

🍠🍠 Fiber

spiced pork scallops with fruit chutney

1	teaspoon ground cumin
3/4	teaspoon ground coriander
1/4	teaspoon ground cinnamon
1/4	teaspoon salt
1/4	teaspoon freshly ground black pepper
4	well-trimmed boneless pork chops (1 pound)
2	tablespoons butter
1	small onion, coarsely chopped
2–3	small tart apples, cored and cut into 3/4" chunks
1/3	cup dried apricots, halved
1/4	cup pitted prunes, halved
1/4	cup water
3	tablespoons frozen apple juice concentrate

In a cup, combine the cumin, coriander, and cinnamon. Reserve 1/2 teaspoon for the chutney. Stir the salt and pepper into the spice mixture in the cup. Rub over both sides of the chops. Place the chops on a plate, cover, and let stand at room temperature.

Meanwhile, melt 1 tablespoon of the butter in a medium saucepan over medium-high heat. Add the onion and cook, stirring frequently, for 3 minutes, or until soft.

Add the apples, apricots, prunes, water, apple juice concentrate, and the reserved 1/2 teaspoon spice mixture. Bring to a boil over high heat. Reduce the heat to low, cover, and simmer, stirring occasionally, for 20 minutes, or until the fruit is very tender and the juices have thickened into a glaze. Remove from the heat and cover to keep warm.

Melt the remaining 1 tablespoon butter in a large nonstick skillet over medium-high heat. Add the chops and cook for 6 minutes, turning once, or until a thermometer inserted in the center of a chop registers 160°F and the juices run clear.

Serve the pork with the chutney.

Makes 4 servings
Per serving: 320 calories, 25 g protein, 33 g carbohydrates, 11 g fat, 5 g saturated fat, 90 mg cholesterol, 4 g dietary fiber, 271 mg sodium

simple ways to eat more fruit

Eating enough fruit may often seem like a chore, but it really can be easy, and fun. Try these tips to easily increase your fruit intake—and add new life to old favorites.

- Add orange sections to your favorite Chinese stir-fry.
- Stir diced apple into curry dishes.
- Toss some raisins or chopped prunes into salads.
- Spread natural peanut butter on half a banana for an energy-boosting snack.
- Halve grapes and add to light chicken dishes.

- Layer thinly sliced pears on meat sandwiches—great with honey-mustard.
- Top ice cream with mashed fresh berries tossed with a bit of sugar.
- Top spicy chicken dishes with chopped mango.
- Use fruit juices instead of wine in savory sauces.
- Fold pineapple chunks into chicken or tuna salad.
- Stir chopped berries into cream cheese before spreading on toast or bagels.
- Stir chopped fruit into yogurt.

Depression

Memory Problems

Aging

Heart Disease

Immunity
Problems

General Vision
Problems

Asthma

Breast Cancer

Cancer

Cataracts

the
healing
factor

🐞🐞🐞 Vitamin C

🐞🐞🐞 Vitamin A

🐞🐞🐞 Thiamin

🐞🐞🐞 Vitamin B₆

🐞🐞🐞 Selenium

🐞🐞 Omega-3
fatty acids

🐞🐞🐞 Phosphorus

🐞🐞 Niacin

🐞🐞🐞 Vitamin K

🐞🐞🐞 Potassium

pork and pepper stir-fry

Photograph on page 52

2	tablespoons apricot all-fruit spread
2	tablespoons soy sauce (see note)
½	teaspoon crushed red-pepper flakes
1	pound pork tenderloin, cut into ½" strips
4	teaspoons canola oil
½	cup chicken or vegetable broth
1	tablespoon cornstarch
6	cloves garlic, thinly sliced
1	tablespoon grated fresh ginger
2	large red bell peppers, cut into thin strips
2	large green bell peppers, cut into thin strips
1	large onion, cut into wedges

In a medium bowl, combine the all-fruit spread, 1 tablespoon of the soy sauce, and ¼ teaspoon of the red-pepper flakes. Add the pork and toss to coat well. Cover and marinate for 20 minutes at room temperature.

Heat 2 teaspoons of the oil in a large nonstick skillet over high heat. Add the pork mixture and cook, stirring frequently, for 3 minutes, or until the pork is slightly pink in the center. Place in a bowl and keep warm. Wipe the skillet with a paper towel.

In a cup, whisk together the broth and cornstarch and set aside.

Add the remaining 2 teaspoons oil to the same skillet and place over medium-high heat. Add the garlic, ginger, and the remaining ¼ teaspoon red-pepper flakes and cook, stirring constantly, for 2 minutes, or until the garlic is golden.

Add the bell peppers, onion, and the remaining 1 tablespoon soy sauce and cook, stirring, for 6 minutes, or until tender.

Add the pork and any accumulated juices to the pepper mixture. Stir the cornstarch mixture and add to the skillet. Cook, stirring constantly, for 1 minute, or until thickened.

Makes 4 servings
Per serving: 285 calories, 27 g protein, 25 g carbohydrates, 9 g fat, 2 g saturated fat, 74 mg cholesterol, 4 g dietary fiber, 665 mg sodium

HEALTH NOTE
People with depression who take monoamine oxidase inhibitors (MAO inhibitors) should not use alcohol or other fermented products, such as the soy sauce in this recipe. Substitute broth for the soy sauce.

Depression
Memory Problems
Aging
Immunity
Problems
Stress/Fatigue
General Vision
Problems
Dental Problems
Osteoporosis

the 🌿
healing factor

🐞🐞🐞 Vitamin A
🐞🐞🐞 Vitamin C
🐞🐞🐞 Thiamin
🐞🐞🐞 Manganese
🐞🐞🐞 Selenium
🐞🐞🐞 Vitamin B$_6$
🐞🐞🐞 Calcium
🐞🐞🐞 Niacin
🐞🐞🐞 Folate
🐞🐞🐞 Phosphorus

spicy pork strips with garlic greens

Greens

1	tablespoon extra-virgin olive oil
1	large red bell pepper, chopped
6	large cloves garlic, minced
2	packages (10 ounces each) frozen chopped collard greens, thawed, with juices reserved
½	cup water
2	tablespoons cider vinegar (see note)
¼	teaspoon salt

Pork

1	pound pork tenderloin, cut into ½" strips
1–2	serrano chile peppers, most seeds removed, finely chopped (wear plastic gloves when handling)
½	teaspoon coarsely ground black pepper
¼	teaspoon salt
1	tablespoon extra-virgin olive oil

To make the greens: Heat the oil in a large nonstick skillet over medium heat. Add the pepper and garlic and cook, stirring often, for 2 minutes, or until lightly browned.

Add the greens and water and bring to a boil. Reduce the heat to low, cover, and simmer, stirring occasionally, adding additional water if needed, for 20 minutes, or until tender. Stir in the vinegar and salt.

Place the greens in a serving dish and keep warm. Wipe the skillet with a paper towel.

To make the pork: While the greens are cooking, in a medium bowl, combine the pork, chile peppers, black pepper, and salt.

Heat the oil in the same skillet over high heat. Add the pork mixture and cook, stirring constantly, for 3 minutes, or until slightly pink in the center.

Spoon the pork strips on top of the greens and serve.

Makes 4 servings
Per serving: 271 calories, 32 g protein, 15 g carbohydrates, 10 g fat, 2 g saturated fat, 67 mg cholesterol, 5 g dietary fiber, 421 mg sodium

HEALTH NOTE
People with depression who take monoamine oxidase inhibitors (MAO inhibitors) should not use alcohol or other fermented products, such as the vinegar in this recipe. Substitute apple juice for the vinegar.

pork tenderloin with vegetables

Stroke

Depression

Stress/Fatigue

Aging

Immunity
Problems

Memory Problems

Heart Disease

Diabetes

General Vision
Problems

Cancer

1	pound small red potatoes, cut into 1"-thick wedges
3	large carrots, cut into 1" chunks
1	tablespoon grated lemon peel
2	teaspoons dried rosemary, crushed, + rosemary sprigs for garnish
1	teaspoon fennel seeds, crushed
3/4	teaspoon cracked black pepper
1/2	teaspoon salt
1	pound pork tenderloin
1	teaspoon +1 tablespoon extra-virgin olive oil
4	medium plum tomatoes, each cut into 4 wedges
1	onion, cut into 1/2"-thick wedges
1/3	cup chicken broth

the 🌿
healing factor

🍅🍅🍅 Vitamin A

🍅🍅🍅 Thiamin

🍅🍅🍅 Vitamin C

🍅🍅🍅 Chromium

🍅🍅🍅 Vitamin B$_6$

🍅🍅🍅 Selenium

🍅🍅🍅 Potassium

🍅🍅🍅 Niacin

🍅🍅🍅 Phosphorus

🍅🍅🍅 Manganese

Preheat the oven to 450°F. Coat a roasting pan with cooking spray.

Place a steamer basket in a large saucepan with 1/2" of water. Place the potatoes and carrots in the steamer. Bring to a boil over high heat. Reduce the heat to medium, cover, and cook for 5 minutes, or until the potatoes are just tender. Remove from the heat.

Meanwhile, in a large bowl, combine the lemon peel, dried rosemary, fennel, pepper, and salt. Rub the pork with 2 teaspoons of the herb mixture. Place the pork in the center of the prepared roasting pan and drizzle with 1 teaspoon of the oil.

Add the potatoes and carrots, tomatoes, and onion to the herb mixture remaining in the bowl. Add the remaining 1 tablespoon oil and toss to coat well. Arrange the vegetables around the roast. Drizzle the vegetables with the broth.

Roast for 30 minutes, or until a thermometer inserted in the center reaches 155°F, the juices run clear, and the vegetables are tender and lightly browned on the edges. Place the pork on a cutting board and let stand for 5 minutes.

Slice the pork on the diagonal and place on a platter with the vegetables. Drizzle with the pan juices and garnish with rosemary sprigs.

Makes 4 servings
Per serving: 320 calories, 29 g protein, 31 g carbohydrates, 9 g fat, 2 g saturated fat, 74 mg cholesterol, 6 g dietary fiber, 427 mg sodium

treat

Aging
Memory Problems
Stress/Fatigue
Immunity
Problems

the healing factor

🐞🐞🐞 Thiamin

🐞🐞🐞 Selenium

🐞🐞🐞 Vitamin B$_6$

🐞🐞🐞 Niacin

🐞🐞🐞 Riboflavin

🐞🐞🐞 Phosphorus

🐞🐞🐞 Zinc

🐞🐞 Vitamin B$_{12}$

🐞🐞 Potassium

chinese barbecued pork chops

quick

1/3	cup tomato sauce
1/4	cup hoisin sauce
3	tablespoons rice wine vinegar or white wine vinegar
2	tablespoons dry sherry or chicken broth
3	cloves garlic, minced
1	tablespoon grated fresh ginger
4	boneless center-cut pork chops (4 ounces each), trimmed of all visible fat

Coat a grill rack or broiler-pan rack with cooking spray. Preheat the grill or broiler.

In a small saucepan, combine the tomato sauce, hoisin sauce, vinegar, sherry or broth, garlic, and ginger. Bring to a boil over medium-high heat. Cook, stirring often, for 3 minutes, or until reduced to a syrupy consistency. Set aside.

Meanwhile, grill or broil the chops 4" from the heat for 8 minutes, turning once. Cook, brushing with the reserved sauce and turning occasionally, for 3 minutes longer, or until a thermometer inserted in the center of a chop registers 160°F and the juices run clear.

Makes 4 servings
Per serving: 239 calories, 23 g protein, 10 g carbohydrates, 10 g fat, 3 g saturated fat, 73 mg cholesterol, 1 g dietary fiber, 457 mg sodium

bbq butterflied leg of lamb

Photograph on page 40

¼	cup extra-virgin olive oil
⅓	cup lemon juice
10	cloves garlic, minced
2	tablespoons chopped fresh rosemary or 2 teaspoons dried, crushed
1	tablespoon grated lemon peel
1¼	teaspoons salt
1¼	teaspoons freshly ground black pepper
1	butterflied, well-trimmed leg of lamb (4 pounds)

In a large shallow baking dish or a large bowl, combine the oil, lemon juice, garlic, rosemary, lemon peel, salt, and pepper.

Add the lamb and turn to coat well. Cover and refrigerate, turning the lamb several times, overnight or for at least 2 hours.

Preheat a grill. Place the lamb on the grill rack and drizzle with any remaining marinade. Grill, turning 2 or 3 times, for 25 to 35 minutes, or until a thermometer inserted in the thickest part registers 145°F for medium-rare. (Thinner parts will be more well-done.)

Place the lamb on a cutting board and let stand for 10 minutes. Cut into thin slices.

Makes 16 servings
Per serving: 180 calories, 23 g protein, 1 g carbohydrates, 9 g fat, 2 g saturated fat, 73 mg cholesterol, 0 g dietary fiber, 253 mg sodium

the
healing factor

🐾🐾🐾 Vitamin B$_{12}$
🐾🐾🐾 Niacin
🐾🐾🐾 Zinc
🐾🐾🐾 Phosphorus
🐾🐾 Riboflavin
🐾🐾 Iron
🐾🐾 Thiamin
🐾🐾 Vitamin B$_6$
🐾🐾 Potassium

Aging
Heart Disease
Depression
Memory Problems
General Vision Problems
Anemia
Diabetes
Stress/Fatigue
Constipation

the
healing factor

🍒🍒🍒 Omega-3 fatty acids

🍒🍒🍒 Niacin

🍒🍒🍒 Phosphorus

🍒🍒🍒 Vitamin B$_{12}$

🍒🍒🍒 Fiber

🍒🍒🍒 Iron

🍒🍒🍒 Folate

🍒🍒🍒 Vitamin C

🍒🍒🍒 Zinc

🍒🍒🍒 Magnesium

minted lamb chops with white beans

Photograph on page 44

3	anchovy fillets, rinsed and patted dry
1	teaspoon extra-virgin olive oil
3	tablespoons chopped fresh mint or 3 teaspoons dried, crushed
½	teaspoon freshly ground black pepper
4	lamb loin chops (about 1¼ pounds), well-trimmed
4	plum tomatoes, coarsely chopped
1	clove garlic, crushed
3	cups rinsed and drained canned cannellini beans
2	tablespoons beef broth
¼	teaspoon salt
	Mint sprigs + additional chopped mint for garnish (optional)

Coat a broiler-pan rack with cooking spray. Preheat the broiler.

On a cutting board, finely chop the anchovies. Sprinkle with the oil, 1 tablespoon of the fresh mint or 1 teaspoon dried, and ¼ teaspoon of the pepper, then mash to a paste with the flat side of a chef's knife or a fork. Place the chops on the prepared rack and rub the anchovy paste over both sides of the chops. Let stand at room temperature

Meanwhile, in a medium nonstick skillet, combine the tomatoes and garlic and cook, stirring frequently, over medium-high heat for 2 minutes, or until the tomatoes begin to give up their juices. Reduce the heat to medium, cover, and cook for 3 minutes, or until the tomatoes are very soft.

Stir in the beans, broth, salt, 2 tablespoons of the remaining fresh mint or 2 teaspoons dried, and the remaining ¼ teaspoon pepper. Bring to a boil over high heat. Reduce the heat to low, cover, and simmer, stirring occasionally, for 10 minutes to blend the flavors.

While the beans are simmering, broil the lamb chops 4" from the heat for 8 minutes per side, or until a thermometer inserted in the center registers 145°F for medium-rare.

To serve, evenly divide the bean mixture among 4 plates and top each with a lamb chop. Garnish with the mint, if using.

Makes 4 servings
Per serving: 476 calories, 47 g protein, 45 g carbohydrates, 13 g fat, 4 g saturated fat, 98 mg cholesterol, 12 g dietary fiber, 667 mg sodium

Depression

Aging

Memory Problems

Immunity
Problems

Stress/Fatigue

General Vision
Problems

lamb kebabs

2	tablespoons lemon juice
1	tablespoon olive oil
2	tablespoons chopped fresh oregano
1	pound leg of lamb, trimmed of all visible fat and cut into 1" cubes
16	cherry tomatoes
2	yellow bell peppers, each cut into 8 pieces
2	zucchini, each cut into 8 pieces
1	large red onion, cut into 16 chunks
1/2	teaspoon salt
1/4	teaspoon freshly ground black pepper

In a medium bowl, combine the lemon juice, oil, and oregano. Add the lamb and toss to coat well. Cover and refrigerate for at least 2 hours or up to 8 hours.

Coat a grill rack or broiler-pan rack with cooking spray. Preheat the grill or broiler.

Evenly divide the lamb onto 4 metal skewers, leaving 1/4" space between the pieces of meat. Discard the marinade.

Evenly divide the tomatoes, bell peppers, zucchini, and onion onto 8 metal skewers, alternating the vegetables. Sprinkle the meat and vegetables with the salt and black pepper.

Cook the skewers 4" from the heat for 8 minutes, turning occasionally, or until the lamb is pink inside and the vegetables are tender.

Makes 4 servings
Per serving: 284 calories, 31 g protein, 15 g carbohydrates, 11 g fat, 3 g saturated fat, 90 mg cholesterol, 3 g dietary fiber, 368 mg sodium

the
healing
factor

🍒🍒🍒 Vitamin C

🍒🍒🍒 Vitamin B₁₂

🍒🍒🍒 Niacin

🍒🍒🍒 Omega-3
fatty acids

🍒🍒🍒 Zinc

🍒🍒🍒 Phosphorus

🍒🍒🍒 Potassium

🍒🍒🍒 Vitamin B₆

🍒🍒🍒 Vitamin A

🍒🍒🍒 Riboflavin

Orange Beef and Broccoli

Photograph on page 35

This stir-fry packs a power-punch of nutrients to help keep stress at bay.

- ¼ cup chicken broth
- 3 tablespoons dry sherry or chicken broth
- ½ cup orange juice
- 2 tablespoons soy sauce
- 1 tablespoon grated fresh ginger
- 2 teaspoons cornstarch
- 1 teaspoon toasted sesame oil
- ½ teaspoon crushed red-pepper flakes
- ¾ pound beef sirloin, trimmed of all visible fat and cut into ¼"-thick strips
- 2 teaspoons vegetable oil
- 1 large bunch broccoli, cut into florets
- 1 bunch scallions, cut into ¼"-thick diagonal slices
- 3 cloves garlic, minced
- 2 cups cooked basmati rice

In a medium bowl, combine the broth, sherry or broth, orange juice, soy sauce, ginger, cornstarch, sesame oil, and red-pepper flakes. Add the beef, tossing to coat. Let stand for 10 minutes.

Heat 1 teaspoon of the vegetable oil in a large skillet over medium-high heat. Add the beef to the skillet; reserve the marinade. Cook the beef, stirring, for 3 minutes, or until browned. Remove to a plate.

Add the remaining 1 teaspoon vegetable oil to the skillet. Add the broccoli, scallions, and garlic; cook, stirring, for 2 minutes. Add 2 tablespoons water. Cover and cook for 2 minutes, or until the broccoli is tender-crisp. Add the reserved marinade and cook, stirring, for 3 minutes, or until the mixture boils and thickens slightly. Return the beef to the pan and cook, stirring, for 2 minutes, or until heated through. Serve over the rice.

Makes 4 servings
Per serving: 395 calories, 25 g protein, 40 g carbohydrates, 15 g fat, 5 g saturated fat, 56 mg cholesterol, 7 g dietary fiber, 432 mg sodium

lamb and barley stew

Aging

Stroke

Depression

Immunity
Problems

General Vision
Problems

Cancer

Heart Disease

Dental Problems

Infections

Insomnia

the 🌿
healing
factor

🐞🐞🐞 Vitamin A

🐞🐞🐞 Niacin

🐞🐞🐞 Fiber

🐞🐞🐞 Vitamin B$_{12}$

🐞🐞🐞 Manganese

🐞🐞🐞 Zinc

🐞🐞🐞 Selenium

🐞🐞🐞 Copper

🐞🐞🐞 Phosphorus

🐞🐞🐞 Vitamin C

1	tablespoon olive oil
1	pound cubed lamb
1	large onion, chopped
2	cloves garlic, minced
2	cups low-sodium beef broth
3	cups water
1	cup pearl barley
1	teaspoon dried thyme, crushed
1/4	teaspoon salt
1/4	teaspoon freshly ground black pepper
3	large carrots, sliced
6	ounces shiitake mushrooms, sliced
2	medium tomatoes, chopped
1	cup frozen petite peas

Preheat the oven to 350°F.

Heat the oil in a large saucepot or Dutch oven over medium-high heat. Add the lamb and onion and cook, stirring occasionally, for 5 minutes, or until browned. Add the garlic and cook for 1 minute. Add the broth, water, barley, thyme, salt, and pepper. Bring to a boil over high heat. Reduce the heat to low, cover, and simmer for 1 hour.

Add the carrots, mushrooms, and tomatoes and cook, stirring occasionally, for 45 minutes, or until the barley is tender. Add the peas during the last 5 minutes.

Makes 4 servings
Per serving: 471 calories, 34 g protein, 60 g carbohydrates, 11 g fat, 3 g saturated fat, 74 mg cholesterol, 13 g dietary fiber, 329 mg sodium

poultry
and seafood

Poultry, fish, and shellfish are great sources of low-fat protein. Chicken and turkey are inexpensive, versatile, and simple to prepare, making them a favorite for most cooks. Look for quick-cooking cuts that are readily available, including cutlets, strips for stir-frying, and boneless thighs and drumsticks.

Fish and shellfish are among the healthiest foods that you can eat. Another versatile protein source, fish and shellfish are available in many types to experiment with. Ask your fishmonger to suggest varieties that would be appropriate for your meal plans.

one-pot chicken and rice

Depression
Memory Problems
Stress/Fatigue
Aging
Immunity Problems
Asthma
Anemia
Colds and Flu
Stroke

the  healing factor

🐞🐞🐞 Manganese

🐞🐞🐞 Niacin

🐞🐞🐞 Phosphorus

🐞🐞🐞 Vitamin B₆

🐞🐞🐞 Magnesium

🐞🐞🐞 Vitamin C

🐞🐞🐞 Thiamin

🐞🐞🐞 Selenium

🐞🐞 Pantothenic acid

🐞🐞 Zinc

2	tablespoons olive oil
3	cloves garlic, minced
1	large onion, chopped
1¼	cups brown rice
4	chicken thighs, skin and visible fat removed
1	can (14½ ounces) diced tomatoes, drained
2	cups chicken broth
1	teaspoon dried thyme, crushed
½	teaspoon freshly ground black pepper

Preheat the oven to 325°F.

Heat the oil in an ovenproof Dutch oven over medium heat. Add the garlic and onion and cook, stirring frequently, for 4 minutes, or until softened.

Add the rice and cook, stirring, for 2 minutes, or until it starts to brown. Stir in the chicken, tomatoes, broth, thyme, and pepper. Bring to a boil over high heat.

Cover the pot and place in the oven. Bake for 1 hour and 15 minutes, or until the rice is tender and the liquid is absorbed.

Makes 4 servings
Per serving: 392 calories, 20 g protein, 52 g carbohydrates, 11 g fat, 2 g saturated fat, 57 mg cholesterol, 4 g dietary fiber, 537 mg sodium

chunky chicken chili

treat ⌐

2	tablespoons olive oil
4	cloves garlic, minced
2	jalapeño or serrano chile peppers, partially seeded, and minced (wear plastic gloves when handling)
1	large onion, chopped
1	pound fresh tomatillos, husked, rinsed, and coarsely chopped
2	teaspoons ground cumin
½	teaspoon salt
¼	teaspoon freshly ground black pepper
1½	cups chicken broth
1	pound boneless, skinless chicken breasts, cut into ¾" cubes
2	cups frozen cut leaf spinach (from a bag)
1	can (15½ ounces) whole hominy, drained and rinsed
½	cup chopped fresh cilantro

Heat the oil in a large saucepot or Dutch oven over medium heat. Add the garlic, chile peppers, and onion and cook, stirring frequently, for 8 minutes, or until soft.

Stir in the tomatillos, cumin, salt, and pepper. Reduce the heat to low, cover, and cook, stirring frequently, for 5 minutes, or until the tomatillos are softened.

Stir in the broth, chicken, spinach, and hominy. Bring to a boil over high heat. Reduce the heat to low and cook, stirring occasionally, for 5 minutes, or until the chicken is no longer pink.

Stir in the cilantro.

Makes 6 servings
Per serving: 237 calories, 22 g protein, 20 g carbohydrates, 7 g fat, 1 g saturated fat, 44 mg cholesterol, 6 g dietary fiber, 662 mg sodium

helps prevent

Stress/Fatigue
Aging
Diabetes
Heart Disease
Depression
Dental Problems
Headaches
Immunity Problems
Memory Problems
Anemia

the healing factor

🍐🍐🍐 Vitamin A
🍐🍐🍐 Niacin
🍐🍐🍐 Vitamin C
🍐🍐🍐 Vitamin B₆
🍐🍐🍐 Fiber
🍐🍐🍐 Phosphorus
🍐🍐 Potassium
🍐🍐 Manganese
🍐🍐 Magnesium
🍐🍐 Iron

COOKING TIP
Tomatillos are Mexican green tomatoes. Smaller than their red tomato cousins, they are often sold with a papery husk. Remove and discard the husk before using.

helps
prevent ～

~treat

Stress/Fatigue

Aging

Depression

Memory Problems

Immunity
Problems

Infections

Stroke

Anemia

General Vision
Problems

the ⚘
**healing
factor**

🐞🐞🐞 Vitamin C

🐞🐞🐞 Niacin

🐞🐞🐞 Vitamin B$_6$

🐞🐞🐞 Phosphorus

🐞🐞🐞 Vitamin A

🐞🐞🐞 Zinc

🐞🐞🐞 Pantothenic
acid

🐞🐞🐞 Riboflavin

🐞🐞🐞 Magnesium

🐞🐞🐞 Potassium

oven-fried chicken with red pepper–sweet onion relish

Chicken

$2/3$	cup buttermilk or fat-free plain yogurt
2	tablespoons lime juice
$1/2$	teaspoon salt
$1/2$	teaspoon freshly ground black pepper
$1 1/4$	cups yellow cornmeal
1	cut-up chicken (3 pounds), wings saved for another use, skin and visible fat removed

Relish

1	large red bell pepper, finely chopped
1	small red onion, finely chopped
$1/2$	cup chopped fresh cilantro
2	tablespoons lime juice
1	tablespoon extra-virgin olive oil
$1/8$	teaspoon salt

To make the chicken: Preheat the oven to 425°F. Coat a large baking sheet with sides with cooking spray.

In a large bowl, combine the buttermilk or yogurt, lime juice, salt, and pepper. Place the cornmeal in a pie plate.

Dip the chicken in the buttermilk mixture, turning to coat well. (The chicken may be marinated in the buttermilk mixture in the refrigerator for up to 1 day.)

One at a time, roll the chicken pieces in the cornmeal, pressing to coat thoroughly. Place the chicken, skinned side up, on the prepared baking sheet. Discard any remaining buttermilk mixture and cornmeal.

Coat the chicken well with cooking spray. Bake for 40 minutes, or until a thermometer inserted in the thickest portion registers 170°F and the juices run clear.

To *make the relish:* Meanwhile, in a medium bowl, combine the bell pepper, onion, cilantro, lime juice, oil, and salt. Cover and let stand at room temperature.

Serve the chicken with the relish.

Makes 6 servings
Per serving: 399 calories, 52 g protein, 25 g carbohydrates, 9 g fat, 2 g saturated fat, 161 mg cholesterol, 43 g dietary fiber, 337 mg sodium

Stress/Fatigue

Aging

Memory Problems

Immunity Problems

Anemia

Infections

Leg Cramps

the *✻*
healing factor

🐞🐞🐞 Niacin

🐞🐞🐞 Vitamin C

🐞🐞🐞 Vitamin A

🐞🐞🐞 Vitamin B$_6$

🐞🐞🐞 Phosphorus

🐞🐞🐞 Manganese

🐞🐞🐞 Chromium

🐞🐞 Calcium

🐞🐞 Potassium

🐞🐞 Magnesium

california chicken

Photograph on page 43

1	tablespoon whole grain mustard
1	egg white
1	cup fresh whole wheat bread crumbs
1/3	cup (1 1/2 ounces) freshly grated Parmesan cheese
1	teaspoon grated lemon peel
4	boneless, skinless chicken breast halves, pounded to 1/2" thickness
1/4	cup chopped fresh basil
1	tablespoon balsamic vinegar
2	teaspoons extra-virgin olive oil
1/8	teaspoon salt
2	bunches watercress or arugula
3	large plum tomatoes, chopped
1/2	small red onion, finely chopped

Coat a broiler-pan rack with cooking spray. Preheat the broiler.

In a shallow bowl, combine the mustard and egg white. In another shallow bowl, combine the bread crumbs, cheese, and lemon peel. Dip the chicken into the mustard mixture, turning to coat, and then into the bread-crumb mixture, pressing to coat thoroughly with crumbs. Place the chicken on the prepared rack.

Broil 6" from the heat for 10 minutes, turning once, or until golden brown and a thermometer inserted in the thickest portion registers 160°F and the juices run clear. If the chicken browns too quickly, turn off the broiler and bake the chicken in a 350°F oven for 15 minutes, or until golden brown and a thermometer inserted in the thickest portion registers 160°F and the juices run clear.

Meanwhile, in a medium bowl, whisk together the basil, vinegar, oil, and salt. Add the watercress or arugula, tomatoes, and onion, and toss to coat well. Evenly divide the salad among 4 plates. Top each with a chicken breast.

Makes 4 servings
Per serving: 264 calories, 34 g protein, 15 g carbohydrates, 8 g fat, 3 g saturated fat, 72 mg cholesterol, 3 g dietary fiber, 483 mg sodium

simple ways to sneak vegetables into your favorite dishes

Getting the recommended amount of vegetables into your meals can often be a challenge. Here are some surefire ways to help you reach your health goals.

- Stir shredded carrots and zucchini into your favorite meat loaf.
- Spike your rice, mashed potatoes, or grains with a mixture of garlic, onions, carrots, and celery sautéed in olive oil. Splash with some balsamic vinegar before stirring into the dish.
- Stir thawed and squeezed-dry frozen chopped spinach into meatballs or burgers.

- Add frozen, thawed corn kernels into meat taco filling.
- Stir steamed cauliflower into macaroni and cheese before baking.
- Place carrot and celery sticks on the table with meals and watch them disappear.
- Sauté chopped onion and bell pepper and add to scrambled eggs.
- Cook diced potatoes with cream soups to thicken upon pureeing.
- Stir thawed frozen corn kernels and chopped roasted red peppers into cornbread or muffins.
- Add frozen mixed vegetables to tuna noodle casserole.

Stress/Fatigue
Aging
Depression
Diabetes
Heart Disease
Dental Problems
Immunity Problems
Anemia
Prostate Problems

chicken breasts arrabbiata

1	tablespoon extra-virgin olive oil
1	large red bell pepper, chopped
1	large onion, chopped
¼	cup seeded, rinsed, and chopped pepperoncini
3	cloves garlic, crushed
1	teaspoon dried basil, crushed
½	teaspoon freshly ground black pepper
¼	teaspoon salt
3	cups coarsely chopped plum tomatoes
¼	cup chicken broth
1	tablespoon balsamic vinegar (see note)
1	tablespoon tomato paste
4	boneless, skinless chicken breast halves

Heat the oil in a large skillet over medium-high heat. Add the bell pepper, onion, pepperoncini, garlic, basil, black pepper, and salt; cook, stirring, for 4 minutes, or until the vegetables are tender. Add the tomatoes, broth, vinegar, and tomato paste. Increase the heat to medium-high and cook, stirring, for 3 minutes, or until the tomatoes start to release their juices.

Add the chicken, reduce the heat to medium-low, cover, and simmer for 15 minutes, or until a thermometer inserted in the thickest portion registers 160°F and the juices run clear.

Makes 4 servings
Per serving: 225 calories, 30 g protein, 14 g carbohydrates, 6 g fat, 1 g saturated fat, 66 mg cholesterol, 3 g dietary fiber, 491 mg sodium

the healing factor

- 🍎🍎🍎 Vitamin C
- 🍎🍎🍎 Niacin
- 🍎🍎🍎 Vitamin A
- 🍎🍎🍎 Vitamin B₆
- 🍎🍎🍎 Phosphorus
- 🍎🍎 Fiber
- 🍎🍎 Potassium
- 🍎🍎 Iron
- 🍎🍎 Pantothenic acid
- 🍎🍎 Magnesium

HEALTH NOTE
People with depression who take monoamine oxidase inhibitors (MAO in-hibitors) should not use the vinegar in this recipe. Substitute broth for the vinegar.

baked chicken with prunes

4	boneless, skinless chicken breast halves
¼	cup red wine (see note)
16	pitted prunes
1	teaspoon finely chopped fresh rosemary
¼	teaspoon salt
⅛	teaspoon freshly ground black pepper

Preheat the oven to 350°F. Coat a 13" × 9" baking dish with cooking spray.

Place the chicken in the prepared baking dish.

In a small microwaveable measuring cup, combine the wine and prunes. Microwave on high power for 1 minute, or until the wine boils. Pour over the chicken. Sprinkle with the rosemary, salt, and pepper.

Bake for 30 minutes, or until a thermometer inserted in the thickest portion registers 160°F and the juices run clear.

Makes 4 servings
Per serving: 228 calories, 25 g protein, 21 g carbohydrates, 4 g fat, 1 g saturated fat, 79 mg cholesterol, 2 g dietary fiber, 236 mg sodium

HEALTH NOTE
People with depression who take monoamine oxidase inhibitors (MAO inhibitors) should not use alcohol or other fermented products, such as the wine in this recipe. Substitute apple juice for the wine.

Stress/Fatigue
Aging
Depression
Memory Problems
Headaches
Anemia
Immunity Problems
Insomnia
Constipation

the healing factor

- 🍐🍐🍐 Niacin
- 🍐🍐🍐 Vitamin B₆
- 🍐🍐🍐 Phosphorus
- 🍐🍐 Vitamin A
- 🍐🍐 Potassium
- 🍐🍐 Pantothenic acid
- 🍐🍐 Riboflavin
- 🍐🍐 Zinc
- 🍐🍐 Iron
- 🍐🍐 Magnesium

helps
prevent

Memory Problems
Depression
Stress/Fatigue
Aging
General Vision
Problems
Cataracts
Anemia

treat

chicken piccata with escarole

4	boneless, skinless chicken breast halves
½	teaspoon dried thyme, crushed
¼	teaspoon freshly ground black pepper
¼	teaspoon salt
2	cloves garlic, minced
5	cups loosely packed cut-up escarole
1	cup cherry tomatoes, halved
½	cup fat-free chicken broth
2	teaspoons cornstarch
½	teaspoon grated lemon peel
1	tablespoon lemon juice
1	tablespoon butter

Coat the broiler-pan rack with cooking spray. Preheat the broiler.

Season both sides of the chicken breasts with the thyme, pepper, and ⅛ teaspoon of the salt. Place the chicken on the broiler-pan rack and broil 2" to 3" from the heat for 5 minutes per side, or until a thermometer inserted in the thickest portion registers 160°F and the juices run clear. Place the chicken on a platter and keep warm.

Meanwhile, heat a large skillet coated with cooking spray over medium-high heat. Add the garlic and cook, stirring constantly, for 30 seconds, or until fragrant. Add the escarole and cook, stirring frequently, for 3 minutes, or until the greens begin to wilt. Add the tomatoes and the remaining ⅛ teaspoon salt and cook for 3 minutes, or until the tomatoes are soft and

the
healing
factor

🐞🐞🐞 Vitamin K
🐞🐞🐞 Niacin
🐞🐞🐞 Vitamin A
🐞🐞🐞 Vitamin C
🐞🐞🐞 Vitamin B₆
🐞🐞🐞 Folate
🐞🐞🐞 Phosphorus
🐞🐞 Manganese
🐞🐞 Potassium
🐞🐞 Pantothenic
acid

the escarole is completely wilted. Place the vegetables on the platter with the chicken.

In a cup, combine the broth and cornstarch and stir until dissolved. In the same skillet, whisk together the cornstarch mixture, lemon peel, and lemon juice and bring to a boil over high heat, stirring constantly. Cook, stirring, for 1 minute, or until the sauce is slightly thickened. Add the butter and any juices that have collected on the platter and return to a boil, stirring constantly. Cook just until the butter is melted and the sauce has thickened. Pour the sauce over the chicken and vegetables.

Makes 4 servings
Per serving: 151 calories, 21 g protein, 6 g carbohydrates, 4 g fat, 2 g saturated fat, 58 mg cholesterol, 3 g dietary fiber, 257 mg sodium

the healing factor

🐦🐦🐦 Niacin

🐦🐦🐦 Vitamin A

🐦🐦🐦 Vitamin B$_6$

🐦🐦🐦 Vitamin C

🐦🐦🐦 Phosphorus

🐦🐦 Potassium

🐦🐦 Iron

🐦🐦 Thiamin

🐦🐦 Pantothenic acid

🐦🐦 Magnesium

jerk chicken with mango

2	jalapeño chile peppers, halved and seeded (wear plastic gloves when handling)
½	small onion, halved
2	cloves garlic, minced
1	slice (¼" thick) peeled fresh ginger
1	tablespoon olive oil
1	tablespoon white wine vinegar (see note)
1½	teaspoons dried thyme, crushed
1	teaspoon ground allspice
¼	teaspoon salt
4	skinless bone-in chicken breast halves
1	mango, peeled and diced
1	tablespoon chopped fresh mint

Preheat the oven to 450°F. Coat a 13" × 9" baking pan with cooking spray.

In a food processor, combine the peppers, onion, garlic, ginger, oil, vinegar, thyme, allspice, and salt. Process until very finely chopped, stopping the machine a few times to scrape down the sides of the container.

Spread the jalapeño mixture on both sides of the chicken breasts. Place them, skinned side up, in the prepared baking pan.

Bake for 30 minutes, or until a thermometer inserted in the thickest portion registers 170°F and the juices run clear.

Place the chicken on plates and scatter the mango on top. Sprinkle with the mint.

Makes 4 servings
Per serving: 199 calories, 26 g protein, 12 g carbohydrates, 5 g fat, 1 g saturated fat, 64 mg cholesterol, 2 g dietary fiber, 220 mg sodium

HEALTH NOTE
People with depression who take monoamine oxidase inhibitors (MAO inhibitors) should not use alcohol or other fermented products, such as the vinegar in this recipe. Substitute broth for the vinegar.

Stress/Fatigue

Memory Problems

Depression

Immunity
Problems

Infections

Colds and Flu

General Vision
Problems

Anemia

Prostate Problems

the ❀
**healing
factor**

🍋🍋🍋 Vitamin C

🍋🍋🍋 Vitamin A

🍋🍋🍋 Niacin

🍋🍋🍋 Vitamin B$_6$

🍋🍋🍋 Phosphorus

🍋🍋🍋 Zinc

🍋🍋🍋 Potassium

🍋🍋🍋 Pantothenic
acid

🍋🍋🍋 Riboflavin

🍋🍋🍋 Magnesium

baked chicken barbecue

1	medium red bell pepper, cut into thin strips
1	medium green bell pepper, cut into thin strips
1	small onion, halved and sliced
2	cloves garlic, minced
2	tablespoons chicken broth
2	tablespoons water
2	cans (8 ounces each) tomato sauce
1/4	cup raisins
3	tablespoons molasses
1	tablespoon cider vinegar (see note)
1/2–1	teaspoon hot-pepper sauce
1	teaspoon mustard powder
1/2	teaspoon freshly ground black pepper
1/4	teaspoon salt
4	whole chicken legs, separated into thighs and drumsticks

Preheat the oven to 425°F. Coat a roasting pan with cooking spray.

In a medium saucepan, combine the bell peppers, onion, garlic, broth, and water. Bring to a boil over high heat. Reduce the heat to medium, cover, and simmer, stirring occasionally, for 5 minutes, or until the vegetables are tender-crisp.

Stir in the tomato sauce, raisins, molasses, vinegar, hot-pepper sauce, mustard powder, black pepper, and salt. Bring to a boil over high heat.

Place the chicken pieces in the prepared roasting pan. Spoon the sauce over the chicken, turning to coat.

Bake, turning the pieces and basting occasionally with the sauce, for 30 minutes, or until a thermometer inserted in the thickest portion registers 170°F and the juices run clear.

Makes 4 servings
Per serving: 380 calories, 44 g protein, 33 g carbohydrates, 8 g fat, 2 g saturated fat, 159 mg cholesterol, 4 g dietary fiber, 761 mg sodium

HEALTH NOTE
People with depression who take monoamine oxidase inhibitors (MAO inhibitors) should not use alcohol or other fermented products, such as the vinegar in this recipe. Substitute apple juice for the vinegar.

Stress/Fatigue
Memory Problems
Depression
Aging
Stroke
Colds and Flu
Immunity Problems

rosemary roast chicken with pan gravy

1	broiler-fryer chicken (3 pounds)
3	teaspoons dried rosemary, crushed
1	lemon, sliced
¼	teaspoon salt
1	small onion, chopped
4	cups chicken broth
1	tablespoon cornstarch
⅓	cup Madeira wine (see note)

the
healing factor

🦴🦴🦴 Niacin

🦴🦴🦴 Vitamin C

🦴🦴🦴 Vitamin B₆

🦴🦴🦴 Phosphorus

🦴🦴 Pantothenic acid

🦴🦴 Zinc

🦴🦴 Potassium

Preheat the oven to 450°F. Coat a roasting rack and roasting pan with cooking spray.

Season the cavity of the chicken with 1 teaspoon of the rosemary. Place the lemon inside the cavity. Place the chicken, breast side up, on the prepared rack. Rub 1 teaspoon of the remaining rosemary and the salt over the breast meat under the skin of the chicken. Scatter the onion around the bottom of the pan. Add 2 cups of the broth.

Roast the chicken for 20 minutes, basting with the pan juices occasionally. Reduce the heat to 350°F. Roast, basting every 15 minutes, for 55 minutes longer, or until a thermometer inserted in a breast registers 180°F and the juices run clear. Place the chicken on a cutting board and keep warm. Skim the fat from the pan juices.

In a small bowl, whisk together the cornstarch and ¼ cup of the remaining broth until smooth.

Place the roasting pan on the stove top over medium-high heat. Add the wine. Boil for 3 minutes, stirring to loosen browned bits from the pan, or until reduced to ¼ cup. Add the remaining 1¾ cups broth and bring to a boil. Add the reserved cornstarch mixture and the remaining 1 teaspoon rosemary. Cook, stirring constantly, for 2 minutes, or until slightly thickened.

Carve the chicken, removing and discarding the skin before eating. Serve with the gravy.

Makes 6 servings
Per serving: 166 calories, 25 g protein, 5 g carbohydrates, 4 g fat, 1 g saturated fat, 79 mg cholesterol, 1 g dietary fiber, 566 mg sodium

HEALTH NOTE
People with depression who take monoamine oxidase inhibitors (MAO inhibitors) should not use alcohol or other fermented products, such as the wine in this recipe. Substitute apple juice for the wine.

southwestern chicken sauté

1	tablespoon chili powder
1 1/4	teaspoons ground cumin
1/4	teaspoon salt
1/8	teaspoon ground red pepper
2	teaspoons olive oil
4	boneless, skinless chicken breast halves
1/2	cup chicken broth
1	tablespoon cider vinegar (see note)
2	plum tomatoes, diced
1	cup frozen corn kernels
1	can (4 ounces) mild green chiles, drained
1/4	cup chopped fresh cilantro

In a cup, combine the chili powder, cumin, salt, and red pepper. Rub both sides of the chicken breasts with 1 tablespoon of the spice mixture.

Heat the oil in a large nonstick skillet over medium-high heat. Add the chicken and cook, turning once, for 6 minutes, or until the spice coating is browned and the surface of the chicken is opaque. Place the chicken on a plate and keep warm.

Add the broth, vinegar, and the remaining spice mixture to the skillet. Bring to a boil over high heat, stirring to loosen the browned bits from the pan. Boil for 2 minutes, or until the liquid is slightly reduced.

Return the chicken to the skillet, adding any juices that have collected on the plate. Add the tomatoes, corn, and chiles and bring to a boil. Reduce the heat to medium, cover, and simmer for 5 minutes, or until a thermometer inserted in the thickest portion of the chicken registers 160°F and the juices run clear. Sprinkle with the cilantro.

Makes 4 servings
Per serving: 342 calories, 57 g protein, 14 g carbohydrates, 6 g fat, 1 g saturated fat, 137 mg cholesterol, 3 g dietary fiber, 460 mg sodium

HEALTH NOTE
People with depression who take monoamine oxidase inhibitors (MAO inhibitors) should not use alcohol or other fermented products, such as the vinegar in this recipe. Substitute broth for the vinegar.

spicy chicken with cool green dipping sauce

Memory Problems

Aging

Immunity Problems

Infections

Stress/Fatigue

General Vision Problems

Cataracts

Colds and Flu

Asthma

the
healing factor

🍏🍏🍏 Niacin

🍏🍏🍏 Vitamin B$_6$

🍏🍏🍏 Phosphorus

🍏🍏🍏 Vitamin C

🍏🍏🍏 Vitamin K

🍏🍏 Vitamin E

🍏🍏 Vitamin A

🍏🍏 Magnesium

🍏🍏 Zinc

🍏🍏 Riboflavin

1	teaspoon oregano
1	teaspoon ground cumin
¼	teaspoon salt
⅛	teaspoon ground red pepper
8	bone-in chicken drumsticks, skin and visible fat removed
½	cup loosely packed fresh cilantro sprigs
¼	cup loosely packed parsley sprigs
¼	cup blanched slivered almonds
1	clove garlic
1	serrano chile pepper, seeded (or leave half the seeds in for a spicier sauce); wear plastic gloves when handling
⅛	teaspoon salt
2	tablespoons lime juice
2	tablespoons flaxseed oil or olive oil
2	tablespoons water

Preheat the grill or broiler. Coat a grill rack or broiler-pan rack with cooking spray.

In a cup, combine the oregano, cumin, salt, and red pepper. Cut two ½"-deep slashes in each side of the drumsticks. Rub the spice mixture over the drumsticks, pressing it into the slits. Place the drumsticks in a baking pan and coat completely with cooking spray. Let stand for 10 minutes.

In a food processor, combine the cilantro, parsley, almonds, garlic, chile pepper, and salt. Process until chopped. While the processor is running, add the lime juice and oil through the feed tube, stopping the machine once or twice to scrape down the sides of the container until the sauce is smooth. Pour the sauce into a bowl. Stir in the water, cover, and chill until ready to serve.

Place the drumsticks on the prepared rack and grill or broil 6" from the heat, turning several times, for 25 minutes, or until a thermometer inserted in the thickest portion registers 170°F and the juices run clear.

Serve with the sauce.

Makes 4 servings
Per serving: 268 calories, 29 g protein, 4 g carbohydrates, 15 g fat, 2 g saturated fat, 89 mg cholesterol, 2 g dietary fiber, 346 mg sodium

the **healing factor**

🌿🌿🌿 Niacin
🌿🌿🌿 Vitamin B₆
🌿🌿🌿 Phosphorus
🌿🌿 Potassium
🌿🌿 Zinc
🌿🌿 Riboflavin
🌿🌿 Vitamin B₁₂
🌿🌿 Magnesium

orange and sage roast turkey breast with pan gravy

1½	tablespoons rubbed sage
1	teaspoon salt
1	teaspoon coarsely ground black pepper
1	bone-in turkey breast (6½–7 pounds)
½	cup orange juice
1	tablespoon extra-virgin olive oil
1	cup + 2 tablespoons water
1¾	cups chicken broth
2	tablespoons cornstarch
2	tablespoons butter, cut into small pieces
1	tablespoon balsamic vinegar (see note)
½	teaspoon freshly grated orange peel

Preheat the oven to 350°F. Place a rack in a roasting pan.

In a cup, combine the sage, salt, and pepper. Gently loosen the skin on the turkey breast, working your hand underneath it from the bottom of the breast. Rub some of the herb mixture under the turkey skin. Rub the remainder all over the turkey. Place the turkey breast on the rack in the roasting pan.

In a cup, combine the orange juice and oil.

Roast the turkey breast, basting with the juice mixture and the pan juices every 15 minutes, for 2 to 2½ hours, or until a thermometer inserted in the thickest part (not touching the bone) registers 170°F.

Remove the turkey from the oven and place on a cutting board. Let stand for 15 minutes.

Add 1 cup of the water to the roasting pan and stir to loosen browned bits from the pan. Strain the pan juices into a measuring cup. Let settle for 10 minutes, then skim off the fat that rises to the surface.

Pour the pan juices and the broth into the roasting pan. Place on the stove top and bring to a boil over high heat. Reduce the heat to medium-low and simmer for 5 minutes.

In a cup, combine the cornstarch with the remaining 2 tablespoons water. Add the mixture to the pan and bring to a boil, stirring constantly, until the sauce is thickened.

Whisk in the butter until melted and smooth. Remove from the heat and stir in the vinegar and orange peel. Pour into a gravy boat. Slice the turkey and serve with the gravy.

Makes 12 servings
Per serving: 188 calories, 33 g protein, 3 g carbohydrates, 4 g fat, 2 g saturated fat, 88 mg cholesterol, 0 g dietary fiber, 364 mg sodium

HEALTH NOTE
People with depression who take monoamine oxidase inhibitors (MAO inhibitors) should not use alcohol or other fermented products, such as the vinegar in this recipe. Substitute broth for the vinegar.

helps
prevent
treat

Stress/Fatigue
Memory Problems
Aging
Insomnia
Anemia

the
healing
factor

🌑🌑🌑 Niacin
🌑🌑🌑 Manganese
🌑🌑🌑 Riboflavin
🌑🌑🌑 Phosphorus
🌑🌑🌑 Vitamin B₆
🌑🌑🌑 Pantothenic acid
🌑🌑🌑 Copper
🌑🌑🌑 Potassium
🌑🌑🌑 Zinc
🌑🌑 Thiamin

turkey-sage cutlets with mushrooms

¼	ounce (⅓ cup) dried porcini mushrooms
1	cup boiling water
1	tablespoon all-purpose flour
1	tablespoon freshly grated Parmesan cheese
¼	teaspoon salt
¼	teaspoon freshly ground black pepper
4	thin-sliced turkey cutlets
4	teaspoons olive oil
12	ounces white button mushrooms, sliced
3	tablespoons dry Marsala wine or 3 tablespoons white grape juice
1	tablespoon chopped fresh sage or 1 teaspoon rubbed

Place the dried mushrooms and boiling water in a bowl and let stand for 15 minutes. Meanwhile, line a small strainer with cheesecloth and place over a small bowl.

Using a slotted spoon, remove the mushrooms from the soaking liquid to a cutting board and chop. Pour the soaking liquid through the strainer. Reserve about ¼ cup of the soaking liquid.

In a shallow bowl, combine the flour, cheese, salt, and pepper. Place the cutlets in the flour mixture, pressing to coat thoroughly.

Heat 2 teaspoons of the oil in a large nonstick skillet over medium-high heat. Add the cutlets and cook for 8 minutes, turning once, or until no longer pink and the juices run clear. Remove to a platter and keep warm.

Add the remaining 2 teaspoons oil to the skillet and heat over medium-high heat. Add the fresh mushrooms and softened dried mushrooms and cook, stirring frequently, for 2 minutes. Add the wine or grape juice and 2 tablespoons of the reserved soaking liquid and cook, stirring frequently, for 3 minutes, or until the mushrooms are tender and the liquid is absorbed. Add a little more soaking liquid if the pan gets too dry.

Pour any juices from the platter over the mushrooms, sprinkle with the sage, and simmer for 30 seconds. Top the cutlets with the sauce and mushrooms.

Makes 4 servings
Per serving: 233 calories, 29 g protein, 7 g carbohydrates, 10 g fat, 2 g saturated fat, 75 mg cholesterol, 1 g dietary fiber, 255 mg sodium

Memory Problems
Stress/Fatigue
Heart Disease
Depression
Cancer
Immunity Problems
Anemia
Insomnia
General Vision Problems

the healing factor

🍒🍒🍒 Vitamin A
🍒🍒🍒 Vitamin K
🍒🍒🍒 Fiber
🍒🍒🍒 Phosphorus
🍒🍒🍒 Folate
🍒🍒🍒 Niacin
🍒🍒🍒 Vitamin B$_6$
🍒🍒🍒 Vitamin C
🍒🍒🍒 Magnesium
🍒🍒 Iron

turkey and bean soft tacos (quick)

8	corn tortillas (6" diameter)
8	ounces (2 cups) shredded cooked turkey breast
1	cup drained and rinsed canned kidney or pinto beans
1¼	cups mild or medium-spicy salsa + additional for topping
½	teaspoon ground cumin
1½	cups finely shredded cabbage
1	large carrot, shredded
¼	cup finely chopped sweet white onion
¼	cup reduced-fat cucumber ranch dressing

Preheat the oven to 350°F.

Stack the tortillas and wrap them in foil. Place the tortillas in the oven and heat for 10 minutes.

Meanwhile, heat a large skillet coated with cooking spray over high heat. Add the turkey, beans, 1¼ cups of the salsa, and cumin and bring to a boil. Reduce the heat to low, cover, and simmer, stirring, for 10 minutes, or until heated through.

In a medium bowl, combine the cabbage, carrot, onion, and ranch dressing.

Spoon about ⅓ cup of the turkey filling into a tortilla. Top with ¼ cup of the cabbage mixture and fold over. Repeat with the remaining tortillas, turkey filling, and cabbage mixture. Top with the remaining salsa.

Makes 4 servings
Per serving: 330 calories, 24 g protein, 44 g carbohydrates, 6 g fat, 1 g saturated fat, 47 mg cholesterol, 8 g dietary fiber, 676 mg sodium

teriyaki tuna burgers

1¼ pounds tuna steak, skin and dark edges trimmed

2 tablespoons lite teriyaki marinade and sauce

1 scallion, chopped

2 teaspoons grated fresh ginger

2 cloves garlic, minced

2 slices (2 ounces) low-fat mozzarella cheese, halved

4 sesame seed sandwich buns

4 leaves lettuce

1 can (6 ounces) unsweetened pineapple slices

Coat a grill rack or broiler-pan rack with cooking spray. Preheat the grill or broiler.

Finely chop the tuna to the consistency of ground meat. Place in a bowl. Add the teriyaki sauce, scallion, ginger, and garlic. Stir just until blended. Shape into 4 burgers. Coat lightly with cooking spray.

Grill or broil the burgers 6" from the heat for 6 minutes, turning once, or until no longer pink. Remove to a plate and keep warm.

Place ½ slice cheese on the bottom half of each bun. Place, cheese side up, on the rack and grill or broil for 1 minute, or until the cheese melts. Top each with lettuce, a burger, and a slice of pineapple.

Makes 4 servings
Per serving: 354 calories, 42 g protein, 29 g carbohydrates, 6 g fat, 2 g saturated fat, 71 mg cholesterol, 2 g dietary fiber, 570 mg sodium

treats / helps prevent

Aging

Memory Problems

Stroke

Stress/Fatigue

PMS

Anemia

Psoriasis

Osteoporosis

Menopausal Problems/Hot Flashes

the healing factor

🍐🍐🍐 Vitamin B₁₂

🍐🍐🍐 Selenium

🍐🍐🍐 Omega-3 fatty acids

🍐🍐🍐 Niacin

🍐🍐🍐 Manganese

🍐🍐🍐 Phosphorus

🍐🍐🍐 Thiamin

🍐🍐🍐 Vitamin B₆

🍐🍐🍐 Riboflavin

🍐🍐🍐 Calcium

Depression
Memory Problems
Stress/Fatigue
Aging
Immunity Problems
Anemia
Psoriasis
Gallstones

pesto salmon (quick)

1 ¼	cups loosely packed fresh basil
1	clove garlic
3	tablespoons chicken broth
1	tablespoon blanched slivered almonds
1	tablespoon lemon juice
2	teaspoons freshly grated Parmesan cheese (see note)
2	teaspoons extra-virgin olive oil
¼	teaspoon salt
¼	teaspoon freshly ground black pepper
1	pound skinned salmon fillet, cut into 4 pieces
	Lemon wedges (optional)
	Basil sprigs (optional)

Place the basil, garlic, broth, almonds, lemon juice, cheese, oil, salt, and pepper in a blender. Process until pureed.

Place the salmon on a plate. Spoon 3 tablespoons of the pesto over the salmon and turn to coat both sides. Cover with plastic wrap and let stand for 15 minutes. Reserve the remaining pesto.

Meanwhile, preheat the broiler. Spray a jelly-roll pan with cooking spray.

Place the salmon in the prepared pan. Spread any of the pesto remaining on the plate on top of each piece. Broil the salmon 4" to 5" from the heat for 6 to 8 minutes, or just until opaque.

Place the salmon pieces on 4 plates and top each piece with some of the reserved pesto. Garnish with lemon wedges and basil sprigs, if using.

Makes 4 servings
Per serving: 203 calories, 24 g protein, 2 g carbohydrates, 11 g fat, 2 g saturated fat, 63 mg cholesterol, 1 g dietary fiber, 242 mg sodium

the healing factor

🐟🐟🐟 Omega-3 fatty acids
🐟🐟🐟 Vitamin B₁₂
🐟🐟🐟 Selenium
🐟🐟🐟 Vitamin B₆
🐟🐟 Niacin
🐟🐟 Riboflavin
🐟🐟 Phosphorus
🐟🐟 Pantothenic acid
🐟🐟 Potassium
🐟🐟 Thiamin

HEALTH NOTE
People with depression who take monoamine oxidase inhibitors (MAO inhibitors) should not use alcohol or other fermented or aged products, such as the cheese in this recipe.

penne with salmon and roasted vegetables

Photograph on page 39

12	ounces penne
2	pounds leeks
1	red bell pepper, cut into strips
¼	cup chicken broth
2	tablespoons lemon juice
1	tablespoon olive oil
2	teaspoons dried thyme, crushed
¼	teaspoon freshly ground black pepper
1	yellow summer squash, halved and cut into ¼" slices
¼	cup pitted kalamata olives
1	salmon fillet (½ pound), skinned

Preheat the oven to 400°F. Prepare the pasta according to package directions.

Meanwhile, cut the leeks into 2" lengths and quarter them lengthwise. Rinse the leeks completely. Place the leeks and bell pepper in a 13" × 9" baking dish. Add the broth, lemon juice, 2 teaspoons of the oil, thyme, and black pepper. Cover with foil and bake for 15 minutes.

Add the squash, olives, and salmon to the baking dish and drizzle with the remaining 1 teaspoon oil. Cover and bake for 30 minutes, or until the salmon is opaque and the vegetables are tender.

Place the penne in a large serving bowl. Break the salmon into bite-size pieces and add to the penne with the vegetables.

Makes 6 servings
Per serving: 402 calories, 18 g protein, 68 g carbohydrates, 7 g fat, 1 g saturated fat, 21 mg cholesterol, 5 g dietary fiber, 121 mg sodium

treat ↗ helps prevent

Depression
Memory Problems
Immunity Problems
Stroke
Anemia
Heart Disease
Cataracts
Gallstones
Eczema
Psoriasis

the healing factor

🍏🍏🍏 Vitamin C
🍏🍏🍏 Thiamin
🍏🍏🍏 Manganese
🍏🍏🍏 Vitamin B$_6$
🍏🍏🍏 Niacin
🍏🍏🍏 Iron
🍏🍏🍏 Vitamin B$_{12}$
🍏🍏🍏 Vitamin A
🍏🍏🍏 Omega-3 fatty acids
🍏🍏🍏 Riboflavin

Memory Problems

Aging

Depression

Immunity
Problems

Heart Disease

General Vision
Problems

Anemia

Asthma

Cancer

the healing factor

🍐🍐🍐 Selenium

🍐🍐🍐 Vitamin B$_{12}$

🍐🍐🍐 Phosphorus

🍐🍐🍐 Vitamin B$_6$

🍐🍐🍐 Niacin

🍐🍐 Vitamin K

🍐🍐 Vitamin A

🍐🍐 Vitamin C

🍐🍐 Potassium

🍐🍐 Riboflavin

orange roughy veracruz (quick)

Photograph on page 56

4	orange roughy or red snapper fillets (5 ounces each)
1	tablespoon lime juice
1	teaspoon dried oregano, crushed
1	tablespoon olive oil
1	onion, chopped
1	clove garlic, minced
1	can (15 ounces) Mexican-style diced tomatoes
12	pimiento-stuffed olives, coarsely chopped
2	tablespoons chopped parsley

Preheat the oven to 350°F. Coat a 9" × 9" baking dish with cooking spray. Place the fillets in the baking dish. Sprinkle with the lime juice and oregano.

Heat the oil in a medium skillet over medium heat. Add the onion and garlic and cook, stirring occasionally, for 5 minutes, or until soft. Add the tomatoes (with juice), olives, and parsley. Cook, stirring occasionally, for 5 minutes, or until thickened. Spoon over the fillets. Cover tightly with foil.

Bake for 15 minutes, or until the fish flakes easily.

Makes 4 servings
Per serving: 185 calories, 22 g protein, 11 g carbohydrates, 6 g fat, 1 g saturated fat, 28 mg cholesterol, 2 g dietary fiber, 510 mg sodium

pan-seared red (quick) snapper with olive crust

treat ʃ

helps
prevent

Stroke

Heart Disease

Immunity
Problems

Memory Problems

Stress/Fatigue

PMS

Psoriasis

1⅓	cups fresh bread crumbs
¼	cup chopped fresh oregano, basil, or thyme
16	pitted and finely chopped kalamata olives
2	tablespoons freshly grated Parmesan cheese
½	teaspoon freshly ground black pepper
4	red snapper fillets (5 ounces each)

In a shallow bowl, combine the bread crumbs; oregano, basil, or thyme; olives; cheese; and pepper. Firmly press the fillets into the mixture to coat evenly on both sides. Coat the top of the fillets with cooking spray.

Heat a large cast-iron skillet coated with cooking spray over medium-high heat. Add the fillets and cook, turning once, for 6 minutes, or until the fish flakes easily.

Makes 4 servings
Per serving: 204 calories, 31 g protein, 6 g carbohydrates, 6 g fat, 1 g saturated fat, 54 mg cholesterol, 1 g dietary fiber, 295 mg sodium

COOKING TIP
Here's a quick sauce to serve with the fish. In a food processor, combine 1 can (14½ ounces) stewed tomatoes, 1 tablespoon chopped fresh oregano, and 1 tablespoon balsamic vinegar. Process until the mixture is chunky. Warm the sauce on the stove top or in the microwave.

the
healing
factor

- Selenium
- Vitamin B_{12}
- Omega-3 fatty acids
- Phosphorus
- Vitamin B_6
- Potassium
- Magnesium
- Manganese
- Pantothenic acid

the
**healing
factor**

🍐🍐🍐 Niacin
🍐🍐 Phosphorus
🍐🍐 Thiamin
🍐🍐 Potassium
🍐🍐 Vitamin A

blackened snapper (quick)

1	teaspoon paprika
½	teaspoon dried oregano, crushed
¼	teaspoon garlic powder
¼	teaspoon onion powder
¼	teaspoon salt
¼	teaspoon ground black pepper
⅛	teaspoon ground red pepper
4	red snapper fillets (5 ounces each)
2	teaspoons olive oil

In a small bowl, combine the paprika, oregano, garlic powder, onion powder, salt, black pepper, and red pepper.

Coat a large cast-iron skillet with cooking spray and heat over high heat. Brush both sides of the snapper with the oil and rub with the spice mixture. Place in the skillet and cook, turning once, for 6 minutes, or until the fish flakes easily.

Makes 4 servings
Per serving: 175 calories, 30 g protein, 1 g carbohydrates, 6 g fat, 1 g saturated fat, 53 mg cholesterol, 0 g dietary fiber, 266 mg sodium

COOKING TIP
Almost any firm, white-fleshed fish can be used in this recipe. Try grouper, sea bass, redfish (red drum), or pompano in place of the snapper.

cod steaks (quick) sicilian-style

1	tablespoon extra-virgin olive oil
1	medium onion, halved and thinly sliced
1	cup thinly sliced fennel
2	cloves garlic, minced
½	teaspoon dried thyme, crushed
¼	teaspoon salt
¼	teaspoon freshly ground black pepper
1	tablespoon balsamic vinegar (see note)
1	can (16 ounces) crushed tomatoes
½	cup orange juice
4	cod steaks (1¼ pounds)

Preheat the oven to 425°F.

Heat the oil in a large nonstick skillet over medium-high heat. Add the onion, fennel, garlic, thyme, salt, and pepper and cook, stirring frequently, for 4 minutes, or until the vegetables are tender-crisp. Add the vinegar and cook for 30 seconds.

Stir in the tomatoes and orange juice and bring to a boil. Reduce the heat to medium-low and simmer for 5 minutes, or until the sauce is slightly thickened.

Place the cod steaks in a 9" × 9" baking dish. Spoon the sauce over the fish. Bake for 12 minutes, or until the fish flakes easily.

Makes 4 servings
Per serving: 221 calories, 28 g protein, 15 g carbohydrates, 6 g fat, 1 g saturated fat, 61 mg cholesterol, 3 g dietary fiber, 592 mg sodium

treat ↳ helps prevent

Depression
Asthma
Memory Problems
Headaches
Psoriasis
Diabetes
PMS
Anemia
Infections

the healing factor

- Selenium
- Vitamin C
- Phosphorus
- Potassium
- Vitamin B$_6$
- Vitamin B$_{12}$
- Omega-3 fatty acids
- Niacin
- Iron
- Magnesium

HEALTH NOTE
People with depression who take monoamine oxidase inhibitors (MAO inhibitors) should not use the vinegar in this recipe. Substitute orange juice for the vinegar.

salmon over noodles

helps
prevent
treat

Memory Problems

Aging

Stress/Fatigue

Immunity Problems

Cancer

Osteoporosis

Psoriasis

Breast Cancer

PMS

the
healing factor

🐟🐟🐟 Omega-3 fatty acids

🐟🐟🐟 Vitamin B$_{12}$

🐟🐟🐟 Selenium

🐟🐟🐟 Niacin

🐟🐟🐟 Vitamin B$_6$

🐟🐟🐟 Phophorus

🐟🐟🐟 Thiamin

🐟🐟🐟 Manganese

🐟🐟🐟 Riboflavin

🐟🐟🐟 Vitamin K

4	skinned salmon fillets (6 ounces each)
3	tablespoons reduced-sodium soy sauce
2	tablespoons dry sherry
2	tablespoons canola oil
2	large cloves garlic, minced
3	scallions, thinly sliced on the diagonal
3	tablespoons grated fresh ginger
1	teaspoon dark Asian sesame oil
2	tablespoons chopped fresh cilantro
8	ounces buckwheat noodles, cooked

Preheat the oven to 400°F. Tear off four 14" pieces of foil and coat with cooking spray. Place a salmon fillet in the center of each piece.

In a small bowl, combine the soy sauce and sherry. Spoon 1 tablespoon over each fillet. Crimp the foil and seal into packets. Reserve the remaining soy sauce mixture. Place the packets on a baking sheet and bake for 12 minutes, or until the salmon is just opaque in the thickest part.

Meanwhile, heat the canola oil in a small nonstick skillet over medium heat. Add the garlic, scallions, and ginger and cook, stirring, for 2 minutes, or until the scallions have wilted. Add the sesame oil and the remaining soy sauce mixture and bring just to a boil. Stir in the cilantro.

Divide the hot noodles among 4 plates. Open the packets and place the salmon and juices over the noodles. Top with the scallion mixture.

Makes 4 servings
Per serving: 530 calories, 43 g protein, 46 g carbohydrates, 19 g fat, 3 g saturated fat, 94 mg cholesterol, 3 g dietary fiber, 979 mg sodium

Grilled Swordfish with Blueberry Salsa

Photograph on page 32

Swordfish is stocked with nutrients that are recommended to battle depression, including vitamin B_6 and omega-3 fatty acids.

1	cup blueberries, chopped
1	cup chopped watermelon
1	small tomato, seeded and chopped
½	small red onion, minced
½	yellow bell pepper, minced
⅓	cup chopped roasted red peppers
1	jalapeño chile pepper, seeded and minced
2	tablespoons chopped fresh basil
2	tablespoons orange juice
2	limes
1	orange
6	scallions, chopped
1	clove garlic, minced
1	tablespoon olive oil
4	swordfish fillets (5 ounces each)

In a bowl, combine the blueberries, watermelon, tomato, onion, peppers, basil, and juice. Cover and refrigerate for at least 2 hours.

Grate 1 teaspoon lime rind and 2 teaspoons orange rind into a 9" × 9" baking dish. Squeeze ¼ cup lime juice and ⅓ cup orange juice into the dish. Add the scallions, garlic, and oil. Place the fish in the mixture and turn to coat. Cover and marinate in the refrigerator for 1 hour, turning once. Remove 15 minutes before cooking.

Coat a grill rack with cooking spray. Preheat the grill. Remove the fish from the marinade; discard the marinade. Cook, turning once, for 8 minutes, or until the fish flakes easily. Serve with the salsa.

Makes 4 servings
Per serving: 294 calories, 30 g protein, 23 g carbohydrates, 10 g fat, 2 g saturated fat, 55 mg cholesterol, 5 g dietary fiber, 232 mg sodium

Stroke
Depression
Heart Disease
Memory Problems
Aging
Insomnia
Diabetes
Asthma
Anemia
Cancer

fish stew (quick) with couscous

Photograph on page 49

the
healing factor

🐦🐦🐦 Selenium
🐦🐦🐦 Fiber
🐦🐦🐦 Phosphorus
🐦🐦🐦 Vitamin B$_{12}$
🐦🐦🐦 Manganese
🐦🐦🐦 Niacin
🐦🐦🐦 Magnesium
🐦🐦🐦 Vitamin B$_6$
🐦🐦🐦 Folate
🐦🐦🐦 Copper

2	cloves garlic, minced
1	onion, halved and thinly sliced
1	teaspoon ground cumin
1/4	teaspoon ground cinnamon
1	can (15 ounces) chopped tomatoes
1	can (14–19 ounces) chickpeas, rinsed and drained
1	cup chicken broth
1/3	cup pitted prunes, chopped
1/4	cup pitted halved kalamata olives
4	orange roughy or halibut fillets (4 ounces each)
1	box (10 ounces) couscous

Coat a large nonstick skillet with cooking spray. Add the garlic, onion, cumin, and cinnamon. Coat with cooking spray and place over medium heat. Cook, stirring, for 8 minutes, or until soft.

Add the tomatoes, chickpeas, broth, prunes, and olives. Cook, stirring occasionally, for 5 minutes. Push the mixture to the edges of the skillet. Add the fish. Spoon the chickpea mixture over the fish. Cover, reduce the heat to low, and cook for 10 minutes, or until the fish flakes easily.

Meanwhile, cook the couscous according to package directions. Fluff with a fork. Evenly divide among 4 plates and top with the fish and chickpea mixture.

Makes 4 servings
Per serving: 576 calories, 34 g protein, 101 g carbohydrates, 5 g fat, 0 g saturated fat, 23 mg cholesterol, 12 g dietary fiber, 680 mg sodium

five-alarm shrimp (quick)

Photograph on page 40

¼	cup cornstarch
½	teaspoon salt
1	pound jumbo shrimp, peeled and deveined
1	tablespoon canola oil
4	scallions, coarsely chopped
2	red or yellow bell peppers, cut into thin strips
2	tablespoons chopped fresh cilantro or parsley
2	cloves garlic, minced
1	serrano chile pepper, seeded and chopped (wear plastic gloves when handling)
1	tablespoon lime juice
3	tablespoons water
¾	teaspoon crushed black peppercorns

In a shallow bowl, combine the cornstarch and salt. Add the shrimp and toss to coat well.

Heat the oil in a large nonstick skillet over medium-high heat. Add the shrimp and cook for 3 minutes, or until just opaque. Add the scallions, bell peppers, cilantro or parsley, garlic, and chile pepper and cook, stirring often, for 1 minute. Add the lime juice, water, and peppercorns. Cook, stirring constantly, for 1 minute, or until the shrimp are opaque.

Makes 4 servings
Per serving: 203 calories, 24 g protein, 14 g carbohydrates, 6 g fat, 1 g saturated fat, 172 mg cholesterol, 2 g dietary fiber, 464 mg sodium

treat

helps prevent

Depression
Aging
Immunity Problems
Memory Problems
General Vision Problems
Anemia
Heart Disease
Insomnia
Psoriasis

the
healing factor

- Vitamin C
- Selenium
- Vitamin A
- Omega-3 fatty acids
- Vitamin K
- Phosphorus
- Vitamin B$_{12}$
- Iron
- Copper
- Niacin

shrimp with chard and red beans

*Immunity
Problems*

*General Vision
Problems*

Heart Disease

Depression

Aging

Insomnia

Psoriasis

the 🐚 healing factor

🐚🐚🐚 Vitamin K

🐚🐚🐚 Vitamin C

🐚🐚🐚 Selenium

🐚🐚🐚 Vitamin A

🐚🐚🐚 Phosphorus

🐚🐚🐚 Fiber

🐚🐚🐚 Iron

🐚🐚🐚 Magnesium

🐚🐚🐚 Omega-3
fatty acids

🐚🐚🐚 Copper

4	cloves garlic, minced
1½	teaspoons paprika
1	teaspoon dried thyme, crushed
½	teaspoon freshly ground black pepper
¼	teaspoon salt
¼	teaspoon ground red pepper
1	pound large shrimp, peeled and deveined, tails left on
2	tablespoons olive oil
2	ribs celery, thinly sliced
1	large onion, chopped
1	large green bell pepper, chopped
¾	cup chicken broth
3	cups green or red Swiss chard, thinly sliced
1	can (14–19 ounces) red kidney beans

In a medium bowl, combine the garlic, paprika, thyme, black pepper, salt, and red pepper. Remove about half of the mixture to a small bowl. Add the shrimp to the medium bowl and toss to coat well.

Heat 1 tablespoon of the oil in a large saucepot or Dutch oven over medium heat. Add the celery, onion, and bell pepper. Cook, stirring frequently, for 6 minutes, or until tender-crisp.

Add the reserved spice mixture and cook, stirring frequently, for 2 minutes. Add ¼ cup of the broth. Cover and cook, stirring often, for 5 minutes.

Add the chard and cook, stirring frequently, for 2 minutes, or until wilted. Stir in the beans, shrimp, and the remaining ½ cup broth and bring to a boil over high heat. Reduce the heat to low, cover, and simmer for 4 minutes, or until the shrimp are opaque.

Makes 4 servings
Per serving: 306 calories, 31 g protein, 26 g carbohydrates, 9 g fat, 1 g saturated fat, 172 mg cholesterol, 9 g dietary fiber, 733 mg sodium

the power of FISH

Adding more fish to our meals is an easier task these days since most supermarkets now offer a selection of fine fresh fish. Try to eat fish at least twice a week. Not only is it a lower-fat protein dish than most meat, but fish also contains omega-3 fatty acids—a type of fat that helps prevent heart disease, may fight colon and breast cancers, and may protect from depression. Try fresh or canned salmon (not smoked), mackerel, rainbow trout, tuna, whitefish (fresh, not smoked), sardines, and pickled Atlantic herring. Also choose canned white (albacore) tuna packed in water, but look for the most grams of fat per serving; the more total fat, the more omega-3 fatty acids.

Osteoporosis
Dental Problems
Aging
Memory Problems
Stress/Fatigue
Insomnia
PMS
Menopausal
Problems/Hot
Flashes

the 🌿
healing
factor

🐞🐞🐞 Phosphorus
🐞🐞🐞 Vitamin K
🐞🐞🐞 Riboflavin
🐞🐞🐞 Potassium
🐞🐞 Calcium
🐞🐞 Niacin
🐞🐞 Copper
🐞🐞 Vitamin A
🐞🐞 Manganese
🐞🐞 Vitamin D

baked scallops (quick) newburg

Photograph on page 39

¼	cup whole wheat bread crumbs
2	teaspoons butter, melted
1	pound bay scallops, rinsed, drained, and patted dry
8	ounces mushrooms, sliced
3	scallions, sliced
2	tablespoons chopped fresh tarragon or 2 teaspoons dried, crushed
2	tablespoons whole wheat or whole grain pastry flour
¼	teaspoon salt
⅛	teaspoon ground red pepper
1½	cups 1% milk
1	egg yolk

Preheat the oven to 400°F. Place 4 small baking dishes (8 ounces each) on a baking sheet. Coat the dishes with cooking spray.

In a small bowl, combine the bread crumbs and butter.

Heat a large skillet coated with cooking spray over medium heat. Add the scallops and cook, stirring, for 3 minutes, or until opaque. Remove to a plate with a slotted spoon and keep warm.

Add the mushrooms and cook, stirring occasionally, for 3 minutes, or until they release liquid. Add the scallions and tarragon and cook for 1 minute, or until the mushrooms are soft. Remove to the plate with the scallops.

Add the flour, salt, and pepper and cook, stirring constantly, for 1 minute. Gradually whisk in the milk until blended.

Cook, stirring often, for 5 minutes, or until thickened. Add the egg yolk and cook, stirring constantly, for 2 minutes, or until the mixture bubbles. Add the scallops and mushroom mixture and stir to coat well. Spoon the mixture into the prepared baking dishes. Sprinkle with the reserved bread crumb mixture.

Bake for 8 minutes, or until golden and bubbly.

Makes 4 servings
Per serving: 226 calories, 25 g protein, 13 g carbohydrates, 9 g fat, 2 g saturated fat, 98 mg cholesterol, 1 g dietary fiber, 707 mg sodium

Memory Problems
Depression
Aging
Anemia
Cancer
Heart Disease
Stress/Fatigue
General Vision
Problems

the ☙
healing
factor

🐞🐞🐞 Vitamin B$_{12}$
🐞🐞🐞 Iron
🐞🐞🐞 Manganese
🐞🐞🐞 Vitamin C
🐞🐞🐞 Selenium
🐞🐞🐞 Vitamin K
🐞🐞 Phosphorus
🐞🐞🐞 Copper
🐞🐞 Riboflavin
🐞🐞🐞 Folate

HEALTH NOTE
People with depres-
sion who take
monoamine oxidase
inhibitors (MAO in-
hibitors) should not
use alcohol or other
fermented products
such as the wine in
this recipe. Substitute
broth for the wine.

linguine with clams
Photograph on page 39

12	ounces spinach linguine
1	tablespoon olive oil
2	shallots, chopped
1	clove garlic, minced
1	cup chopped plum tomatoes
1	cup dry white wine or alcohol-free wine (see note)
1½	cups chicken broth
¼	cup + 2 tablespoons chopped Italian parsley
3	dozen littleneck clams, scrubbed

Prepare the linguine according to package directions.

Meanwhile, heat the oil in a large saucepot or Dutch oven over medium-high heat. Add the shallots and garlic and cook, stirring often, for 4 minutes, or until soft. Add the tomatoes and cook for 1 minute. Add the wine and bring to a boil. Cook for 2 minutes. Add the broth and parsley. Bring to a boil.

Add the clams, cover, and cook for 5 minutes, or until the clams open. (Discard any unopened clams.)

Remove the clams to a bowl with a slotted spoon. Return the broth mixture to the heat and bring to a boil. Boil for 4 minutes, or until reduced by one-third. Remove 24 of the clams from their shells and mince; discard those shells. Keep the remaining 12 clams in their shells.

Add the minced clams and pasta to the pot. Toss to combine. Add the clams in the shells.

Makes 4 servings
Per serving: 312 calories, 23 g protein, 32 g carbohydrates, 6 g fat, 1 g saturated fat, 76 mg cholesterol, 3 g dietary fiber, 425 mg sodium

grains and legumes

Whole grains and beans are powerful foods.
Packed with complex carbohydrates, fiber, vitamins,
and minerals, they're low in fat and sodium and
contain no cholesterol. Whole grains are more readily
available than ever, and they're inexpensive and easy to
use. Experiment with grains ranging from the familiar
brown rice to the out-of-the-ordinary quinoa. Fill your
shelves with a large selection of canned or dried
legumes such as quick-cooking lentils or slower but
exciting dried selections such as adzuki beans. Try to
include these healthy plant foods in your meals daily.

the healing factor

🐛🐛🐛 Vitamin C
🐛🐛🐛 Manganese
🐛🐛🐛 Vitamin A
🐛🐛🐛 Fiber
🐛🐛🐛 Vitamin K
🐛🐛 Potassium
🐛🐛 Magnesium
🐛🐛 Folate
🐛🐛 Thiamin
🐛🐛 Niacin

tabbouleh with fruit

Photograph on page 29

1	cup orange juice
½	cup medium-grain bulgur
1	large tomato, seeded and finely chopped
½	small cantaloupe, finely chopped
1	cup finely chopped hulled fresh strawberries
½	pint fresh blueberries
½	pint fresh raspberries
¼	cup chopped flat-leaf parsley
½	small red onion, finely chopped
1	tablespoon chopped fresh mint
2	tablespoons lemon juice
1	tablespoon extra-virgin olive oil
¾	teaspoon ground cumin
½	teaspoon ground cinnamon
¼	teaspoon salt
¼	teaspoon freshly ground black pepper

In a medium bowl, combine the orange juice and bulgur. Let stand for 30 minutes, or until tender and softened.

Drain the bulgur and place in a large bowl. Add the tomato, cantaloupe, strawberries, blueberries, raspberries, parsley, onion, mint, lemon juice, oil, cumin, cinnamon, salt, and pepper and toss to coat well. Let stand for at least 15 minutes to allow the flavors to blend.

Makes 4 servings
Per serving: 193 calories, 4 g protein, 37 g carbohydrates, 5 g fat, 1 g saturated fat, 0 mg cholesterol, 9 g dietary fiber, 162 mg sodium

spiced brown rice with cashews

½	tablespoon olive oil
1	medium onion, chopped
1	cup brown basmati or long-grain brown rice
3–4	whole cardamom pods or ½ teaspoon ground cardamom
1	stick cinnamon (4"), broken in half, or ¼ teaspoon ground cinnamon
2	cups chicken broth
⅓	cup unsalted cashews, toasted

Heat the oil in a large saucepan over medium heat. Add the onion and cook, stirring frequently, for 4 minutes, or until soft. Add the rice, cardamom, and cinnamon and cook, stirring, for 2 minutes, or until the rice just starts to brown lightly. Add the broth and bring to a boil over high heat. Reduce the heat to low, cover, and simmer for 50 minutes, or until the liquid is absorbed and the rice is very tender. Stir in the cashews. Remove from the heat and let stand for 5 minutes. Remove and discard the cardamom pods and cinnamon stick.

Makes 6 servings
Per serving: 241 calories, 5 g protein, 39 g carbohydrates, 8 g fat, 1 g saturated fat, 0 mg cholesterol, 3 g dietary fiber, 288 mg sodium

treat · helps prevent

Insomnia
Stress/Fatigue
Cancer
Constipation
High Cholesterol

the
healing
factor

Copper
Thiamin
Magnesium
Manganese
Fiber
Iron
Niacin

Diabetes

Cancer

Heart Disease

Stroke

Dental Problems

Depression

Memory Problems

General Vision Problems

Prostate Problems

the 🌿
healing factor

🍑🍑🍑 Manganese

🍑🍑🍑 Vitamin C

🍑🍑🍑 Fiber

🍑🍑🍑 Magnesium

🍑🍑🍑 Phosphorus

🍑🍑🍑 Folate

🍑🍑🍑 Chromium

🍑🍑🍑 Vitamin A

🍑🍑 Thiamin

🍑🍑 Iron

cilantro and tomato rice

1	cup short-grain brown rice
2	cups water
½	teaspoon salt
1	pound tomatoes, coarsely chopped
⅓	cup chopped fresh cilantro
1	tablespoon extra-virgin olive oil
1	tablespoon lime juice or lemon juice
1	clove garlic, minced
1	teaspoon ground cumin
¼	teaspoon freshly ground black pepper
1	can (14–19 ounces) chickpeas, rinsed and drained
¼	cup slivered almonds, toasted

Place the rice, water, and ¼ teaspoon of the salt in a medium saucepan. Bring to a boil over high heat. Reduce the heat to low, cover, and simmer for 50 minutes, or until the rice is tender and the liquid is absorbed.

Meanwhile, in a medium bowl, combine the tomatoes, cilantro, oil, lime juice or lemon juice, garlic, cumin, pepper, and the remaining ¼ teaspoon salt. Cover and let stand at room temperature. Stir in the rice and chickpeas and top with the almonds.

Makes 4 servings
Per serving: 405 calories, 12 g protein, 68 g carbohydrates, 11 g fat, 1 g saturated fat, 0 mg cholesterol, 10 g dietary fiber, 472 mg sodium

millet pilaf

1	cup millet
1½	cups water
1	cup chicken broth
¼	teaspoon salt
½	cup golden raisins
2	tablespoons dry sherry (see note)
1	tablespoon extra-virgin olive oil
⅓	cup natural almonds, coarsely chopped
1½	teaspoons chopped fresh rosemary
2	tablespoons chopped flat-leaf parsley

In a medium saucepan over medium-high heat, cook the millet, stirring frequently, for 4 minutes, or until the grains are fragrant, browned in spots, and just beginning to crackle.

Add the water, broth, and salt. Bring to a boil over high heat. Reduce the heat to low, cover, and simmer for 25 minutes, or until the millet is tender, some grains have burst, and the water has evaporated. Remove from the heat and let stand, covered, for 10 minutes.

Meanwhile, in a small bowl, soak the raisins in the sherry.

Heat the oil in a small skillet over medium heat. Add the almonds and cook, stirring frequently, for 4 minutes, or until lightly toasted. Stir in the rosemary and raisins and cook, stirring, for 30 seconds. Remove from the heat.

Fluff the millet with a fork. Stir in the almond mixture and sprinkle with the parsley.

Makes 4 servings
Per serving: 359 calories, 8 g protein, 55 g carbohydrates, 11 g fat, 1 g saturated fat, 0 mg cholesterol, 7 g dietary fiber, 299 mg sodium

treat ⌇ helps prevent

Memory Problems
Cancer
High Cholesterol
Heart Disease
Stroke
Depression
Diabetes
Insomnia
Cataracts

the
healing factor

🌿🌿🌿 Manganese
🌿🌿🌿 Copper
🌿🌿🌿 Folate
🌿🌿🌿 Fiber
🌿🌿🌿 Magnesium
🌿🌿🌿 Phosphorus
🌿🌿🌿 Vitamin-E
🌿🌿 Thiamin
🌿🌿 Riboflavin
🌿🌿 Iron

HEALTH NOTE
People with depression who take monoamine oxidase inhibitors (MAO inhibitors) should not use alcohol or other fermented products, such as the sherry in this recipe. Substitute apple juice for the sherry.

Heart Disease
Cancer
Diabetes
Aging
Stress/Fatigue
General Vision
Problems
Dental Problems
Overweight
Constipation
Diverticulosis

the
**healing
factor**

 Vitamin C

 Fiber

 Vitamin A

 Potassium

kamut, orange, and fennel salad

Photograph on page 48

1	cup whole grain kamut, spelt, or wheat berries
2½	cups water
1	cup chicken or vegetable broth
3	medium navel oranges
2	tablespoons extra-virgin olive oil
1	tablespoon balsamic vinegar
½	teaspoon salt
¼	teaspoon freshly ground black pepper
1	medium bulb fennel, chopped
1	large red bell pepper, chopped
1	small red onion, chopped
¼	cup sliced pitted kalamata olives

Place the kamut, spelt, or wheat berries in a sieve and rinse until the water runs clear. Place in a bowl with 2 cups of the water. Let stand for 8 hours or overnight. Drain.

Place the kamut, spelt, or wheat berries, the remaining ½ cup water, and the broth in a medium saucepan and bring to a boil over high heat. Reduce the heat to low, cover, and simmer for 45 minutes, or until tender and some of the grains have burst.

Drain in a colander and place in a medium bowl. Let stand for 30 minutes, or until cooled.

Cut off the peel and most of the white membrane from 2 of the oranges. Cut each orange in half through the top end and place the half flat on a cutting board. Cut the half lengthwise into ½" slices. Juice the remaining orange. In a small bowl, whisk together the orange juice, oil, vinegar, salt, and black pepper.

Add the fennel, bell pepper, onion, and olives to the kamut, spelt, or wheat berries. Add the orange juice mixture and toss to coat well. Add the oranges and toss gently.

Serve immediately or cover and chill to serve later.

Makes 8 servings
Per serving: 149 calories, 4 g protein, 27 g carbohydrates, 5 g fat, 1 g saturated fat, 0 mg cholesterol, 5 g dietary fiber, 272 mg sodium

kasha with onions

1	egg
1	cup medium-grain kasha
1	tablespoon extra-virgin olive oil
4	scallions, thinly sliced
3	large shallots, thinly sliced
1	large onion, chopped
1	medium leek, white and green parts, halved lengthwise, rinsed, and sliced ¼" thick
2	cloves garlic, minced
1	tablespoon coarsely chopped fresh thyme or 1 teaspoon dried
½	teaspoon salt
¼	teaspoon freshly ground black pepper
2	cups vegetable or chicken broth
¼	cup coarsely chopped pecans or walnuts

In a medium bowl, beat the egg with a fork. Add the kasha and stir until the grains are coated. Heat a large nonstick skillet over medium heat. Add the kasha and cook, stirring frequently, for 4 minutes, or until the grains are dry and separate. Place in a bowl; set aside. Wipe the skillet with a paper towel.

Heat the oil in the same skillet over medium-high heat. Add the scallions, shallots, onion, leek, and garlic. Cook, stirring frequently, for 6 minutes, or until tender. Stir in the thyme, salt, and pepper and remove from the heat.

Stir the kasha and broth into the onion mixture. Bring to a boil over medium-high heat. Reduce the heat to low, cover, and simmer for 15 minutes, or until the liquid is absorbed.

Sprinkle the kasha with the nuts.

Makes 6 servings
Per serving: 182 calories, 7 g protein, 27 g carbohydrates, 7 g fat, 1 g saturated fat, 35 mg cholesterol, 4 g dietary fiber, 437 mg sodium

10 ways to pump up pasta

Pasta has become a favorite fast food in many households, and why not? It's delicious, low in fat, and can often be ready in just 10 minutes. Here are 10 simple ways to increase the nutritional value of any pasta dish. Be sure to use whole wheat pasta for the most nutritious start to any of these dishes.

1. Increase your antioxidant intake by stirring 2 cups broccoli florets into the pasta water during the last 5 minutes of cooking. Drain with the pasta and top with your favorite sauce.

2. Pack your favorite tomato sauce (even if it's out of a jar) with calcium. Heat the sauce to a simmer, remove from the heat, and let cool for 1 minute. Stir in plain yogurt, reduced-fat sour cream, or part-skim ricotta cheese.

3. For added fiber, rinse and drain a can of beans (chickpeas or cannellini beans work well with Italian dishes) and add to the simmering sauce just before tossing with the pasta.

4. Bathe your pasta in a flavorful, high-iron sauce. Sauté minced garlic in olive oil until fragrant. Add fresh spinach and sauté just until wilted (be sure to use enough; spinach shrinks to about one-quarter of its volume when wilted).

Toss with hot cooked pasta and top with freshly grated Romano cheese.

5. Get more vitamin E by topping your pasta dishes with some toasted almonds or sunflower seeds.

6. Benefit from the vitamin C in red bell peppers by adding them to your favorite sauce. Or, make a red pepper sauce. Sauté red bell pepper strips and some shallots in olive oil until browned. Add some vegetable broth and simmer until very tender. Puree in the blender and toss over hot pasta.

7. Add to your soy intake by dicing firm or smoked tofu into bits and adding to a vegetable sauce.

8. Be sure to get your share of omega-3 fatty acids by tossing a light pasta dish with grilled or broiled salmon.

9. Fight disease with the phytochemicals in green tea. Add some tea bags to the pasta water when cooking the pasta. Reserve some of the liquid to add to the sauce.

10. Use pasta as a bed for stir-fried vegetables. Forgo long-cooking brown rice when you're in a rush and top whole wheat spaghetti with stir-fried veggies and fish or chicken.

treat

Diabetes
Stress/Fatigue
Stroke
Aging
Heart Disease
Dental Problems
Immunity
Problems
Memory Problems
Prostate Problems

the
**healing
factor**

🌱🌱🌱 Vitamin C
🌱🌱🌱 Chromium
🌱🌱🌱 Vitamin A
🌱🌱🌱 Phosphorus
🌱🌱🌱 Fiber
🌱🌱🌱 Manganese
🌱🌱 Magnesium
🌱🌱 Thiamin
🌱🌱 Potassium
🌱🌱 Vitamin B$_6$

polenta with fresh tomato sauce

6	cups water
¾	teaspoon salt
2	cups coarse yellow cornmeal
½	cup (2 ounces) freshly grated Parmesan cheese
1	tablespoon extra-virgin olive oil
1	large clove garlic, minced
¼	teaspoon dried oregano, crushed
¼	teaspoon fennel seeds, crushed
8	plum tomatoes, coarsely chopped
⅛	teaspoon freshly ground black pepper
2	tablespoons tomato paste

Preheat the oven to 400°F. Coat a 9" × 9" baking dish with cooking spray.

Bring the water to a boil in a large saucepan over high heat. Stir in ½ teaspoon of the salt. Add the cornmeal in a slow, steady stream, whisking constantly. Bring to a boil. Stir in the cheese.

Remove from the heat and pour into the prepared baking dish. Bake for 35 minutes, or until firm.

Meanwhile, heat the oil in a large nonstick skillet over medium heat. Add the garlic, oregano, and fennel seeds and cook, stirring, for 3 minutes, or until fragrant.

Stir in the tomatoes, the remaining ¼ teaspoon salt, and pepper. Increase the heat to high and bring to a boil. Reduce the heat to medium-low and simmer, stirring frequently, for 8 minutes, or until the tomatoes are cooked down and juicy. Add the tomato paste and cook, stirring, for 2 minutes, or until the sauce is slightly thickened. Cover and keep warm.

Serve the polenta with the sauce.

Makes 6 servings
Per serving: 246 calories, 8 g protein, 40 g carbohydrates, 7 g fat, 2 g saturated fat, 7 mg cholesterol, 5 g dietary fiber, 497 mg sodium

Pesto Pasta

The herb basil has a reputation for easing a variety of digestive disorders, especially gas. This pesto is bursting with basil. It's great over pasta, or you can freeze it for up to 3 months in an airtight container (you'll have about 1 cup). Thaw in the refrigerator.

- 8   ounces linguine
- 2½ cups packed fresh basil
- ¾   cup packed parsley
- 2   tablespoons olive oil
- 3   cloves garlic
- 2   tablespoons toasted pine nuts or walnuts
- ¼   cup freshly grated Parmesan cheese
- ¼   cup chicken broth

Prepare the pasta according to package directions.

Meanwhile, in a food processor or blender, combine the basil, parsley, oil, garlic, and nuts. Pulse to finely chop. Sprinkle with the cheese. With the machine running, add the broth, 1 tablespoon at a time, until the mixture is the consistency of prepared mustard.

Toss the pesto with the pasta and serve.

Makes 4 servings
Per serving: 286 calories, 11 g protein, 34 g carbohydrates, 12 g fat, 2 g saturated fat, 5 mg cholesterol, 3 g dietary fiber, 365 mg sodium

Aging
Memory Problems
Stress/Fatigue
Cancer
Heart Disease
Stroke
Dental Problems
Cataracts
Immunity Problems
Menopausal Problems/Hot Flashes

the ❀
healing factor

🍎🍎🍎 Vitamin C
🍎🍎🍎 Vitamin A
🍎🍎🍎 Omega-3 fatty acids
🍎🍎 Folate
🍎🍎 Thiamin
🍎🍎 Vitamin B₆
🍎🍎 Fiber
🍎🍎 Calcium
🍎 Iron
🍎🍎 Riboflavin

garlic and red pepper grits

3¾	cups water
½	teaspoon salt
¾	cup quick-cooking grits
1	tablespoon canola oil
3	cloves garlic, minced
2	large red bell peppers, chopped
½	teaspoon paprika
½	teaspoon dried thyme, crushed
¼	teaspoon freshly ground black pepper
⅓	cup (1½ ounces) shredded Monterey Jack cheese

Bring the water to a boil in a medium saucepan over high heat. Add the salt and slowly stir in the grits. Reduce the heat to medium-low and cook, stirring occasionally, for 20 minutes, or until the grits are creamy and thickened. Remove from the heat.

Meanwhile, heat the oil in a medium nonstick skillet over medium-low heat. Add the garlic and cook, stirring, for 2 minutes, or until fragrant. Add the bell peppers, paprika, thyme, and black pepper and cook, stirring frequently, for 8 minutes, or until very tender. (Add a tablespoon of water to the pan if it gets dry.)

Stir the bell pepper mixture and the cheese into the grits, stirring until the cheese melts.

Makes 4 servings
Per serving: 185 calories, 6 g protein, 27 g carbohydrates, 7 g fat, 2 g saturated fat, 10 mg cholesterol, 3 g dietary fiber, 358 mg sodium

wheat-berry salad

1	cup wheat berries or whole grain spelt
3½	cups water
2	cups chicken or vegetable broth
3	cups small broccoli florets
2	tablespoons extra-virgin olive oil
2	cloves garlic, minced
1	tablespoon fresh herb, such as basil, rosemary, or marjoram, or 1 teaspoon dried, crushed
2	cups halved mixed red and yellow cherry tomatoes
1	cup fresh, drained canned, or frozen corn kernels
¼	teaspoon salt
¼	teaspoon freshly ground black pepper

Place the wheat berries or spelt in a sieve and rinse until the water runs clear. Place in a bowl with 2 cups of the water. Let stand for 8 hours or overnight. Drain.

Place the remaining 1½ cups water and broth in a medium saucepan and bring to a boil over high heat. Add the wheat berries or spelt and return to a boil. Reduce the heat to low, cover, and simmer for 45 minutes, or until tender, adding the broccoli during the last 5 minutes. Drain and place in a large bowl.

Meanwhile, heat the oil in a skillet over medium-high heat. Add the garlic and herb and cook, stirring, for 1 minute. Add the tomatoes, corn, salt, and pepper and cook, stirring frequently, for 3 minutes, or until the tomatoes begin to collapse. Serve over the wheat berries or spelt.

Makes 6 servings
Per serving: 256 calories, 11 g protein, 47 g carbohydrates, 9 g fat, 1 g saturated fat, 0 mg cholesterol, 12 g dietary fiber, 460 mg sodium

treat helps prevent

Diabetes
Cancer
Heart Disease
Dental Problems
Memory Problems
Osteoporosis
Stress/Fatigue
General Vision Problems
Overweight
Constipation

the healing factor

- Vitamin K
- Vitamin C
- Fiber
- Vitamin A
- Folate
- Manganese
- Vitamin B₆
- Potassium
- Chromium

Stress/Fatigue
Aging
Memory Problems
Cancer
Heart Disease
Headaches
Cataracts
Constipation
Prostate Problems
Menopausal Problems/Hot Flashes

the
healing factor

🍇🍇🍇 Vitamin C
🍇🍇🍇 Fiber
🍇🍇🍇 Vitamin A
🍇🍇🍇 Calcium
🍇🍇🍇 Iron
🍇🍇🍇 Phosphorus
🍇🍇 Riboflavin
🍇🍇 Omega-3 fatty acids
🍇🍇 Thiamin
🍇🍇 Vitamin B₆

tamale pie

1	tablespoon olive oil
2	large red and/or green bell peppers, chopped
4–5	teaspoons chili powder
2	cans (14–19 ounces each) kidney beans, rinsed and drained
1	can (14½ ounces) diced tomatoes with green chiles
1	can (14½ ounces) diced tomatoes, drained
1	cup yellow cornmeal
¾	cup whole grain pastry flour
1	teaspoon baking powder
½	teaspoon baking soda
¼	teaspoon salt
1	cup (8 ounces) fat-free plain yogurt
1	cup (4 ounces) shredded reduced-fat Cheddar cheese
1	egg
2	tablespoons olive oil

Preheat the oven to 375°F. Coat an 11" × 7" baking dish with cooking spray.

Heat the oil in a large nonstick skillet over medium-high heat. Add the bell peppers and cook, stirring frequently, for 7 minutes, or until tender. Stir in the chili powder, beans, tomatoes with chiles, and diced tomatoes. Bring to a boil. Place in the prepared baking dish.

Meanwhile, in a large bowl, combine the cornmeal, flour, baking powder, baking soda, and salt. Add the yogurt, cheese, egg, and oil and combine just until blended.

Spoon the cornmeal mixture in spoonfuls over the filling, gently spreading it to cover. Place the baking dish on a baking pan to catch any spillover.

Bake for 25 minutes, or until the crust is lightly browned and firm and the filling is bubbly.

Let stand for 10 minutes before serving.

Makes 6 servings
Per serving: 415 calories, 20 g protein, 57 g carbohydrates, 13 g fat, 4 g saturated fat, 14 mg cholesterol, 13 g dietary fiber, 690 mg sodium

Whole Grain Caprese Pasta

Calcium-rich yogurt is the secret and one of the reasons why this recipe helps fight PMS. The calcium also gives you a bone-healthy bonus.

1   *pound whole wheat pasta shapes, such as twists*
1   *cup (8 ounces) fat-free plain yogurt*
1   *tablespoon + 1 teaspoon extra-virgin olive oil*
½   *teaspoon salt*
1   *large clove garlic*
1   *cup packed fresh basil + additional for garnish*
2   *large tomatoes, chopped*
1   *teaspoon balsamic or red wine vinegar*
6   *ounces reduced-fat mozzarella cheese, cubed*

Prepare the pasta according to package directions.

Meanwhile, place the yogurt, oil, salt, and garlic in a blender. Puree until smooth. Add the basil and puree until completely blended.

Place the tomatoes in a small bowl. Toss with the vinegar and add the cheese.

Place the pasta in a large serving bowl. Top with the basil sauce and tomato mixture. Garnish with additional basil.

Makes 5 servings
Per serving: 495 calories, 26 g protein, 72 g carbohydrates, 13 g fat, 4 g saturated fat, 20 mg cholesterol, 9 g fiber, 431 mg sodium

Cancer
Dental Problems
Overweight
Diabetes
Heart Disease
High Cholesterol
Osteoporosis

the ✍
healing factor

 Fiber

 Calcium

🌶 Potassium

🌶 Vitamin C

botana

1	tablespoon olive oil
5	cloves garlic, minced
¾	teaspoon ground cumin
¾	teaspoon dried oregano, crushed
2	cans (14–19 ounces each) black beans, rinse and drain 1 can, use both beans and liquid from other can
1	can (15 ounces) diced tomatoes with green chiles
¼–½	cup water
½	cup (2 ounces) shredded reduced-fat sharp Cheddar cheese
	Baked tortilla chips or warmed corn tortillas
	Red bell pepper wedges, cucumber spears, and celery sticks for dipping

Heat the oil in a large nonstick skillet over medium heat. Add the garlic, cumin, and oregano and cook, stirring frequently, for 2 minutes, or until fragrant.

Stir in the drained beans and the beans with their liquid and bring to a boil. Remove from the heat. Mash the beans with a potato masher to a coarse-textured puree.

Return to medium heat and stir in the tomatoes and ¼ cup of the water. Bring to a boil, stirring. Reduce the heat to medium-low and cook, stirring frequently, for 5 minutes, or until the beans are heated through and the flavors are blended. Stir in up to ¼ cup additional water if the mixture is too thick.

Place in a serving bowl and sprinkle with the cheese. Serve with the chips or tortillas and vegetables.

Makes 8 servings
Per serving: 103 calories, 6 g protein, 16 g carbohydrates, 3 g fat, 1 g saturated fat, 5 mg cholesterol, 5 g dietary fiber, 494 mg sodium

barley with spring greens

Photograph on page 42

1 ½	cups chicken or vegetable broth
½	cup pearl barley
1	tablespoon extra-virgin olive oil
1	bunch scallions, thinly sliced
3	cloves garlic, slivered
10	cups loosely packed torn mixed greens, such as escarole, Swiss chard, watercress, and arugula
¼	teaspoon salt
⅛	teaspoon freshly ground black pepper

Bring the broth to a boil in a medium saucepan over high heat. Add the barley and return to a boil. Reduce the heat to low, cover, and simmer for 45 minutes, or until tender.

Meanwhile, heat the oil in a large saucepot or Dutch oven over medium-high heat. Add the scallions and garlic and cook, stirring frequently, for 3 minutes, or until the scallions are wilted.

Add the greens, salt, and pepper. Cook, stirring, for 3 minutes, or until just wilted.

Fluff the barley with a fork and stir into the greens.

Makes 4 servings
Per serving: 143 calories, 5 g protein, 24 g carbohydrates, 4 g fat, 1 g saturated fat, 0 mg cholesterol, 7 g dietary fiber, 391 mg sodium

treat ⸱ **helps prevent**

Cancer
Dental Problems
Diabetes
Heart Disease
Osteoporosis
Asthma
High Cholesterol
Overweight
Leg Cramps
Rheumatoid Arthritis

the
healing factor

🐦🐦🐦 Vitamin K
🐦🐦🐦 Vitamin A
🐦🐦🐦 Vitamin C
🐦🐦🐦 Manganese
🐦🐦🐦 Fiber
🐦🐦🐦 Folate
🐦🐦 Selenium
🐦🐦 Potassium
🐦🐦 Calcium
🐦🐦 Magnesium

Aging
Cancer
Heart Disease
Stroke
Dental Problems
Immunity
Problems
Insomnia
Stress/Fatigue
General Vision
Problems
Irritable Bowel
Syndrome

the
**healing
factor**

🐞🐞🐞 Vitamin A
🐞🐞🐞 Fiber
🐞🐞🐞 Manganese
🐞🐞 Selenium
🐞🐞 Iron
🐞🐞 Niacin
🐞🐞 Phosphorus

baked barley with mushrooms and carrots

1	tablespoon butter
3	large carrots, halved lengthwise and thinly sliced
1	large onion, halved and thinly sliced
1 1/4	cups vegetable or chicken broth
10–12	ounces cremini, baby portobello, or white button mushrooms, sliced
2	cups water
1	cup pearl barley
1	teaspoon dried thyme, crushed
1/2	teaspoon salt
1/4	teaspoon freshly ground black pepper

Preheat the oven to 350°F.

Melt the butter in an ovenproof Dutch oven over medium-high heat. Add the carrots, onion, and 1 tablespoon of the broth. Cook, stirring frequently, for 8 minutes, or until tender, adding another 1 tablespoon broth halfway through cooking.

Add the mushrooms and 2 tablespoons of the remaining broth and cook, stirring frequently, for 4 minutes, or until tender.

Stir in the remaining 1 cup broth, the water, barley, thyme, salt, and pepper. Bring to a boil over high heat. Cover the pot and place in the oven. Bake for 45 minutes, or until the barley is tender and the liquid is absorbed.

Makes 6 servings
Per serving: 176 calories, 7 g protein, 33 g carbohydrates, 3 g fat, 1 g saturated fat, 5 mg cholesterol, 8 g dietary fiber, 392 mg sodium

barley risotto

4	cups chicken or vegetable broth
2½	cups water
2	tablespoons extra-virgin olive oil
1	medium leek, both white and green parts, halved, rinsed, and very thinly sliced, or 1 large onion, chopped
1	clove garlic, minced
¾	cup medium pearl barley
½	teaspoon dried tarragon, crushed
¼	teaspoon freshly ground black pepper
½	cup frozen peas, thawed
¼	cup (1 ounce) freshly grated Parmesan cheese
1	tablespoon chopped fresh chives (optional)

Combine the broth and water in a medium saucepan and bring to a boil over high heat. Reduce the heat to low, cover, and simmer.

Heat the oil in a large saucepan over medium heat. Add the leek or onion and garlic. Cook, stirring, for 4 minutes. Add the barley, tarragon, and pepper; stir until the barley is coated.

Begin adding the hot broth mixture, about ½ cup at a time, stirring frequently after each addition and cooking until the liquid is nearly evaporated. Continue adding the broth mixture, ½ cup at a time, until all has been added and the barley is very tender and creamy, about 55 minutes.

Stir in the peas, cheese, and chives, if using. Cook, stirring, for 5 minutes, or until heated through.

Makes 4 servings
Per serving: 250 calories, 8 g protein, 35 g carbohydrates, 9 g fat, 2 g saturated fat, 5 mg cholesterol, 7 g dietary fiber, 719 mg sodium

Insomnia
Aging
Cancer
Headaches
Stress/Fatigue

the healing factor

🌾🌾🌾 Manganese
🌾🌾🌾 Fiber
🌾🌾🌾 Selenium
🌾🌾 Phosphorus
🌾🌾 Magnesium
🌾🌾 Calcium
🌾🌾 Niacin
🌾🌾 Copper
🌾🌾 Iron
🌾🌾 Thiamin

quinoa with peperonata

Aging

Diabetes

Stress/Fatigue

Heart Disease

Dental Problems

Headaches

Immunity Problems

Insomnia

Anemia

Prostate Problems

1	cup quinoa (see tip)
2	cups water
¼	teaspoon salt
2	tablespoons extra-virgin olive oil
3	large red bell peppers, cut into ½" squares
3	cloves garlic, minced
2	inner stalks celery with leaves, thinly sliced
1	medium red onion, chopped
¼	teaspoon salt
¼	teaspoon freshly ground black pepper
1	can (14½ ounces) diced tomatoes, drained, with 2 tablespoons of the liquid reserved
2	strips orange peel (each 2" long), removed with a vegetable peeler
1	tablespoon drained capers, chopped

the healing factor

🍐🍐🍐 Vitamin C

🍐🍐🍐 Vitamin A

🍐🍐🍐 Manganese

🍐🍐🍐 Iron

🍐🍐🍐 Magnesium

🍐🍐🍐 Copper

🍐🍐🍐 Fiber

🍐🍐🍐 Phosphorus

🍐🍐 Vitamin B₆

🍐🍐 Potassium

COOKING TIP
You must thoroughly rinse the quinoa to remove the saponin, a naturally occurring coating on the grain that has a bitter flavor.

Place the quinoa in a fine-mesh strainer and rinse under cold running water until the water runs clear.

Place the water in a medium saucepan and bring to a boil over high heat. Add the quinoa and salt and return to a boil. Reduce the heat to low, cover, and simmer for 20 minutes, or until the quinoa is tender and the water is absorbed.

Meanwhile, heat the oil in a large skillet over medium heat. Add the bell peppers, garlic, celery, onion, salt, and black pepper and cook, stirring frequently, for 8 minutes, or until tender-crisp.

Stir in the tomatoes and the reserved 2 tablespoons tomato liquid, the orange peel, and capers. Bring to a boil over high heat. Reduce the heat to low, cover, and simmer, stirring occasionally, for 12 minutes, or until the vegetables are very tender. Remove and discard the orange peel.

Fluff the quinoa with a fork and spoon into a shallow serving dish. Top with the pepper mixture.

Makes 4 servings
Per serving: 262 calories, 7 g protein, 39 g carbohydrates, 10 g fat, 1 g saturated fat, 0 mg cholesterol, 5 g dietary fiber, 605 mg sodium

the power of

BEANS
Beans contain a healthy dose of fiber—approximately 7 grams per ½ cup—and they can help lower cholesterol, stabilize blood sugar, reduce the risk of breast and prostate cancer, and help prevent heart disease in people with diabetes.

Although dried beans have negligible amounts of sodium, the easy-to-use canned varieties are packed in a salt brine. Look for low-sodium canned beans and always rinse the beans to reduce the sodium content.

To prevent the gas that often follows a bean dish, toss the beans with summer savory, ginger, or cumin. These spices have been shown to reduce beans' gas-producing effects.

Here are some delicious ways to get more beans into your diet.

- Toss into soup or salads.
- Add to stir-fry dishes.
- Add to vegetable dishes during the last 3 minutes of cooking.
- Make guacamole with half mashed beans and half avocado.
- Stir into stews.
- Add to salsa for a hearty dip.
- Mash with minced vegetables and slather on bread topped with lettuce, tomato, and another bread slice.

quinoa with peppers and beans

Photograph on page 41

1	cup quinoa (see tip on page 246)
2½	cups vegetable broth
2	tablespoons extra-virgin olive oil
3	cloves garlic, minced
1	tablespoon finely chopped peeled fresh ginger
¾	teaspoon whole cumin seeds
2	medium red bell peppers, cut into thin strips
1	large onion, cut into thin wedges
1	can (14–19 ounces) black beans, rinsed and drained
¼	cup chopped fresh cilantro

Place the quinoa in a fine-mesh strainer and rinse under cold running water until the water runs clear.

Bring 2 cups of the broth to a boil in a medium saucepan over high heat. Add the quinoa and return to a boil. Reduce the heat to low, cover, and simmer for 20 minutes, or until tender.

Meanwhile, heat the oil in a large nonstick skillet over medium heat. Add the garlic, ginger, and cumin seeds and cook, stirring, for 2 minutes, or until fragrant. Add the bell peppers and onion and cook, stirring, for 8 minutes, or until tender. Stir in the beans and the remaining ½ cup broth and cook for 2 minutes.

Fluff the quinoa with a fork and stir in the cilantro. Place in a serving bowl and top with the pepper mixture.

Makes 4 servings
Per serving: 307 calories, 14 g protein, 50 g carbohydrates, 10 g fat, 1 g saturated fat, 0 mg cholesterol, 9 g dietary fiber, 637 mg sodium

southwestern quinoa and chickpea salad

1	cup quinoa (see tip on page 246)
1¾	cups water
⅛	teaspoon salt
1	cup rinsed and drained canned chickpeas
1	medium tomato, seeded and chopped
1	clove garlic, minced
3	tablespoons lime juice
2	tablespoons finely chopped fresh cilantro
4	teaspoons olive oil
½	teaspoon ground cumin

Place the quinoa in a fine-mesh strainer and rinse under cold running water until the water runs clear.

Bring the water to a boil in a medium saucepan over high heat. Add the quinoa and salt and return to a boil. Reduce the heat to low, cover, and simmer for 20 minutes, or until tender and the liquid is absorbed.

Meanwhile, in a large bowl, combine the chickpeas, tomato, garlic, lime juice, cilantro, oil, and cumin. Add the quinoa and toss to coat well.

Makes 4 servings
Per serving: 283 calories, 9 g protein, 46 g carbohydrates, 8 g fat, 1 g saturated fat, 0 mg cholesterol, 6 g dietary fiber, 200 mg sodium

treat ⌐ **helps prevent**

Stress/Fatigue
Aging
Stroke
Diabetes
Cancer
High Cholesterol
Heart Disease
Depression
General Vision Problems

the **healing factor**

🍎🍎🍎 Manganese
🍎🍎🍎 Iron
🍎🍎🍎 Magnesium
🍎🍎🍎 Phosphorus
🍎🍎🍎 Fiber
🍎🍎🍎 Vitamin C
🍎🍎 Copper
🍎🍎 Folate
🍎🍎 Zinc
🍎🍎 Potassium

helps
prevent ↴

treat

Aging

Cancer

Dental Problems

Depression

Diabetes

Immunity
Problems

Memory Problems

General Vision
Problems

Constipation

the *healing factor*

🍐🍐🍐 Vitamin A

🍐🍐🍐 Vitamin C

🍐🍐 Omega-3
fatty acids

🍐🍐🍐 Folate

🍐🍐🍐 Fiber

🍐🍐🍐 Manganese

🍐🍐🍐 Vitamin B₆

🍐🍐🍐 Potassium

🍐🍐🍐 Phosphorus

🍐🍐 Copper

bahamian bean and corn stew with sweet potatoes

1	cup dried appaloosa, calypso, pinto, or cranberry beans, sorted and rinsed
½	teaspoon dried thyme, crushed
2	tablespoons canola oil
5	cloves garlic, minced
1	large onion, chopped
1	large red bell pepper, chopped
1	habanero or Scotch bonnet chile pepper or 2 jalapeño chile peppers, seeded and minced (optional); wear plastic gloves when handling
3	cups chicken or vegetable broth
1	large sweet potato, peeled and cut into 1" chunks
1	tablespoon minced fresh ginger
2	teaspoons turmeric
1	teaspoon paprika
1	teaspoon ground coriander
¼	teaspoon salt
2	cups fresh or frozen corn kernels
1	can (5½ ounces) pineapple tidbits packed in juice
	Lime wedges (optional)

Place the beans in a bowl. Add water to cover by 2", cover, and let stand overnight. Drain and rinse the beans.

Place the soaked beans in a medium saucepan. Add water to cover by 2". Bring to a boil over high heat. Skim off the foam and stir in the thyme. Reduce the heat to low, cover, and simmer, stirring occasionally, for 1¼ hours, or until tender. Drain the beans, return to the pot, and set aside. (This may be done 1 to 3 days ahead. Store in the refrigerator.)

Heat the oil in a Dutch oven over medium-high heat. Add the garlic, onion, bell pepper, and chile pepper (if using) and cook, stirring occasionally, for 6 minutes, or until the vegetables are tender.

Stir in the broth, sweet potato, beans, ginger, turmeric, paprika, coriander, and salt. Bring to a boil over high heat. Reduce the heat to low, partially cover, and simmer for 25 minutes, or until the sweet potatoes are tender.

Stir in the corn, cover, and simmer for 5 minutes longer, or until tender. Remove from the heat and stir in the pineapple (with juice).

Ladle the stew into bowls and serve with lime wedges, if using.

Makes 4 servings
Per serving: 435 calories, 15 g protein, 81 g carbohydrates, 8 g fat, 1 g saturated fat, 0 mg cholesterol, 17 g dietary fiber, 597 mg sodium

Stress/Fatigue
Aging
Depression
Diabetes
Headaches
Insomnia
Memory Problems
Constipation
Diverticulosis

the
healing factor

🌰🌰🌰 Fiber
🌰🌰🌰 Folate
🌰🌰🌰 Manganese
🌰🌰🌰 Phosphorus
🌰🌰🌰 Magnesium
🌰🌰🌰 Iron
🌰🌰🌰 Thiamin
🌰🌰🌰 Copper
🌰🌰 Potassium
🌰🌰 Vitamin B$_6$

mediterranean baked beans

1	cup great Northern beans, picked over and rinsed
1	cup red kidney beans, picked over and rinsed
2	cups chicken broth
1½	cups water
6	cloves garlic, minced
2	tablespoons extra-virgin olive oil
1	large sprig fresh sage or ½ teaspoon dried, crushed
½	teaspoon freshly ground black pepper

Place the great Northern and kidney beans in a bowl. Add cold water to cover by 2". Cover and let stand overnight.

Preheat the oven to 325°F.

Drain the beans and place in an ovenproof Dutch oven. Add the broth, water, garlic, oil, sage, and pepper.

Cover and bake for 1 hour and 45 minutes, or until the beans are very creamy and tender. (Add a little more water during baking, if needed.)

Makes 4 servings
Per serving: 292 calories, 15 g protein, 42 g carbohydrates, 8 g fat, 1 g saturated fat, 0 mg cholesterol, 16 g dietary fiber, 408 mg sodium

adzuki beans with miso dressing

1¼	cups dried adzuki beans, small red beans, or black beans, picked over and rinsed
¼	teaspoon freshly ground black pepper
2	tablespoons mellow white miso
3	tablespoons orange juice
2	tablespoons lemon juice
2	tablespoons olive oil
½	teaspoon grated fresh ginger
3	scallions, diagonally sliced
2	medium cucumbers, peeled, halved, seeded, and cut into thin diagonal slices
1	small carrot, shredded
¼	cup coarsely chopped walnuts

Place the beans in a bowl. Add water to cover by 2". Cover and let stand overnight.

Drain the beans and place in a medium saucepan. Add water to cover by 2" and bring to a boil over high heat. Stir in the pepper. Reduce the heat to low, cover, and simmer, stirring, for 30 minutes, or until very tender.

Drain the beans and place in a serving bowl for 20 minutes.

Meanwhile, in a large bowl, whisk together the miso, orange juice, lemon juice, oil, and ginger. Stir in the scallions, cucumbers, carrot, walnuts, and beans.

Let stand for 15 minutes to blend the flavors.

Makes 4 servings
Per serving: 351 calories, 15 g protein, 49 g carbohydrates, 12 g fat, 2 g saturated fat, 0 mg cholesterol, 10 g dietary fiber, 327 mg sodium

treat ↗ **helps prevent**

Diabetes
Cancer
High Cholesterol
Heart Disease
Dental Problems
Kidney Stones
Memory Problems
Osteoporosis
General Vision Problems

the 🌿
healing factor

🍓🍓🍓 Folate
🍓🍓🍓 Vitamin A
🍓🍓🍓 Manganese
🍓🍓🍓 Copper
🍓🍓🍓 Fiber
🍓🍓🍓 Vitamin K
🍓🍓🍓 Phosphorus
🍓🍓🍓 Potassium
🍓🍓🍓 Vitamin C
🍓🍓🍓 Magnesium

COOKING TIP
Though perfect as a main course, these hearty beans are also well-suited as a side dish. Just halve the portions to get 8 tasty side-dish servings.

helps
prevent

treat

Stress/Fatigue

Memory Problems

Aging

High Cholesterol

Heart Disease

Diabetes

Constipation

Irritable Bowel
Syndrome

Overweight

the
healing factor

🍐🍐🍐 Fiber

🍐🍐🍐 Vitamin B$_6$

🍐🍐🍐 Manganese

🍐🍐🍐 Iron

🍐🍐🍐 Phosphorus

🍐🍐🍐 Vitamin C

🍐🍐🍐 Copper

🍐🍐🍐 Vitamin K

🍐🍐🍐 Thiamin

🍐🍐🍐 Potassium

lentils with tomatoes

1½	cups brown lentils, picked over and rinsed
3½	cups water
¼	teaspoon ground allspice
½	teaspoon freshly ground black pepper
¾	teaspoon salt
2	tablespoons extra-virgin olive oil
2	cloves garlic, minced
3	medium tomatoes, cut into 1½" chunks
½	cup (4 ounces) fat-free plain yogurt
2	tablespoons snipped fresh chives or scallion greens

In a large saucepan, combine the lentils, water, allspice, and ¼ teaspoon of the pepper. Bring to a boil over high heat. Reduce the heat to low, cover, and simmer for 25 minutes, or until the lentils are tender but still hold their shape. Remove from the heat and stir in ½ teaspoon of the salt.

Meanwhile, heat the oil in a large nonstick skillet over medium-high heat. Add the garlic and cook, stirring, for 30 seconds, or until fragrant. Add the tomatoes, the remaining ¼ teaspoon salt, and the remaining ¼ teaspoon pepper. Cook, stirring occasionally, for 2 minutes, or until the tomatoes just start to release their juices. Remove from the heat.

Drain the lentils and place in a shallow serving dish. Spoon the tomato mixture over the lentils, top with the yogurt, and sprinkle with the chives or scallion greens.

Makes 4 servings
Per serving: 344 calories, 23 g protein, 49 g carbohydrates, 8 g fat, 1 g saturated fat, 1 mg cholesterol, 23 g fiber, 482 mg sodium

vegetables

From artichokes to zucchini, vegetables are a
powerhouse of healing nutrients. They are
high in fiber, vitamins, minerals, and complex
carbohydrates. They're also colorful, easy to prepare,
and versatile enough that you can enjoy them every
night of the week. Fresh veggies contain lots of
nutrients, but don't forget the frozen option.
Flash-frozen soon after the vegetables are picked at
the peak of their season, they are a great healing
food, especially in the winter months.

Stroke
Stress/Fatigue
Depression
Diabetes
Memory Problems
Heart Disease
Dental Problems
Immunity
Problems
General Vision
Problems
Cataracts

the healing factor

🍎🍎🍎 Vitamin A
🍎🍎🍎 Vitamin C
🍎🍎🍎 Manganese
🍎🍎🍎 Vitamin B₆
🍎🍎🍎 Fiber
🍎🍎 Potassium
🍎🍎 Chromium
🍎🍎 Copper
🍎🍎 Thiamin
🍎🍎 Riboflavin

rosemary-roasted potatoes

1	very large sweet potato (1 pound), peeled and cut into ¾" chunks
4	small red or white new potatoes, scrubbed and cut into ¾" chunks
4	teaspoons extra-virgin olive oil
2	teaspoons chopped fresh rosemary or ½ teaspoon dried, crushed
½	teaspoon grated orange peel
¼	teaspoon salt
⅛	teaspoon freshly ground black pepper

Preheat the oven to 425°F. Coat a 13" × 9" baking pan with cooking spray.

Place the sweet potatoes, potatoes, oil, rosemary, orange peel, salt, and pepper in the prepared baking pan. Toss to coat well. Spread the potatoes in a single layer.

Roast, turning the potatoes several times, for 45 minutes, or until very tender and browned.

Makes 4 servings
Per serving: 222 calories, 4 g protein, 41 g carbohydrates, 5 g fat, 1 g saturated fat, 0 mg cholesterol, 5 g dietary fiber, 163 mg sodium

spicy oven fries

2	medium russet potatoes, scrubbed and cut into long ¼"-thick strips
1	tablespoon canola oil
1	tablespoon roasted garlic and red pepper spice blend
¼	teaspoon salt
¼	teaspoon freshly ground black pepper

Preheat the oven to 425°F. Coat a 13" × 9" baking pan with cooking spray.

Place the potatoes in a mound in the prepared baking pan and sprinkle with the oil, spice blend, salt, and pepper. Toss to coat well. Spread the potatoes in a single layer.

Bake, turning the potatoes several times, for 40 minutes, or until crisp and lightly browned.

Makes 4 servings
Per serving: 115 calories, 3 g protein, 18 g carbohydrates, 4 g fat,
0 g saturated fat, 0 mg cholesterol, 2 g dietary fiber, 144 mg sodium

treat ⌐ helps prevent

Stroke
Aging
Heart Disease
Diabetes
Depression
Immunity Problems
Stress/Fatigue
Psoriasis

the
healing factor

Vitamin C
Omega-3 fatty acids
Chromium
Potassium
Vitamin B$_6$
Manganese

Heart Disease

Dental Problems

Diabetes

Immunity Problems

Osteoporosis

Breast Cancer

Cancer

General Vision Problems

Stress/Fatigue

Leg Cramps

the
healing factor

🐞🐞🐞 Vitamin A

🐞🐞🐞 Omega-3 fatty acids

🐞🐞🐞 Vitamin C

🐞🐞🐞 Chromium

🐞🐞🐞 Fiber

🐞🐞 Potassium

🐞🐞 Calcium

🐞🐞 Vitamin K

🐞🐞 Manganese

🐞🐞 Vitamin B$_6$

indian-spiced potatoes and spinach

2	medium russet potatoes, scrubbed and cut into ½" chunks
2	tablespoons canola oil
3	large cloves garlic, minced
1	medium onion, chopped
1¾	teaspoons ground cumin
¾	teaspoon ground coriander
½	teaspoon ground turmeric
¼	teaspoon ground ginger
¼	teaspoon salt
¼	teaspoon freshly ground black pepper
⅛	teaspoon ground cinnamon
2	cups frozen cut leaf spinach (from a bag)
2–4	tablespoons water
½	cup (4 ounces) fat-free plain yogurt

Place a steamer basket in a large saucepan with ½" of water. Place the potatoes in the steamer. Bring to a boil over high heat. Reduce the heat to medium, cover, and cook for 20 minutes, or until the potatoes are very tender.

Place the potatoes in a bowl and keep warm. Drain and dry the saucepan.

Heat the oil in the same saucepan over medium heat. Add the garlic and onion and cook, stirring frequently, for 5 minutes, or until soft. Add the cumin, coriander, turmeric, ginger, salt, pepper, and cinnamon and cook, stirring, for 30 seconds to cook the spices.

Add the potatoes and cook, stirring frequently, for 5 minutes, or until crisp and golden.

Add the spinach and 2 tablespoons water. Cover and cook, tossing gently, adding additional water 1 tablespoon at a time, if needed, for 5 minutes, or until heated through.

Place in a serving bowl. Spoon the yogurt on top, but don't stir it in, and serve hot.

Makes 4 servings
Per serving: 195 calories, 8 g protein, 24 g carbohydrates, 7 g fat, 1 g saturated fat, 1 mg cholesterol, 6 g dietary fiber, 350 mg sodium

Diabetes
Stress/Fatigue
Stroke
Depression
Memory Problems
Aging
Heart Disease
Cancer

the
healing factor

🍐🍐🍐 Vitamin C
🍐🍐🍐 Chromium
🍐🍐🍐 Potassium
🍐🍐🍐 Manganese
🍐🍐 Vitamin B$_6$
🍐🍐 Fiber
🍐🍐 Thiamin
🍐🍐 Phosphorus
🍐🍐 Niacin
🍐🍐 Magnesium

fluffy garlic mashed potatoes

4	medium russet or Yukon gold potatoes, cut into 1" chunks
8	cloves garlic
½	cup buttermilk
1	tablespoon butter
½	teaspoon salt
¼	teaspoon freshly ground black pepper
1	tablespoon snipped fresh chives, dill, or scallion greens

Place a steamer basket in a large saucepan with ½" of water. Place the potatoes and garlic in the steamer. Bring to a boil over high heat. Reduce the heat to medium, cover, and cook for 20 minutes, or until the potatoes are very tender.

Place the potatoes and garlic in a bowl and mash with a potato masher. Add the buttermilk, butter, salt, pepper, and chives, dill, or scallion greens; mash until well-blended.

Makes 4 servings
Per serving: 172 calories, 6 g protein, 30 g carbohydrates, 4 g fat, 2 g saturated fat, 9 mg cholesterol, 3 g dietary fiber, 360 mg sodium

Baked Stuffed Potatoes with Spinach and Cannellini Beans

Photograph on page 45

Take comfort from your stress with America's all-time favorite comfort food: potatoes. Spuds contain nutrients—including vitamin C and iron—that help combat stress and fatigue. If you're not a big spinach fan, substitute broccoli florets for even more vitamin C.

> 4   *large russet potatoes, pricked several times with a fork*
> 4   *ounces low-fat goat cheese*
> ¼   *cup (2 ounces) reduced-fat sour cream*
> 1   *tablespoon extra-virgin olive oil*
> 2   *teaspoons fat-free milk*
> ½   *teaspoon salt*
> ½   *teaspoon freshly ground black pepper*
> 1   *package (10 ounces) frozen chopped spinach, thawed and squeezed dry*
> 2   *scallions, thinly sliced*
> 1   *can (14–19 ounces) cannellini beans, rinsed and drained*

Preheat the oven to 425°F.

Place the potatoes directly on the oven rack and bake for 1 hour, or until soft when squeezed (wear an oven mitt).

Remove the potatoes from the oven and cut each lengthwise in half. Let stand until easily handled but still warm.

Scoop out the potato pulp into a large bowl, leaving a ¼"-thick shell. Place the potato shells in a 13" × 9" baking pan.

With a potato masher, mash the pulp with the cheese, sour cream, oil, milk, salt, and pepper. Fold in the spinach, scallions, and beans. Spoon into the potato shells. Bake for 20 minutes, or until lightly browned.

Makes 8 servings
Per serving: 227 calories, 11 g protein, 31 g carbohydrates, 7 g fat, 4 g saturated fat, 14 mg cholesterol, 6 g dietary fiber, 368 mg sodium

Stroke

Stress/Fatigue

Aging

Depression

Memory Problems

Diabetes

Immunity Problems

General Vision Problems

Cataracts

Breast Cancer

the 🌿
healing factor

🐛🐛🐛 Vitamin A

🐛🐛🐛 Vitamin C

🐛🐛🐛 Manganese

🐛🐛🐛 Vitamin B$_6$

🐛🐛🐛 Fiber

🐛🐛 Riboflavin

🐛🐛 Copper

🐛🐛 Potassium

🐛🐛 Pantothenic acid

🐛🐛 Phosphorus

root vegetable mash

Photograph on page 50

3	pounds sweet potatoes, peeled and cut into small chunks
1	pound celery root, peeled and cut into small chunks
2	cloves garlic
1	small onion, peeled and chopped
1/3	cup 1% milk, warmed
1 1/2	tablespoons olive oil
1/2	teaspoon salt

Place a steamer basket in a large saucepan with ½" of water. Place the sweet potatoes, celery root, and garlic in the steamer. Bring to a boil over high heat. Reduce the heat to medium, cover, and cook for 10 minutes. Add the onion, cover, and cook for 10 minutes longer, or until the onion and celery root are very tender.

Place the vegetables in a bowl and mash with a potato masher. Add the milk, oil, and salt. Mash to blend.

Makes 8 servings
Per serving: 221 calories, 4 g protein, 45 g carbohydrates, 3 g fat, 1 g saturated fat, 0 mg cholesterol, 6 g dietary fiber, 207 mg sodium

roasted beets with herbs and garlic

2	pounds small beets, scrubbed
2	tablespoons chicken or vegetable broth
1	tablespoon extra-virgin olive oil
2	cloves garlic, minced
1	large shallot, finely chopped
½	teaspoon dried sage, crushed
	Pinch of ground allspice
⅛	teaspoon salt
⅛	teaspoon freshly ground black pepper

Preheat the oven to 400°F.

Cut each beet into 8 wedges. Place the beets, broth, oil, garlic, shallot, sage, allspice, salt, and pepper in an 11" × 7" baking dish. Toss to coat well.

Cover tightly with foil and bake, stirring occasionally, for 1 hour, or until the beets are very tender.

Makes 4 servings
Per serving: 132 calories, 4 g protein, 23 g carbohydrates, 4 g fat, 1 g saturated fat, 0 mg cholesterol, 5 g dietary fiber, 288 mg sodium

treat ↘ helps prevent

Stroke
Diabetes
Cancer
High Cholesterol
Heart Disease
Stress/Fatigue
Anemia
Aging

the
healing
factor

🌱🌱🌱 Folate
🌱🌱🌱 Manganese
🌱🌱🌱 Potassium
🌱🌱🌱 Fiber
🌱🌱🌱 Vitamin C
🌱🌱 Magnesium
🌱🌱 Iron

Stroke

Aging

Cancer

Heart Disease

Diabetes

High Cholesterol

Dental Problems

Memory Problems

Stress/Fatigue

the
**healing
factor**

🐀🐀🐀 Vitamin C

🐀🐀🐀 Chromium

🐀🐀 Manganese

🐀🐀 Fiber

🐀🐀 Potassium

🐀🐀 Vitamin B$_6$

🐀🐀 Calcium

🐀🐀 Folate

🐀🐀 Phosphorus

stuffed vidalia onions

Photograph on page 51

4	Vidalia or sweet onions
½	teaspoon olive oil
2	medium zucchini, shredded
3	cloves garlic, minced
1	teaspoon dried thyme, crushed
1	teaspoon dried basil, crushed
3	tablespoons plain dry bread crumbs
1½	tablespoons chopped toasted pine nuts
3	tablespoons freshly grated Parmesan cheese
¼	teaspoon salt
¼	teaspoon freshly ground black pepper

Preheat the oven to 400°F. Line a small baking pan with foil.

Cut ½" off the top of each onion; slightly trim the bottoms so that the onions stand upright. Place the onions, cut side up, in the prepared baking pan and coat with cooking spray. Bake for 1 hour, or until soft. Set aside for 15 minutes, or until cool enough to handle.

Reduce the oven temperature to 350°F.

Remove and discard the onion peels. Using a spoon, scoop out the onion centers, leaving a ½" shell. Chop the centers and reserve 1 cup for the stuffing; save the remainder for another use.

Heat the oil in a large nonstick skillet over medium heat. Add the zucchini, garlic, thyme, basil, and the 1 cup chopped onions. Cook for 6 minutes, or until the zucchini is softened and most of the liquid has evaporated. Remove from the heat and stir in the bread crumbs, pine nuts, 2½ tablespoons of the cheese, salt, and pepper.

Divide the filling among the onion shells. Place the onion shells in the same baking pan and top with the remaining ½ tablespoon cheese.

Bake for 20 minutes, or until golden.

Makes 4 servings
Per serving: 122 calories, 6 g protein, 18 g carbohydrates, 4 g fat, 1 g saturated fat, 3 mg cholesterol, 4 g dietary fiber, 262 mg sodium

Thyme and Rosemary Potatoes

The vitamin C in the potatoes and the mixture of herbs and garlic are great for combating a stuffy nose. So delicious and versatile, they're a wonderful accompaniment to any meat, fish, or chicken dish.

- 2 *pounds potatoes, scrubbed and sliced*
- 1 *tablespoon olive oil*
- 1 *tablespoon chopped fresh rosemary or 1 teaspoon dried, crushed*
- 1 *tablespoon chopped fresh thyme or 1 teaspoon dried, crushed*
- 2 *cloves garlic, minced*
- ¼ *teaspoon salt*
- ¼ *teaspoon freshly ground black pepper*

Preheat the oven to 425°F.

Place the potatoes in a 13" × 9" baking dish. Add the oil, rosemary, thyme, garlic, salt, and pepper and toss to coat well.

Bake for 40 minutes, or until golden and tender.

Makes 8 servings
Per serving: 140 calories, 3 g protein, 29 g carbohydrates, 2 g fat, 0 g saturated fat, 0 mg cholesterol, 3 g dietary fiber, 82 mg sodium

Remedy Recipe for Stuffy Nose

sweet potato stew

Diabetes
Stress/Fatigue
Dental Problems
Insomnia
Memory Problems
Osteoporosis
Breast Cancer
Anemia
General Vision Problems
Aging

the
healing
factor

🍒🍒🍒 Vitamin A
🍒🍒🍒 Vitamin K
🍒🍒🍒 Vitamin C
🍒🍒🍒 Manganese
🍒🍒🍒 Fiber
🍒🍒🍒 Chromium
🍒🍒🍒 Potassium
🍒🍒🍒 Iron
🍒🍒🍒 Magnesium
🍒🍒🍒 Niacin

1½	cups brown rice
1	tablespoon olive oil
3	cloves garlic, minced
2	red bell peppers, cut into 1" chunks
1	large onion, chopped
1	tablespoon minced fresh ginger
½	teaspoon ground allspice
¼	teaspoon ground red pepper
4	cups vegetable broth
2	large sweet potatoes, peeled and cut into 1" chunks
½	cup natural peanut butter
1	cup boiling water
⅓	cup tomato paste
1	can (10½–15 ounces) chickpeas, rinsed and drained
1	pound spinach, coarsely chopped

Prepare the rice according to package directions.

Meanwhile, heat the oil in a Dutch oven over medium-high heat. Add the garlic, bell peppers, and onion; cook for 3 minutes. Add the ginger, allspice, and ground red pepper; cook for 1 minute.

Add the broth and potatoes; bring to a boil. Reduce the heat to low, cover, and simmer for 15 minutes, or until tender.

In a bowl, whisk the peanut butter and water. Add to the pan with the tomato paste, chickpeas, and spinach. Cook for 10 minutes, or until heated through. Serve over the rice.

Makes 6 servings
Per serving: 426 calories, 19 g protein, 61 g carbohydrates, 16 g fat, 3 g saturated fat, 0 mg cholesterol, 16 g dietary fiber, 669 mg sodium

roasted carrots and parsnips

1	pound carrots, cut into 1" chunks
1	pound parsnips, cut into 1" chunks
4	small red onions, cut into wedges
6	cloves garlic
½	tablespoon olive oil
½	teaspoon salt
½	teaspoon grated lemon peel

Preheat the oven to 375°F. Coat a medium baking pan with cooking spray. Add the carrots, parsnips, onions, garlic, oil, salt, and lemon peel. Toss to coat well.

Bake, stirring occasionally, for 40 minutes, or until golden and tender.

Makes 6 servings
Per serving: 113 calories, 2 g protein, 24 g carbohydrates, 2 g fat, 0 g saturated fat, 0 mg cholesterol, 7 g dietary fiber, 229 mg sodium

treat ⌐ helps prevent

Stroke

Heart Disease

Depression

Cancer

General Vision Problems

Macular Degeneration

Night Blindness

Dental Problems

Diabetes

Rheumatoid Arthritis

the healing factor

🥕🥕🥕 Vitamin A
🥕🥕🥕 Vitamin C
🥕🥕🥕 Manganese
🥕🥕🥕 Fiber
🥕🥕 Potassium
🥕🥕 Folate
🥕🥕 Thiamin
🥕🥕 Vitamin B$_6$
🥕🥕 Phosphorus

Heart Disease
Dental Problems
Memory Problems
Immunity
Problems
Breast Cancer
Cancer
Diabetes
Infections
Colds and Flu
Aging

the ✿
healing factor

🍎🍎🍎 Vitamin C
🍎🍎🍎 Vitamin A
🍎🍎🍎 Vitamin K
🍎🍎 Fiber
🍎🍎 Vitamin B₆

COOKING TIP
To cook this dish
indoors, coat a
broiler-pan rack with
cooking spray and
preheat the broiler.
Place the vegetables
on the rack and broil,
turning often, for 10
minutes, or until
browned.

grilled portobellos, peppers, and onions

¼	cup chopped flat-leaf parsley
3	tablespoons lemon juice
2	tablespoons extra-virgin olive oil
3	cloves garlic, minced
1	teaspoon dried Italian herb seasoning, crushed
½	teaspoon freshly ground black pepper
¼	teaspoon salt
2	large red bell peppers, cut into strips
6	ounces portobello mushrooms, sliced
1	large sweet white onion, halved and cut into 1"-thick slices

Coat a grill rack with cooking spray. Preheat the grill to medium-hot.

In a large bowl, combine the parsley, lemon juice, oil, garlic, Italian seasoning, black pepper, and salt. Add the bell peppers, mushrooms, and onion and toss to coat well. (The mixture can be prepared ahead to this point and refrigerated up to 2 days.)

Place a vegetable basket or grill screen on the grill rack and place the vegetables on the basket or screen. Grill, turning often, for 15 minutes, or until very tender and lightly charred.

Makes 4 servings
Per serving: 110 calories, 3 g protein, 10 g carbohydrates, 7 g fat,
1 g saturated fat, 0 mg cholesterol, 3 g dietary fiber, 155 mg sodium

soybeans with sesame and scallions

1	bag (12 ounces) frozen shelled green soybeans (edamame)
1	tablespoon soy sauce
½	cup water
1½	teaspoons sesame oil
	Dash of hot-pepper sauce (optional)
2	tablespoons minced scallions
⅛	teaspoon freshly ground black pepper

In a medium saucepan over high heat, bring the soybeans, soy sauce, and water to a boil, stirring occasionally. Reduce the heat to low and simmer for 12 minutes, or until tender. If any liquid remains, cook, stirring occasionally, over medium-high heat until the liquid has evaporated.

Remove from the heat. Stir in the oil, hot-pepper sauce (if using), scallions, and black pepper.

Makes 4 servings
Per serving: 132 calories, 9 g protein, 11 g carbohydrates, 5 g fat, 0 g saturated fat, 0 mg cholesterol, 5 g dietary fiber, 280 mg sodium

High Cholesterol
Heart Disease
Stroke
Stress/Fatigue
Overweight
Diabetes
Osteoporosis
Rheumatoid
Arthritis

the
healing
factor

- Vitamin C
- Folate
- Omega-3 fatty acids
- Manganese
- Thiamin
- Iron
- Calcium
- Phosphorus
- Potassium
- Fiber

Heart Disease
Diabetes
Memory Problems
Breast Cancer
Cancer
Headaches
Osteoporosis
Immunity Problems
Prostate Problems

the *healing factor*

🍏🍏🍏 Vitamin K
🍏🍏🍏 Vitamin C
🍏🍏🍏 Vitamin A
🍏🍏🍏 Manganese
🍏🍏🍏 Fiber
🍏🍏 Folate
🍏🍏 Potassium
🍏🍏 Magnesium
🍏🍏 Iron
🍏🍏 Thiamin

stewed vegetables

2	teaspoons extra-virgin olive oil
1	large onion, halved and thinly sliced
3	cloves garlic, thinly sliced
1	can (16 ounces) whole tomatoes
1/2	teaspoon dried thyme, crushed
1/4	teaspoon salt
1	pound green beans, halved
1	medium zucchini, halved lengthwise and thinly sliced
1/2	cup fresh basil leaves, cut into thin strips

Heat the oil in a large nonstick skillet over medium heat. Add the onion and garlic and cook, stirring occasionally, for 4 minutes, or until tender.

Add the tomatoes (with juice), thyme, and salt, stirring to break up the tomatoes. Bring to a boil over high heat. Add the green beans. Reduce the heat to low, cover, and simmer, stirring occasionally, for 10 minutes, or until the beans are tender.

Add the zucchini and cook, stirring occasionally, for 5 minutes, or until tender. Remove from the heat and stir in the basil.

Makes 4 servings
Per serving: 95 calories, 4 g protein, 16 g carbohydrates, 3 g fat, 0 g saturated fat, 0 mg cholesterol, 6 g dietary fiber, 465 mg sodium

artichoke gratin

treat ⸻ helps **prevent**

2	packages (9 ounces each) frozen artichoke hearts
1	tablespoon lemon juice
3	tablespoons plain dry bread crumbs
1	tablespoon freshly grated Parmesan cheese
1	teaspoon dried Italian herb seasoning, crushed
1	clove garlic, minced
1	teaspoon olive oil

Preheat the oven to 375°F. Coat a 9" glass pie plate with cooking spray.

Place the artichokes in a colander and rinse well with cold water to separate. Drain well, then pat dry with paper towels. Place in the prepared pie plate and sprinkle with the lemon juice.

In a small bowl, combine the bread crumbs, cheese, Italian seasoning, garlic, and oil. Sprinkle the mixture evenly over the artichokes.

Bake for 15 minutes, or until the topping is golden.

Makes 4 servings
Per serving: 102 calories, 6 g protein, 18 g carbohydrates, 2 g fat, 0 g saturated fat, 1 mg cholesterol, 7 g dietary fiber, 184 mg sodium

Stroke

Diabetes

Cancer

High Cholesterol

Heart Disease

Insomnia

Kidney Stones

Stress/Fatigue

the
healing factor

🍏🍏🍏 Fiber

🍏🍏🍏 Vitamin C

🍏🍏 Magnesium

🍏🍏 Manganese

🍏🍏 Folate

🍏🍏 Copper

🍏🍏 Potassium

🍏🍏 Phosphorus

🍏🍏 Iron

Depression
Memory Problems
Stress/Fatigue
Aging
Heart Disease
Immunity
Problems
Breast Cancer
High Cholesterol
Infections
Overweight

stir-fried asparagus with ginger, sesame, and soy

1½	pounds thin asparagus, cut diagonally into 2" pieces
2	teaspoons canola oil
½	large red bell pepper, cut into thin strips
1	tablespoon chopped fresh ginger
1	tablespoon reduced-sodium soy sauce (see note)
⅛	teaspoon crushed red-pepper flakes
1	teaspoon toasted sesame oil
1	teaspoon sesame seeds, toasted

Bring ¼" water to a boil in a large nonstick skillet over high heat. Add the asparagus and return to a boil. Reduce the heat to low, cover, and simmer for 5 minutes, or until tender-crisp. Drain in a colander and cool briefly under cold running water. Wipe the skillet dry with a paper towel.

Heat the canola oil in the same skillet over high heat. Add the bell pepper and cook, stirring constantly, for 3 minutes, or until tender-crisp. Add the asparagus, ginger, soy sauce, and red-pepper flakes and cook for 2 minutes, or until heated through. Remove from the heat and stir in the sesame oil and sesame seeds.

Makes 4 servings
Per serving: 79 calories, 5 g protein, 7 g carbohydrates, 5 g fat, 0 g saturated fat, 0 mg cholesterol, 4 g dietary fiber, 157 mg sodium

HEALTH NOTE
People with depression who take monoamine oxidase inhibitors (MAOs) should not use alcohol or other fermented products, such as the soy sauce in this recipe. Substitute broth for the soy sauce.

the
healing factor

🌿🌿🌿 Vitamin K
🌿🌿🌿 Vitamin C
🌿🌿🌿 Vitamin A
🌿🌿 Omega-3 fatty acids
🌿🌿 Thiamin
🌿🌿 Riboflavin
🌿🌿 Fiber
🌿🌿 Potassium
🌿🌿 Manganese
🌿🌿 Vitamin B₆

cinnamon carrot coins

helps
prevent

treat

6	medium carrots, thinly sliced
6	tablespoons orange juice
1½	teaspoons unsalted butter
¾	teaspoon ground cinnamon
⅛	teaspoon freshly ground black pepper

Place the carrots and orange juice in a medium saucepan. Cover and cook over medium-low heat for 6 minutes, or until the carrots are tender-crisp.

Add the butter, cinnamon, and pepper. Cook for 1 minute, stirring to coat.

Makes 4 servings
Per serving: 64 calories, 1 g protein, 12 g carbohydrates, 2 g fat, 1 g saturated fat, 4 mg cholesterol, 3 g dietary fiber, 33 mg sodium

Stroke
Dental Problems
Diabetes
Breast Cancer
Immunity Problems
Infections
General Vision Problems
Cataracts
Night Blindness

the
healing
factor

Vitamin A
Vitamin C
Fiber
Potassium
Manganese

Memory Problems
Heart Disease
Depression
Diabetes
Stress/Fatigue
Aging
Cancer
Breast Cancer

braised italian peppers with onions and thyme

1	tablespoon extra-virgin olive oil
6–8	Italian frying peppers, cut into 2" chunks
1	large red onion, cut into wedges
1	tablespoon balsamic vinegar (see note)
2	teaspoons coarsely chopped fresh thyme or 1/4 teaspoon dried, crushed
1/8	teaspoon salt
1/8	teaspoon freshly ground black pepper
2	plum tomatoes, cut into 1/2" chunks
3	tablespoons chicken or vegetable broth or water

Heat the oil in a large skillet over medium heat. Add the frying peppers and onion and cook, stirring occasionally, for 5 minutes, or until the onion starts to soften.

Add the vinegar, thyme, salt, and black pepper and cook for 1 minute. Add the tomatoes and broth or water. Reduce the heat to low, cover, and simmer, stirring occasionally, for 8 minutes, or until the vegetables are very tender.

Makes 4 servings
Per serving: 90 calories, 2 g protein, 14 g carbohydrates, 4 g fat, 1 g saturated fat, 0 mg cholesterol, 3 g dietary fiber, 134 mg sodium

HEALTH NOTE
People with depression who take monoamine oxidase inhibitors (MAO inhibitors) should not use alcohol or other fermented products, such as the vinegar in this recipe. Substitute broth for the vinegar.

the 🌿
healing
factor

🐞🐞🐞 Vitamin C
🐞🐞🐞 Chromium
🐞🐞🐞 Vitamin K
🐞🐞🐞 Vitamin A
🐞🐞 Vitamin B$_6$
🐞🐞 Fiber
🐞🐞 Potassium
🐞🐞 Thiamin
🐞🐞 Folate
🐞🐞 Manganese

cauliflower with red pepper and garlic

Photograph on page 53

1	large head cauliflower, cut into small florets
1	large red bell pepper, cut into 1" squares
2	tablespoons extra-virgin olive oil
4	cloves garlic, minced
1	tablespoon red wine vinegar (see note)
2	teaspoons chopped fresh thyme or ¼ teaspoon dried, crushed
¾	teaspoon paprika
½	teaspoon salt

Place a steamer basket in a large saucepan with ½" of water. Place the cauliflower and pepper in the steamer. Bring to a boil over high heat. Reduce the heat to medium, cover, and cook for 4 minutes, or until tender-crisp. Place in a serving bowl.

Heat the oil in a small skillet over medium heat. Remove from the heat and stir in the garlic. When the sizzling stops, stir in the vinegar, thyme, paprika, and salt. Add to the vegetables and toss to coat well.

Makes 4 servings
Per serving: 122 calories, 4 g protein, 12 g carbohydrates, 7 g fat, 1 g saturated fat, 0 mg cholesterol, 5 g dietary fiber, 345 mg sodium

HEALTH NOTE
People with depression who take monoamine oxidase inhibitors (MAO inhibitors) should not use alcohol or other fermented products, such as the vinegar in this recipe. Substitute broth for the vinegar.

Depression
Stroke
Stress/Fatigue
Memory Problems
Heart Disease
High Cholesterol
Aging
Immunity Problems
General Vision Problems
Breast Cancer

the healing factor

- Vitamin C
- Vitamin A
- Folate
- Vitamin B₆
- Fiber
- Potassium
- Manganese
- Omega-3 fatty acids
- Thiamin
- Riboflavin

Heart Disease

High Cholesterol

Depression

*Immunity
Problems*

Memory Problems

*General Vision
Problems*

Breast Cancer

Diabetes

Constipation

Diverticulosis

the
**healing
factor**

🍃🍃🍃 Vitamin A

🍃🍃🍃 Vitamin C

🍃🍃🍃 Fiber

🍃🍃🍃 Potassium

🍃🍃🍃 Folate

🍃🍃 Vitamin B$_6$

🍃🍃 Manganese

🍃🍃 Vitamin K

🍃🍃 Omega-3
fatty acids

curried cauliflower and carrots with beans

Photograph on page 34

1	large head cauliflower, cut into small florets
2	large carrots, cut into ½"-thick diagonal slices
2	tablespoons olive oil
1	medium onion, chopped
1	tablespoon finely chopped fresh ginger
2	cloves garlic, minced
1	tablespoon unbleached all-purpose flour
1½–2	teaspoons curry powder
1	cup chicken or vegetable broth
2	tablespoons dry white wine (see note)
1	can (14–19 ounces) black beans or chickpeas, rinsed and drained
½	cup chopped fresh cilantro or flat-leaf parsley

Place a steamer basket in a large saucepan with ½" of water. Place the cauliflower and carrots in the steamer. Bring to a boil over high heat. Reduce the heat to medium, cover, and cook for 10 minutes, or until tender. Place in a bowl and keep warm. Rinse and dry the saucepan.

Heat the oil in the same saucepan over medium heat. Add the onion, ginger, and garlic and cook, stirring frequently, for 3 minutes, or until soft.

In a cup, combine the flour and curry powder. Add to the saucepan and cook, stirring, for 1 minute.

Gradually stir in the broth and wine and bring to a boil. Reduce the heat to low and simmer, stirring frequently, for 5 minutes, or until the sauce is lightly thickened.

Add the beans or chickpeas and cook, stirring, for 3 minutes, or until heated through. Add to the vegetables in the bowl and toss gently just until combined. Sprinkle with the cilantro or parsley.

Makes 6 servings
Per serving: 140 calories, 6 g protein, 22 g carbohydrates, 5 g fat, 1 g saturated fat, 0 mg cholesterol, 8 g dietary fiber, 281 mg sodium

the power of CARROTS

Carrots are so commonly used that we often forget what a nutrient powerhouse they are. Carrots contain rich stores of the antioxidant beta-carotene, which improves night vision and protects against heart disease, cancer, and macular degeneration (the leading cause of blindness in older adults).

When purchasing carrots with the tops still on, trim off the greenery before storing to prevent leaves from leaching nutrients from roots. To help release the beta-carotene, try juicing or lightly cooking carrots. Eating them with a little fat also helps boost absorption. Here are a few ideas to get you started.

- Cut 1 pound carrots into julienne strips and sauté in 2 teaspoons olive oil until tender. Add 1 teaspoon balsamic vinegar and ¼ teaspoon cardamom and cook until syrupy. Serve as a bed for grilled chicken or fish.
- Make risotto using fresh carrot juice in place of the broth.
- Sauté 1 pound shredded carrots and ½ pound shredded cabbage in 1 tablespoon toasted sesame oil for 4 minutes. Place in a bowl and cool slightly. Toss with ⅓ cup orange juice, 1 tablespoon rice wine vinegar, ½ tablespoon grated fresh ginger, and ⅛ teaspoon salt.
- Start the day off right by juicing 3 carrots, ½ apple, and a 1" piece of fresh ginger.
- Roast whole or chopped carrots in a touch of olive oil. When done, toss with apricot preserves.
- Turn your favorite green beans amandine recipe into carrots amandine.

HEALTH NOTE
People with depression who take monoamine oxidase inhibitors (MAO inhibitors) should not use alcohol or other fermented products, such as the wine in this recipe. Substitute broth for the wine.

Memory Problems
General Vision Problems
Aging
High Cholesterol
Heart Disease
Immunity Problems
Infections
Prostate Problems
Cancer
Overweight

the
healing factor

🍐🍐🍐 Vitamin K
🍐🍐🍐 Vitamin C
🍐🍐🍐 Omega-3 fatty acids
🍐🍐🍐 Manganese
🍐🍐🍐 Vitamin A
🍐🍐 Riboflavin
🍐🍐🍐 Folate
🍐🍐🍐 Phosphorus
🍐🍐🍐 Copper
🍐🍐 Potassium

stir-fried broccoli and mushrooms with tofu

Photograph on page 55

⅓	cup chicken or vegetable broth
1	tablespoon apricot all-fruit spread
1	tablespoon reduced-sodium soy sauce
1	tablespoon dry sherry
2	teaspoons cornstarch
1	tablespoon canola oil
1	large bunch broccoli, cut into small florets
4	cloves garlic, minced
1	tablespoon finely chopped fresh ginger
4	ounces mushrooms, sliced
1	cup halved cherry and/or yellow pear tomatoes
8	ounces firm tofu, drained and cut into ¼" cubes

In a cup, whisk together the broth, all-fruit spread, soy sauce, sherry, and cornstarch. Set aside.

Heat the oil in a large nonstick skillet over medium-high heat. Add the broccoli, garlic, and ginger and cook, stirring constantly, for 1 minute. Add the mushrooms and cook, stirring frequently, for 3 minutes, or until tender-crisp and lightly browned.

Add the tomatoes and tofu and cook, stirring frequently, for 2 minutes, or until the tomatoes begin to collapse.

Stir the cornstarch mixture and add to the skillet. Cook, stirring, for 2 minutes, or until the mixture boils and thickens.

Makes 4 servings
Per serving: 147 calories, 9 g protein, 15 g carbohydrates, 7 g fat, 1 g saturated fat, 0 mg cholesterol, 4 g dietary fiber, 230 mg sodium

sweet-and-sour red cabbage and apples

 (quick)

1	tablespoon butter
1	tablespoon canola oil
1	large onion, chopped
½	medium head red cabbage, cored and shredded
½	teaspoon salt
¼	teaspoon freshly ground black pepper
¼	teaspoon ground allspice
3	medium sweet-tart apples (such as Golden Delicious), peeled, cored, and cut into thin wedges
¼	cup frozen apple juice concentrate
2	tablespoons red wine vinegar

In a large saucepot or Dutch oven, heat the butter and oil over medium heat until the butter melts. Add the onion and cook, stirring frequently, for 6 minutes, or until soft.

Add the cabbage, salt, pepper, and allspice. Cook, stirring frequently, for 4 minutes, or until the cabbage begins to wilt and the color starts to change.

Add the apples, apple juice concentrate, and vinegar. Bring to a boil. Reduce the heat to low, cover, and simmer, stirring frequently, for 15 minutes, or until the cabbage is very tender.

Makes 6 servings
Per serving: 124 calories, 2 g protein, 21 g carbohydrates, 5 g fat, 1 g saturated fat, 5 mg cholesterol, 4 g dietary fiber, 235 mg sodium

treat 〜 helps prevent

Diabetes
High Cholesterol
Heart Disease
Cancer
Breast Cancer
Aging
Overweight
Stress/Fatigue

the healing factor

- Vitamin K
- Vitamin C
- Omega-3 fatty acids
- Fiber
- Manganese
- Potassium
- Chromium

helps
prevent

treat

Cancer

Aging

Stroke

High Blood
Pressure

Infections

Colds and Flu

Immunity
Problems

Yeast Infections

the
**healing
factor**

🌿 Manganese

🌿 Vitamin B₆

🌿 Vitamin C

roasted garlic

Photograph on page 40

1	large bulb garlic
	Pinch of salt

Preheat the oven to 400°F.

Cut a thin slice from the top of the garlic to expose the cloves. Place the head, cut side up, on a large piece of foil. Seal the top and sides of the foil tightly. Place in the oven and roast for 35 minutes, or until the cloves are very soft and lightly browned. Remove and set aside until cool enough to handle.

Squeeze the garlic cloves into a small bowl. With the back of a spoon, mash the garlic with the salt to make a smooth paste. Use in place of butter on potatoes, rice, or bread.

Makes 4 tablespoons
Per 2 tablespoons: 22 calories, 1 g protein, 5 g carbohydrates, 0 g fat, 0 g saturated fat, 0 mg cholesterol, 0 g dietary fiber, 94 mg sodium

HEALTH NOTE
Although garlic isn't loaded with vitamins and minerals, it is brimming with phytochemicals. You'll get the most by eating your garlic raw, but only one phytochemical is lost in cooking, so eat as much garlic as possible both raw and cooked.

summer squash with walnuts and parmesan

(quick)

treat ∫

helps
prevent

PMS
Aging
Insomnia
Osteoporosis

2	teaspoons butter
2	large cloves garlic, minced
1	medium zucchini, cut into 3"-long spears
1	medium yellow summer squash, cut into 3"-long spears
2	tablespoons chicken or vegetable broth or water
1/8	teaspoon salt
1/8	teaspoon freshly ground black pepper
1/3	cup chopped walnuts, toasted
1/4	cup (1 ounce) shredded Parmesan cheese

the
healing
factor

- 🐾🐾 Vitamin C
- 🐾🐾 Calcium
- 🐾🐾 Phosphorus
- 🐾🐾 Copper
- 🐾🐾 Magnesium
- 🐾🐾 Manganese
- 🐾🐾 Omega-3 fatty acids

Melt the butter in a large nonstick skillet over medium-low heat. Add the garlic and cook, stirring constantly, for 1 minute, or until soft.

Add the zucchini, yellow squash, broth or water, salt, and pepper. Bring to a simmer over medium heat. Cover and simmer, stirring occasionally, for 6 minutes, or until the squash are tender. Remove from the heat. Sprinkle with the walnuts and cheese.

Makes 4 servings
Per serving: 145 calories, 6 g protein, 7 g carbohydrates, 11 g fat, 3 g saturated fat, 10 mg cholesterol, 2 g dietary fiber, 251 mg sodium

Heart Disease
Memory Problems
High Cholesterol
Aging
Cancer
Diabetes
Stress/Fatigue
Osteoporosis

the
healing factor

🐚🐚🐚 Omega-3 fatty acids

🐚🐚🐚 Vitamin C

🐚🐚🐚 Manganese

🐚🐚🐚 Calcium

🐚🐚🐚 Vitamin B$_6$

🐚🐚🐚 Vitamin K

🐚🐚 Phosphorus

🐚🐚 Fiber

🐚🐚 Potassium

🐚🐚 Folate

spaghetti squash casserole

Photograph on page 58

1	spaghetti squash, halved lengthwise and seeded
1	tablespoon vegetable oil
2	cloves garlic, chopped
1	small onion, chopped
1	teaspoon dried basil, crushed
2	plum tomatoes, chopped
8	ounces 1% cottage cheese
½	cup (2 ounces) shredded low-fat mozzarella cheese
¼	cup chopped parsley
¼	teaspoon salt
¼	cup (1 ounce) freshly grated Parmesan cheese
3	tablespoons seasoned dry bread crumbs

Preheat the oven to 400°F. Coat a 13" × 9" baking dish and a baking sheet with cooking spray.

Place the squash, cut side down, on the prepared baking sheet. Bake for 30 minutes, or until tender. With a fork, scrape the squash strands into a large bowl.

Meanwhile, heat the oil in a medium skillet over medium heat. Add the garlic, onion, and basil and cook for 4 minutes, or until soft. Add the tomatoes and cook for 3 minutes, or until the mixture is dry.

To the bowl with the squash, add the cottage cheese, mozzarella, parsley, salt, and the tomato mixture. Toss to coat. Place in the prepared baking dish. Sprinkle with the Parmesan and bread crumbs.

Bake for 30 minutes, or until hot and bubbly.

Makes 6 servings
Per serving: 219 calories, 12 g protein, 28 g carbohydrates, 7 g fat,
3 g saturated fat, 10 mg cholesterol, 4 g dietary fiber, 528 mg sodium

COOKING TIP
Spaghetti squash can also be prepared in the microwave oven. Pierce
the squash in several places with a knife. Place on a microwaveable
plate and cover loosely with a piece of plastic wrap. Cook on high power,
turning twice, for 20 minutes, or until tender when pierced. Remove and
let stand until cool enough to handle.

stuffed acorn squash

Stress/Fatigue
Diabetes
Memory Problems
Heart Disease
Dental Problems
Depression
Cancer
Osteoarthritis
Leg Cramps
Rheumatoid Arthritis

the
healing factor

🐦🐦🐦 Vitamin C
🐦🐦🐦 Manganese
🐦🐦🐦 Potassium
🐦🐦🐦 Thiamin
🐦🐦🐦 Fiber
🐦🐦🐦 Magnesium
🐦🐦🐦 Vitamin B₆
🐦🐦 Vitamin K
🐦🐦 Vitamin A
🐦🐦 Iron

3	acorn squash, halved lengthwise and seeded
⅔	cup quick-cooking barley
2	teaspoons vegetable oil
1	small onion, chopped
1	rib celery, chopped
1	clove garlic, chopped
3	ounces mushrooms, sliced
¼	cup chopped fresh parsley and/or thyme or sage or 2 teaspoons dried, crushed
1	cup coarse fresh bread crumbs
⅔	cup dried cranberries
1	teaspoon grated lemon peel
¼	teaspoon salt
¼–½	cup vegetable broth or apple juice

Preheat the oven to 400°F.

Place the squash, cut side up, on a baking sheet. Coat the cut sides lightly with cooking spray. Bake for 30 minutes, or until fork-tender.

Meanwhile, prepare the barley according to package directions.

Heat the oil in a medium nonstick skillet over medium heat. Add the onion, celery, and garlic and cook for 2 minutes. Add the mushrooms and parsley and/or thyme or sage and cook for 4 minutes, or until the mushrooms are soft. Remove from the heat. Stir in the bread crumbs, cranberries, lemon peel, salt, and barley. Add up to ½ cup broth or apple juice to moisten and bind the stuffing.

Reduce the oven temperature to 350°F. Spoon the stuffing into the squash halves. Bake for 10 minutes, or until heated through.

Makes 6 servings
Per serving: 198 calories, 4 g protein, 44 g carbohydrates, 3 g fat, 0 g saturated fat, 0 mg cholesterol, 6 g dietary fiber, 190 mg sodium

COOKING TIP

Ingredients for savory recipes should be considered options, not dictates. If you don't care for an ingredient in the list, feel free to make substitutions. Any number of grains can take the place of barley in Stuffed Acorn Squash, for example. Try quinoa, millet, cracked wheat berries, or even chunks of whole grain bread. Instead of cranberries, use dried cherries, dried apricots, diced apples, diced pears, or another fresh or dried fruit of your choice. By tailoring recipes to suit your tastes, a healthy eating plan is sure to succeed.

Stroke

Depression

Memory Problems

Stress/Fatigue

Diabetes

Cancer

High Cholesterol

Immunity Problems

General Vision Problems

Osteoarthritis

the
healing factor

🍒🍒🍒 Vitamin A

🍒🍒🍒 Vitamin C

🍒🍒🍒 Manganese

🍒🍒🍒 Potassium

🍒🍒🍒 Magnesium

🍒🍒🍒 Vitamin B$_6$

🍒🍒🍒 Thiamin

🍒🍒🍒 Folate

🍒🍒🍒 Fiber

🍒🍒🍒 Niacin

maple squash with cardamom

1	tablespoon butter, melted
1	tablespoon maple syrup
1	teaspoon ground cardamom
¼	teaspoon salt
1	large butternut squash (3¼ pounds)

Preheat the oven to 400°F. Coat a 13" × 9" baking pan with cooking spray.

In a large bowl, combine the butter, maple syrup, cardamom, and salt.

Pierce the squash in several places with a fork. Place in the microwave and cook for 4 minutes, or until softened. Peel and seed the squash and cut into 1" chunks. Add to the bowl with the butter mixture and toss to coat well. Place the squash mixture in the prepared baking pan.

Bake, tossing occasionally, for 45 minutes, or until browned and tender.

Makes 4 servings
Per serving: 207 calories, 4 g protein, 47 g carbohydrates, 3 g fat, 2 g saturated fat, 8 mg cholesterol, 6 g dietary fiber, 192 mg sodium

desserts

Most people don't think of desserts as healing
foods. However, balance is an important part of a
healthy diet, and all of these recipes are prepared
using the healthiest cooking methods and the
highest-quality ingredients. Though not nutrient-
dense the way vegetables are, the ingredients contain
the most nutrients possible. For example, whole
grain pastry flour is used because it is unprocessed,
so the fiber, vitamins, and minerals remain in the
flour. It is important that you enjoy good-quality
desserts to reduce cravings for less-nutritious sweets.

Aging
High Cholesterol
Constipation
Diverticulosis
Hemorrhoids
Overweight
Osteoporosis

the *healing factor*

- 🌶🌶🌶 Omega-3 fatty acids
- 🌶🌶🌶 Manganese
- 🌶 Fiber
- 🌶 Vitamin K
- 🌶 Phosphorus
- 🌶 Magnesium

oatmeal cookies (quick) with cranberries and chocolate chips

2	cups rolled oats (not quick-cooking)
½	cup whole grain pastry flour
¾	teaspoon baking soda
½	teaspoon ground cinnamon
¼	teaspoon salt
½	cup packed brown sugar
⅓	cup canola oil
3	egg whites
2	teaspoons vanilla extract
¾	cup dried sweetened cranberries
½	cup mini semisweet chocolate chips

Preheat the oven to 350°F. Coat 2 large baking sheets with cooking spray.

In a large bowl, combine the oats, flour, baking soda, cinnamon, and salt. In a medium bowl, whisk the brown sugar, oil, egg whites, and vanilla extract until smooth. Stir in the cranberries and chocolate chips. Add to the flour mixture; stir just until blended.

Drop the batter by scant tablespoons onto the prepared baking sheets. Bake for 10 minutes, or until the cookies are golden brown.

Cool the cookies on racks. Store in an airtight container.

Makes 18 cookies
Per serving: 157 calories, 3 g protein, 23 g carbohydrates, 6 g fat, 1 g saturated fat, 0 mg cholesterol, 2 g dietary fiber, 97 mg sodium

almond coffee drops

⅔	cup almonds
2	egg whites, at room temperature
1	teaspoon vanilla extract
¼	teaspoon cream of tartar
¼	teaspoon salt
½	cup granulated sugar
½	teaspoon instant coffee granules

Preheat the oven to 350°F. Coat 2 baking sheets with cooking spray.

Finely chop the almonds in a food processor or by hand.

Reduce the oven temperature to 325°F.

Place the egg whites, vanilla extract, cream of tartar, and salt in a large bowl. With an electric mixer on high speed, beat until the whites are frothy. Gradually add the sugar, beating until stiff glossy peaks form.

Using a rubber spatula, gently fold in the nuts and coffee granules just until blended.

Drop the batter by rounded teaspoons onto the prepared baking sheets, spacing them about 1" apart. Bake for 20 minutes, or until lightly browned.

Place the cookies on racks and let cool completely. Store in an airtight container.

Makes 10 servings
Per serving: 99 calories, 3 g protein, 12 g carbohydrates, 5 g fat, 0 g saturated fat, 0 mg cholesterol, 1 g dietary fiber, 69 mg sodium

the
healing factor

- Vitamin E
- Magnesium
- Riboflavin
- Copper
- Phosphorus
- Fiber

helps
prevent

Heart Disease
Stroke
Aging
Diabetes
Overweight
Osteoporosis

treat

the
**healing
factor**

🌰🌰🌰 Manganese

🌰🌰🌰 Thiamin

🌰🌰🌰 Phosphorus

🌰🌰🌰 Magnesium

🌰🌰🌰 Selenium

🌰🌰 Omega-3
fatty acids

🌰🌰 Riboflavin

🌰🌰 Copper

🌰🌰 Fiber

🌰🌰 Vitamin E

rich 'n' creamy brown rice pudding

Photograph on page 54

3	cups vanilla soy milk
½	cup uncooked brown rice
½	teaspoon salt
¼	teaspoon freshly grated nutmeg
2	eggs, lightly beaten
½	cup dried cherries

In a medium saucepan, combine the milk, rice, salt, and nutmeg. Bring to a boil over high heat. Reduce the heat to low, cover, and simmer for 45 minutes. Remove from the heat and let cool for 5 minutes.

Stir ½ cup of the rice mixture into the eggs, stirring constantly. Gradually stir the egg mixture into the saucepan. Stir in the cherries.

Place over medium-low heat and cook, stirring constantly, for 5 minutes, or until thickened. Serve warm or refrigerate to serve cold later.

Makes 4 servings
Per serving: 242 calories, 11 g protein, 38 g carbohydrates, 7 g fat, 1 g saturated fat, 106 mg cholesterol, 3 g dietary fiber, 347 mg sodium

summer fruit compote

1	cup water
1	package (6 ounces) mixed whole dried fruit
3	tablespoons frozen orange juice concentrate
2	tablespoons packed brown sugar
3	whole allspice berries
1	bay leaf
1	stick cinnamon or a pinch of ground cinnamon
3	medium peaches, cut into ¾" wedges
3	medium plums, cut into ¾" wedges
1	cup pitted sweet white or red cherries (optional)

In a large saucepan, combine the water, dried fruit, orange juice concentrate, brown sugar, allspice berries, bay leaf, and cinnamon stick or ground cinnamon. Bring to a boil over high heat. Reduce the heat to low, cover, and simmer, stirring occasionally, for 10 minutes, or until the fruit is very tender.

Add the peaches and plums. Cover and simmer for 5 minutes, or until the peaches and plums are tender but not mushy. Stir in the cherries, if using, and cook for 3 minutes. Remove from the heat and place in a serving bowl. Let stand for at least 1 hour, or until the fruit has cooled and the flavors have blended. Remove and discard the bay leaf and cinnamon stick before serving.

Makes 6 servings
Per serving: 217 calories, 3 g protein, 56 g carbohydrates, 1 g fat, 0 g saturated fat, 0 mg cholesterol, 7 g dietary fiber, 5 mg sodium

treat

helps
prevent

Memory Problems
Stress/Fatigue
Aging
Dental Problems
Infections
Cataracts
Cancer
Constipation
Diverticulosis
Wrinkles

the healing factor

- Vitamin C
- Vitamin A
- Fiber
- Potassium
- Vitamin K
- Copper
- Niacin
- Manganese
- Riboflavin

COOKING TIP
Once you've added the fresh fruit, don't let the mixture boil. Let the heat of the liquid gently cook the fruit. Boiling will make it break up.

Breast Cancer

Cancer

High Cholesterol

Heart Disease

Dental Problems

Immunity
Problems

General Vision
Problems

Osteoarthritis

Constipation

broiled peaches and strawberries

5	medium peaches, cut into 1" wedges
1½	pints strawberries, hulled and quartered
2	tablespoons honey
½	teaspoon ground cinnamon
⅛	teaspoon ground allspice or cloves
1	tablespoon butter, cut into small pieces
3	tablespoons slivered fresh mint, lemon verbena, or cinnamon basil (optional)

Preheat the broiler. Coat a large baking sheet with sides with cooking spray.

In a large bowl, combine the peaches, strawberries, honey, cinnamon, and allspice or cloves and toss to coat well. Place the fruit on the prepared baking sheet. Dot with the butter.

Broil, turning the pan 2 or 3 times (no need to turn the fruit), for 4 minutes, or until the fruit is glazed, bubbly, and golden brown in spots. Remove from the oven and let cool slightly.

Sprinkle with the mint, lemon verbena, or cinnamon basil, if using. Serve warm or at room temperature.

Makes 6 servings
Per serving: 111 calories, 1 g protein, 23 g carbohydrates, 3 g fat, 1 g saturated fat, 5 mg cholesterol, 4 g dietary fiber, 23 mg sodium

the
healing
factor

🍊🍊🍊 Vitamin C

🍊🍊🍊 Manganese

🍊🍊 Omega-3
fatty acids

🍊🍊 Fiber

🍊🍊 Vitamin A

🍊🍊 Vitamin K

🍊🍊 Potassium

pear and almond crisp

treat

helps prevent

4	large pears, cored and sliced ½" thick
2	tablespoons maple syrup
1	tablespoon lemon juice
1	teaspoon vanilla extract
½	teaspoon freshly grated nutmeg
1	cup rolled oats (not quick-cooking)
⅓	cup sliced natural almonds
¼	cup packed brown sugar
2	tablespoons whole grain pastry flour
2	tablespoons cold butter, cut into small pieces
2	tablespoons canola oil

Preheat the oven to 350°F.

Combine the pears, maple syrup, lemon juice, vanilla extract, and nutmeg in an 11" × 7" baking dish.

In a medium bowl, combine the oats, almonds, brown sugar, flour, butter, and oil and mix with your fingers to form crumbs. Sprinkle the topping over the pear mixture.

Bake for 40 minutes, or until the pears are tender and bubbly and the topping is lightly browned.

Makes 8 servings
Per serving: 271 calories, 4 g protein, 45 g carbohydrates, 10 g fat, 3 g saturated fat, 8 mg cholesterol, 5 g dietary fiber, 134 mg sodium

Memory Problems
Depression
Stroke
Aging
Stress/Fatigue
Heart Disease
Immunity Problems
General Vision Problems

the healing factor

Vitamin E
Vitamin B₁₂
Vitamin C
Pantothenic acid
Riboflavin
Iron
Zinc
Niacin
Folate
Vitamin B₆

Heart Disease
Stroke
Breast Cancer
Cancer
High Cholesterol
Constipation
Cataracts

the
healing factor

🍐🍐🍐 Vitamin C
🍐🍐🍐 Omega-3 fatty acids
🍐🍐🍐 Manganese
🍐🍐 Fiber

strawberry tart with oat-cinnamon crust

Photograph on page 41

Crust

²⁄₃	cup rolled oats
½	cup whole grain pastry flour
1	tablespoon sugar
1	teaspoon ground cinnamon
¼	teaspoon baking soda
2	tablespoons canola oil
2–3	tablespoons fat-free plain yogurt

Filling

¼	cup strawberry all-fruit spread
½	teaspoon vanilla extract
1½	pints strawberries, hulled

To make the crust: Preheat the oven to 375°F. Coat a baking sheet with cooking spray.

In a medium bowl, combine the oats, flour, sugar, cinnamon, and baking soda. Stir in the oil and 2 tablespoons of the yogurt to make a soft, slightly sticky dough. If the dough is too stiff, add the remaining 1 tablespoon yogurt.

Place the dough on the prepared baking sheet and pat evenly into a 10" circle. If the dough sticks to your hands, coat them lightly with cooking spray.

Place a 9" cake pan on the dough and trace around it with a sharp knife. With your fingers, push up and pinch the dough around the outside of the circle to make a 9" circle with a rim ¼" high.

Bake for 15 minutes, or until firm and golden. Remove from the oven and set aside to cool.

To make the filling: Meanwhile, in a small microwaveable bowl, combine the all-fruit spread and vanilla extract. Microwave on high power for 10 to 15 seconds, or until melted.

Brush a generous tablespoon evenly over the cooled crust. Arrange the strawberries evenly over the crust. Brush the remaining spread evenly over the strawberries, making sure to get some of the spread between the strawberries to secure them.

Refrigerate for at least 30 minutes, or until the spread has jelled.

Makes 6 servings
Per serving: 187 calories, 4 g protein, 31 g carbohydrates, 6 g fat, 0 g saturated fat, 0 mg cholesterol, 3 g dietary fiber, 65 mg sodium

COOKING TIP
For a calcium boost, you can serve the tart with a scoop of fat-free vanilla frozen yogurt on the side.

the power of
BERRIES

Adding more berries to your meals can help prevent cataracts, cancer, and constipation. Berries contain fiber, vitamin C, and the antioxidant ellagic acid.

To get the most nutrients, buy or pick berries at peak freshness and eat them raw. To store for later use, freeze them raw. Do this by placing unwashed berries in a single layer on a baking pan. Freeze completely. Place in a zip-top freezer bag, seal, and freeze for up to 8 months. To use, rinse the frozen berries quickly, then add directly to a recipe.

Aging
Cancer
Dental Problems
Osteoporosis
Overweight
High Cholesterol
General Vision Problems
Menopausal Problems/Hot Flashes

the
healing factor

🐞🐞🐞 Vitamin A
🐞🐞🐞 Omega-3 fatty acids
🐞🐞🐞 Vitamin K
🐞🐞 Calcium
🐞🐞 Riboflavin
🐞🐞 Fiber
🐞🐞 Iron
🐞🐞 Phosphorus

COOKING TIP
To save time on baking day, you can make the dough for this pie 1 to 3 days ahead. Wrap in plastic wrap and refrigerate until ready to use.

ginger pumpkin pie
Photograph on page 58

1 ¼	cups whole grain pastry flour
¼	teaspoon + ⅛ teaspoon salt
3	tablespoons canola oil
2	tablespoons cold butter, cut into small pieces
2–4	tablespoons ice water
½	cup packed brown sugar
1	egg
2	egg whites
1 ½	teaspoons vanilla extract
½	teaspoon ground cinnamon
½	teaspoon ground ginger
¼	teaspoon ground nutmeg
1	can (15 ounces) plain pumpkin
1	cup fat-free evaporated milk

In a food processor, combine the flour and ¼ teaspoon of the salt. Pulse until blended. Add the oil and butter. Pulse until the mixture resembles a fine meal. Add the water, 1 tablespoon at a time, as needed, and pulse just until the dough forms large clumps. Form into a ball and flatten into a disk. Cover and refrigerate for at least 1 hour.

Preheat the oven to 425°F. Coat a 9" pie plate with cooking spray.

Place the dough between 2 pieces of waxed paper and roll into a 12" circle. Remove the top piece of paper and invert the dough into the pie plate. Peel off the second piece of paper. Press the dough into the pie plate and up onto the rim, patching where necessary. Turn under the rim and flute. Chill in the refrigerator.

Meanwhile, in a large bowl, whisk the brown sugar, egg, egg whites, vanilla extract, cinnamon, ginger, nutmeg, and the remaining ⅛ teaspoon salt until well-blended. Whisk in the pumpkin and milk. Pour into the chilled crust. Bake for 15 minutes. Reduce the temperature to 350°F. Bake for 25 minutes, or until a knife inserted off-center comes out clean. Cool on a rack.

Makes 8 servings
Per serving: 252 calories, 7 g protein, 36 g carbohydrates, 9 g fat, 3 g saturated fat, 36 mg cholesterol, 4 g dietary fiber, 217 mg sodium

Red-Pepper Taffy

Here's a tasty, easy-to-make candy that's tough on sore throats.

1 cup sugar

1 cup light corn syrup

⅔ cup water

1 tablespoon cornstarch

2 tablespoons butter

1 teaspoon salt

2 teaspoons butter-flavored sprinkles

1 teaspoon ground red pepper

In a 2-quart saucepan, combine the sugar, corn syrup, water, cornstarch, butter, and salt. Cook, stirring constantly, over medium heat, until a candy thermometer registers 256°F, or until a small amount of the mixture dropped into very cold water forms a hard ball.

Remove from the heat, stir in the butter-flavored sprinkles and pepper. Pour onto a baking sheet. When cool enough to handle, pull the taffy until satiny and stiff. (If too sticky, butter your hands.) Pull into long ½"-wide strips. Cut into 1" pieces with clean scissors. Wrap individually in plastic wrap or waxed paper.

Makes 30 pieces
Per serving: 64 calories, 0 g protein, 15 g carbohydrates, 1 g fat, 1 g saturated fat, 2 mg cholesterol, 0 g dietary fiber, 103 mg sodium

apple crumble with toasted-oat topping

Photograph on page 27

6	medium Jonagold or Golden Delicious apples, cored and thinly sliced
½	cup unsweetened applesauce
¾	cup rolled oats
3	tablespoons toasted wheat germ
3	tablespoons packed light brown sugar
1	teaspoon ground cinnamon
1	tablespoon canola oil
1	tablespoon unsalted butter, cut into small pieces

Preheat the oven to 350°F. Coat a 13" × 9" baking dish with cooking spray.

Combine the apples and applesauce in the prepared baking dish.

In a small bowl, combine the oats, wheat germ, brown sugar, and cinnamon. Add the oil and butter. Mix with your fingers to form crumbs. Sprinkle the oat mixture evenly over the apples.

Bake for 30 minutes, or until the topping is golden and the apples are bubbling.

Makes 6 servings
Per serving: 207 calories, 3 g protein, 38 g carbohydrates, 6 g fat, 2 g saturated fat, 5 mg cholesterol, 6 g dietary fiber, 3 mg sodium

COOKING TIP
Although you can make this recipe with peeled apples, leaving the peels on ensures that you get more fiber as well as the beneficial antioxidant quercetin.

chocolate-zucchini loaf

1 1/3	cups whole grain pastry flour
1/2	cup soy flour
1 1/2	teaspoons baking powder
1 1/2	teaspoons ground cinnamon
1/2	teaspoon baking soda
1/4	teaspoon salt
2	eggs
1/2	cup packed brown sugar
1/2	cup (4 ounces) fat-free plain yogurt
1/3	cup canola oil
2	teaspoons vanilla extract
1 1/2	cups shredded zucchini
1/2	cup mini semisweet chocolate chips

Preheat the oven to 350°F. Coat a 9" × 5" loaf pan with cooking spray.

In a large bowl, combine the pastry flour, soy flour, baking powder, cinnamon, baking soda, and salt.

In a medium bowl, using a wire whisk, beat the eggs, brown sugar, yogurt, oil, and vanilla extract until smooth. Stir in the zucchini and chocolate chips. Add to the flour mixture and stir just until blended. Place in the prepared loaf pan.

Bake for 40 minutes, or until the cake is springy to the touch and a wooden pick inserted in the center comes out clean. Cool in the pan on a rack for 30 minutes. Remove from the pan and cool completely on the rack.

Makes 12 servings
Per serving: 209 calories, 5 g protein, 27 g carbohydrates, 10 g fat, 2 g saturated fat, 36 mg cholesterol, 2 g dietary fiber, 175 mg sodium

helps prevent

Constipation
Diverticulosis
Aging
Memory Problems

the healing factor

- 🍒🍒🍒 Omega-3 fatty acids
- 🍒🍒 Manganese
- 🍒🍒 Vitamin K
- 🍒🍒 Copper
- 🍒🍒 Fiber

helps
prevent ~
~ treat

Aging
Cancer
Heart Disease
Stroke
Depression
Overweight

the
**healing
factor**

🐞🐞 Vitamin C
🐞🐞 Riboflavin
🐞🐞 Selenium
🐞🐞 Fiber
🐞🐞 Manganese

olive oil–cornmeal cake with blueberry and red wine sauce

Photograph on page 49

Cake

1	cup yellow cornmeal
¾	cup sugar
½	cup whole grain pastry flour
1 ¼	teaspoons baking powder
½	teaspoon baking soda
¼	teaspoon salt
2	eggs
2	egg whites
½	cup (4 ounces) fat-free plain yogurt
¼	cup extra-virgin olive oil
1	tablespoon freshly grated orange peel
2	tablespoons orange juice
1	tablespoon confectioners' sugar (optional)

Sauce

1	pint fresh or frozen blueberries
¼	cup dry red wine (see note)
1	tablespoon orange juice
	Pinch of ground nutmeg

To make the cake: Preheat the oven to 350°F. Coat an 8" round cake pan with cooking spray. Line the pan bottom with a round of waxed paper and coat the waxed paper with cooking spray.

In a large bowl, combine the cornmeal, sugar, flour, baking powder, baking soda, and salt.

In a medium bowl, using a wire whisk, beat the eggs, egg whites, yogurt, oil, orange peel, and orange juice. (The mixture may look curdled.) Add to the cornmeal mixture and stir just until blended. Place in the prepared pan.

Bake for 25 minutes, or until browned, firm, and a wooden pick inserted off-center comes out clean.

Cool in the pan on a rack for 30 minutes. Loosen the edges and turn the cake out onto the rack. Peel off the waxed paper and let cool completely.

To make the sauce: In a medium saucepan, combine the blueberries, wine, orange juice, and nutmeg. Bring to a boil over medium-high heat, stirring constantly. Boil for 1 minute.

Reduce the heat to low, cover, and simmer, stirring frequently, for 5 minutes, or until the blueberries are tender and the sauce is thickened.

Place the sauce in a bowl, partially cover, and let cool. Dust the cake with confectioners' sugar, if using, and serve with the sauce.

the power of
ORANGES

So often consumed as a breakfast drink, oranges are packed with vitamin C, which aids healing, boosts immunity, and helps the body absorb iron. They also contain pectin, which helps lower cholesterol and control blood sugar.

Be sure not to peel off the white spongy layer just beneath the skin; it contains half of the fruit's pectin. And stock up on juice concentrate because it's as nutritious as fresh juice. Try these simple tips to use more juice concentrate in your meals.

- Make a glaze for cakes or brownies by blending with confectioners' sugar.
- Decrease the fat in homemade full-fat salad dressings by replacing half the oil with OJ concentrate.
- Use as a base for fruit salad and toss with a variety of chopped fruit and minced fresh mint.
- Make a marinade for chicken or fish by combining with a touch of oil and vinegar and your favorite minced herb.

Makes 8 servings
Per serving: 274 calories, 6 g protein, 43 g carbohydrates, 9 g fat, 1 g saturated fat, 53 mg cholesterol, 3 g dietary fiber, 263 mg sodium

HEALTH NOTE
People with depression who take monoamine oxidase inhibitors (MAO inhibitors) should not use alcohol or other fermented products, such as the wine in this recipe. Substitute fruit juice for the wine.

Osteoporosis

Aging

General Vision Problems

Cataracts

Overweight

Menopausal Problems/Hot Flashes

the
healing factor

🍒🍒🍒 Phosphorus

🍒🍒 Vitamin A

🍒🍒 Riboflavin

🍒🍒 Calcium

🍒🍒 Manganese

🍒🍒 Selenium

lemon cheesecake

Photograph on page 37

1¼	cups graham cracker crumbs
¼	cup pecans, toasted and ground
2¼	cups sugar
3	tablespoons butter, melted
3	egg whites, divided
2	packages (8 ounces each) fat-free cream cheese
1	package (8 ounces) reduced-fat cream cheese
¼	cup all-purpose flour
½	cup lemon juice
2	eggs
2	cups (16 ounces) fat-free sour cream

Preheat the oven to 350°F. Coat a 9" springform pan with cooking spray.

In a large bowl, combine the cracker crumbs, pecans, ¼ cup of the sugar, and butter. Lightly beat 1 of the egg whites in a cup. Add half of the egg white to the bowl; reserve the remainder for another use or discard. Mix well. Press the mixture into the bottom and 1" up the sides of the prepared pan.

Bake for 10 minutes, or until lightly browned. Cool on a rack.

Meanwhile, place the fat-free cream cheese and reduced-fat cream cheese in a food processor. Process for 1 minute, or until smooth. Add the flour and 1½ cups of the remaining sugar. Process for 3 minutes, or until light and fluffy; stop and scrape the sides of the bowl as necessary. Add the lemon juice and process briefly. Add the eggs and the remaining 2 egg whites, one at a time, and process until just incorporated.

Place the mixture in the prepared crust. Bake for 1 hour. Remove from the oven; do not turn off the oven.

In a small bowl, combine the sour cream and the remaining ½ cup sugar. Spread over the hot cheesecake. Bake for 10 minutes. Place on a rack and let cool to room temperature. Cover and refrigerate for at least 8 hours.

Makes 12 servings
Per serving: 358 calories, 12 g protein, 56 g carbohydrates, 10 g fat, 5 g saturated fat, 61 mg cholesterol, 1 g dietary fiber, 448 mg sodium

COOKING TIP
This cheesecake is equally delicious served with a fresh fruit topping. Omit the sour-cream topping. Toss 3 cups berries, sliced peaches, or orange segments with 2 tablespoons melted jam or jelly. Decoratively arrange the fruit on top of the cooled cheesecake.

Osteoporosis
Cancer
Heart Disease
High Cholesterol
Infections
Overweight
Cataracts
Menopausal
Problems/Hot
Flashes

the
**healing
factor**

🍐🍐🍐 Vitamin A

🍐🍐🍐 Omega-3
fatty acids

🍐🍐 Fiber

🍐🍐 Vitamin K

🍐🍐 Riboflavin

🍐🍐 Calcium

🍐🍐 Vitamin E

carrot cake with cream cheese frosting

Photograph on page 31

Cake

2	cups whole grain pastry flour
2	teaspoons baking powder
2	teaspoons baking soda
1	teaspoon ground cinnamon
¼	teaspoon salt
1	cup granulated sugar
2	eggs
2	egg whites
⅓	cup canola oil
2	teaspoons vanilla extract
1	cup buttermilk or fat-free plain yogurt (see note)
2	cups finely shredded carrots
½	cup golden raisins
½	cup well-drained crushed pineapple

Frosting

2	ounces reduced-fat cream cheese, at room temperature
2	tablespoons unsalted butter, at room temperature
1¼	cups confectioners' sugar
½	teaspoon vanilla extract
3	tablespoons chopped walnuts or pecans

To make the cake: Preheat the oven to 350°F. Coat two 8" round cake pans with cooking spray.

In a medium bowl, combine the flour, baking powder, baking soda, cinnamon, and salt.

In a large bowl, using a wire whisk, beat the granulated sugar, eggs, egg whites, oil, and vanilla extract until well-blended and frothy. Whisk in the buttermilk or yogurt. Stir in the carrots, raisins, and pineapple. Add the flour mixture and stir just until blended.

Evenly divide the batter between the prepared cake pans. Bake for 25 minutes, or until a wooden pick inserted in the center comes out clean.

Cool the cakes in the pans on racks for 30 minutes. Loosen the edges and turn the cakes out onto the racks to cool completely.

To make the frosting: In a medium bowl, with an electric mixer on medium-high speed, beat the cream cheese and butter just until blended. Beat in the confectioners' sugar and vanilla extract until light and fluffy.

Place one cake layer on a plate. Spread the top of the layer with frosting, but not the sides. Place the other cake layer on top. Spread the top of the layer with the remaining frosting. Sprinkle with the walnuts or pecans.

Makes 10 servings
Per serving: 445 calories, 7 g protein, 76 g carbohydrates, 13 g fat, 3 g saturated fat, 53 mg cholesterol, 4 g dietary fiber, 467 mg sodium

COOKING TIP
If you don't have buttermilk or yogurt, you can use soured milk instead. To make soured milk, pour the desired amount of 1% milk into a measuring cup. Add 1 tablespoon lemon juice or cider vinegar. Let stand for 10 minutes.

helps
prevent ~ treat

Aging
Anemia
Diabetes
Overweight

the
**healing
factor**

🐞🐞 Magnesium

🐞🐞 Iron

🐞 Phosphorus

🐞 Vitamin E

🐞 Riboflavin

almond and chocolate flourless cake

Photograph on page 47

2	tablespoons unsalted butter
3	tablespoons unsweetened cocoa powder
½	cup blanched almonds
2	tablespoons + ¾ cup sugar
3	ounces bittersweet chocolate
½	cup (4 ounces) reduced-fat sour cream
2	egg yolks
1	teaspoon vanilla extract
¼	teaspoon almond extract (optional)
5	egg whites, at room temperature
¼	teaspoon salt
1	tablespoon toasted slivered almonds (optional)

Preheat the oven to 350°F. Generously coat a 9" springform pan with 2 teaspoons of the butter and dust with 1 tablespoon of the cocoa (don't tap out the excess cocoa; leave it in the pan).

In a food processor, combine the blanched almonds with 2 tablespoons of the sugar. Process until finely ground.

In the top of a double boiler over barely simmering water, melt the chocolate and the remaining 4 teaspoons butter, stirring occasionally, until smooth. Remove from the heat. Place the chocolate mixture in a large bowl. Add the almond mixture, sour cream, egg yolks, vanilla extract, almond extract (if using), ½ cup of the remaining sugar, and the remaining 2 tablespoons cocoa. Stir until well-blended.

In a large bowl, with an electric mixer on high speed, beat the egg whites and salt until frothy. Gradually add the remaining ¼ cup sugar, beating until stiff glossy peaks form.

Stir one-quarter of the beaten whites into the chocolate mixture to lighten it. Gently fold in the remaining whites until no white streaks remain. Place in the prepared pan. Gently smooth the top.

Bake for 30 minutes, or until the cake has risen, is dry on the top, and a wooden pick inserted in the center comes out with a few moist crumbs.

Place in the pan on a rack and cool until warm. The cake will fall dramatically. Loosen the edges of the cake with a knife and remove the pan sides. Sprinkle with the toasted almonds, if using.

Makes 12 servings
Per serving: 184 calories, 5 g protein, 21 g carbohydrates, 10 g fat, 4 g saturated fat, 45 mg cholesterol, 1 g dietary fiber, 81 mg sodium

the
healing factor

🍐🍐🍐 Vitamin C

🍐🍐🍐 Manganese

🍐🍐🍐 Fiber

🍐🍐🍐 Calcium

🍐🍐 Omega-3
fatty acids

fresh berry shortcakes (quick)

Photograph on page 28

2	cups whole grain pastry flour
3	tablespoons + ⅓ cup sugar
2	teaspoons baking powder
¼	teaspoon baking soda
¼	cup butter, cut into small pieces
⅔	cup + 2 tablespoons buttermilk (see tip on page 305)
1½	pints assorted berries
2	tablespoons orange juice
2	cups (16 ounces) fat-free frozen vanilla yogurt

Preheat oven to 400°F. Coat a baking sheet with cooking spray.

In a large bowl, combine the flour, 2 tablespoons of the sugar, baking powder, and baking soda. Cut in the butter until the mixture resembles cornmeal. Add ⅔ cup of the buttermilk, stirring with a fork until the dough comes together.

Turn the dough out onto a lightly floured surface. Pat to ½" thickness. Using a 3" round cutter, cut 8 biscuits. (Pat the dough scraps together to cut out all the biscuits.) Place on the prepared baking sheet. Brush with the remaining 2 tablespoons buttermilk. Sprinkle with 1 tablespoon of the remaining sugar. Bake for 12 minutes, or until golden brown. Remove to a rack to cool.

Meanwhile, in a large bowl, combine the berries, orange juice, and the remaining ⅓ cup sugar. Let stand for 10 minutes.

Split the biscuits crosswise in half. Place a biscuit bottom on each of 8 dessert plates. Top with the berry filling and a scoop of frozen yogurt. Cover with the biscuit tops.

Makes 8 servings
Per serving: 302 calories, 7 g protein, 54 g carbohydrates, 7 g fat, 4 g saturated fat, 19 mg cholesterol, 5 g dietary fiber, 259 mg sodium

eat to beat:
the healing
food finder

Foods go a long way toward making and keeping us all healthy. And depending on your own specific health needs, it may be even more important for you to get certain foods into your diet. The profiles that follow provide you with the knowledge you need to eat the foods that best target whatever ails you. We have highlighted the top foods that contain each nutrient.

For some conditions, all you really need to know is what foods to eat. For others, there may be important information about what *not* to eat as well as food combinations to avoid. Where appropriate, some conditions include details about foods that can interact with medication you may be taking. Because foods may have interactions with many over-the-counter items as well as prescription drugs, tell your pharmacist what medications you are taking. This includes all vitamin, mineral, and other supplements, herb products, and over-the-counter and prescription medications. Finally, be aware that the health benefits of some of the compounds listed here are still being studied. As always, consult your doctor before beginning any new diet or eating plan.

Acne

Acne is an active inflammation of the oil glands on the skin. It shows itself in the form of whiteheads, blackheads, pimples, and even cysts.

What to eat
Eat a well-balanced, low-fat diet that includes a wide variety of foods.

What not to eat
Mangoes may cause dermatitis that resembles acne. Excess iodine, found in foods including fast food, dairy products, shellfish, kelp, and sushi, might cause acne.

Aging

Scientists are unlocking the secrets of aging, discovering why our bodies break down and how to slow this process. Because of advances in medicine, humans are living longer and, in the process, we're expanding the number of years that we can expect to live in robust good health.

What to eat

Your body needs . . .	Some sources include . . .
Anthocyanins	Blackberries, blueberries, strawberries, cherries, grapes
Antioxidants	Fruits and juices, including citrus and tropical fruits and juices; vegetables, especially cruciferous vegetables, dark green leafy vegetables, and deep orange vegetables; wheat germ; whole grains; nuts; seeds; cooking oils
Vitamin B_6	Bananas, figs, prunes, prune juice, avocado, potatoes, sweet potatoes, cabbage, cauliflower, dark green leafy vegetables, acorn squash, beans, chickpeas, meats, poultry, kidney, pork, fish, eggs, walnuts, wheat bran, whole and enriched grains, fortified cereals
Vitamin B_{12}	Any animal product, such as lean meats, liver, poultry, seafood, low-fat dairy products, eggs
Calcium	Low-fat or fat-free dairy products, broccoli, dark green leafy vegetables, sardines and salmon with bones, calcium-fortified foods
Flavonoids	Concord grape juice, apples, blueberries, cranberries, olives, oranges, onions, kale, legumes, wine, green and black tea
Iron	Dried fruit, vegetables, dark green leafy vegetables, lean red meats, poultry, seafood, legumes, eggs, fortified ready-to-eat cereals, cream of wheat
Potassium	Fresh fruit, dried fruit, prune juice, vegetables, lean meats, seafood, legumes, milk
Riboflavin	Dark green leafy vegetables, lean meats, fish, chicken, whole grain breads, milk and milk products
Zinc	Lean meats, liver, seafood, poultry, lentils, whole grains, wheat germ, buckwheat, Brazil nuts

What not to eat

Avoid eating to excess. Eat only adequate amounts, and you may live longer.

Anemia

There are several kinds of anemia. Iron-deficient anemia results when the body does not get enough iron. Folate-deficient anemia, also called megaloblastic or macrocytic anemia, is caused by the body's inability to absorb folate. In vitamin B_{12}-deficient, or pernicious, anemia, the body lacks "intrinsic factor," which is needed to absorb vitamin B_{12}.

(*Note:* People with iron-deficient anemia should follow their doctors' instructions with regard to prescribed medications. Strict vegetarians should take B_{12} supplements to cover their needs.)

What to eat

Iron is best absorbed when combined with vitamin C or other acidic ingredients. Adding citrus fruits or tomatoes to meat and poultry dishes is a simple way to increase iron absorption.

Another boost in iron absorption comes from the combination of heme iron (from animal products) and nonheme iron (from vegetable sources). Serve meat, poultry, or fish dishes with high-iron vegetables and legumes such as broccoli with lentils.

Your body needs . . .	Some sources include . . .
Vitamin B_{12}	Any animal product, such as lean meats, liver, poultry, seafood, low-fat dairy products, eggs
Vitamin C	Cantaloupe, strawberries, citrus fruits, citrus fruit juices, cranberry juice, tropical fruits, vegetables, dark green leafy vegetables, cruciferous vegetables
Iron	Dried fruit, vegetables, dark green leafy vegetables, lean red meats, poultry, seafood, legumes, eggs, fortified ready-to-eat cereals, cream of wheat

What not to eat

Certain foods can prevent iron from being absorbed into the body by binding with the iron. Tannins in tea, coffee, and nuts; calcium and phosphorus in milk; and fiber and phytates in nuts, soy foods, and whole grain cereals can reduce the absorption of nonheme iron. Try to avoid eating these foods together with foods high in nonheme iron.

When to eat

Eat foods high in vitamin C with iron-rich foods to increase iron absorption.

Food/medication interactions

Antacids can interfere with iron absorption. If your iron supplement gives you an upset stomach, take it with food. Take iron supplements 1 hour before or 2 hours after eating bran or high-phytate foods, fiber supplements, tea, coffee, dairy products, or eggs.

Folate supplementation may mask pernicious anemia and result in progression of neuralgic damage.

Asthma

When pollen, pollution, or other airborne irritants enter the lungs, the immune system releases chemicals to "kill" the invaders. These chemicals, meant to defend, can actually cause harm, triggering the airways to become inflamed and swollen, making breathing difficult.

What to eat

Your body needs . . .	Some sources include . . .
Vitamin C	Cantaloupe, strawberries, citrus fruits, citrus fruit juices, cranberry juice, tropical fruits, vegetables, dark green leafy vegetables, cruciferous vegetables

(continued)

What to eat (cont.)

Your body needs...	Some sources include...
Vitamin E	Dark green leafy vegetables; vegetable oils such as cotton seed, peanut, sunflower, and safflower; wheat germ; nuts; seeds; whole grain cereals
Magnesium	Root vegetables, dark green leafy vegetables, seafood, legumes, whole grains, wheat germ, brown rice, ready-to-eat cereals, nuts, seeds
Omega-3 fatty acids	Fish such as anchovies, bluefish, herring, mackerel, salmon, sardines, trout, canned white tuna (not light tuna), canned albacore tuna; canola oil; flaxseed oil; flaxseed
Selenium	Broccoli, fish, seafood, lean meats, chicken, bulgur, whole grain cereals and breads, barley, Brazil nuts
Sulfur compounds	Onions, garlic, chives, shallots, leeks

Herbs to use

Research in China shows that cinnamon tea may stop attacks of bronchial asthma.

Breast Cancer

Research shows that women who adopt lifestyle strategies that reduce the amount of estrogen circulating throughout their bodies may significantly reduce their risk of developing breast cancer. Strategies include maintaining ideal body weight, adopting a low-fat diet, and eating plenty of plant fiber and vegetables.

What to eat

Your body needs...	Some sources include...
Allicin	Garlic, onions
Antioxidants	Fruits and juices, including citrus and tropical fruits and juices; vegetables, especially cruciferous vegetables, dark green leafy vegetables, and deep orange vegetables; wheat germ; whole grains; nuts; seeds; cooking oils

Beta-carotene	Deep orange fruits, tropical fruits, deep orange winter squash, carrots and carrot juice, broccoli, dark green leafy vegetables
Conjugated linoleic acid	Milk (not fat-free) and other dairy products
Vitamin D	Fatty fish, such as herring, salmon, and sardines; fish-liver oil; egg yolks; vitamin D–fortified milk and cereals
Fiber	Fruits (especially with skin), dried fruits, vegetables, cruciferous vegetables, legumes, whole grains and cereals, oats and oat bran products, brown rice
Indoles	Broccoli, Brussels sprouts, cabbage, Daikon radish
Lignans	Flaxseed, flaxseed oil, rye or whole grain crackers such as Wasa or Finn Crisps
Limonoids	White pith and peel of oranges
Lycopene	Tomatoes and tomato products, guavas
Monounsaturated fats	Avocados, olives, olive oil, canola oil, nuts
Nobiletin	Tangerines
Omega-3 fatty acids	Fish such as anchovies, bluefish, herring, mackerel, salmon, sardines, trout, canned white tuna (not light tuna), canned albacore tuna; canola oil; flaxseed oil; flaxseed
Perillyl alcohol	Cherries
Selenium	Broccoli, fish, seafood, lean meats, chicken, bulgur, whole grain cereals and breads, barley, Brazil nuts
Sulforaphane	Broccoli sprouts
Tangeretin	Tangerines

What not to eat

Don't have more than one serving of alcohol a day. A serving consists of 12 ounces of beer, 4 to 5 ounces of wine, or 1½ ounces of hard liquor. Avoid very well done red meat as well as foods containing trans fatty acids, such as french fries. Look for a margarine that doesn't contain trans fatty acids.

Herbs to use

Basil has terpenoids, which may help render cancer-causing cells ineffective.

Cancer (see also *Breast Cancer, Prostate Problems*)

Cancer is a malignant, abnormal cell growth that can spread within the body. Researchers have found that people who eat the most fruits, vegetables, and other plant foods are less likely to get cancer than those who do not. Certain substances found only in plant foods—phytochemicals—have the ability to help prevent cancer.

What to eat

Your body needs...	Some sources include...
Allyl sulfides	Garlic
Anthocyanins	Blackberries, blueberries, strawberries, cherries, grapes
Beta-carotene	Deep orange fruits, tropical fruits, deep orange winter squash, carrots and carrot juice, broccoli, dark green leafy vegetables
Vitamin C	Cantaloupe, strawberries, citrus fruits, citrus fruit juices, cranberry juice, tropical fruits, vegetables, dark green leafy vegetables, cruciferous vegetables
Calcium	Low-fat or fat-free dairy products, broccoli, dark green leafy vegetables, sardines and salmon with bones, calcium-fortified foods
Carotenoids	Cantaloupe, oranges, carrots, tomatoes, sweet potatoes, winter squash, dark green leafy vegetables
Catechins	Green tea
Chlorogenic acid	Pineapple, strawberries, tomatoes, carrots, green bell peppers

Coumaric acid	Pineapple, strawberries, tomatoes, carrots, green bell peppers
Vitamin E	Dark green leafy vegetables; vegetable oils such as cotton seed, peanut, sunflower, and safflower; wheat germ; nuts; seeds; whole grain cereals
Fiber	Fruits (especially with skin), dried fruits, vegetables, cruciferous vegetables, legumes, whole grains and cereals, oats and oat bran products, brown rice
Folate	Fruits, dark green leafy vegetables, legumes
Indoles	Broccoli, Brussels sprouts, cabbage, Daikon radish
Isothiocyanate (mustard oils)	Watercress, broccoli
Lignans	Flaxseed, flaxseed oil, rye or whole grain crackers such as Wasa or Finn Crisps
Lycopene	Tomatoes and tomato products, guavas
Phenols	Olives, wine
Selenium	Broccoli, fish, seafood, lean meats, chicken, bulgur, whole grain cereals and breads, barley, Brazil nuts

Food/medication interactions

Citrus fruits, such as oranges, grapefruit, and tangerines, increase the effectiveness of tamoxifen, an anticancer drug. Citrus fruits also contain flavonoids that assist tamoxifen in halting growth of cancer cells. Methotrexate is used to treat cancer, and because its structure is similar to that of folate, the drug competes with folic acid for binding sites, so a severe deficiency of folic acid may occur. In these cases, doctors may prescribe folic acid supplements. It's also a good idea to try to eat more foods containing folate to help compensate.

Herbs to use

Rosemary contains carnosol, rosmarinic acid, and other compounds that stimulate enzymes that may help fight cancer. Basil contains compounds called terpenoids, which may help make cancer-causing substances ineffective. Sage contains monoterpenes, which can slow some cancers.

Cataracts

Cataracts are cloudy or opaque spots in the lens of the eye that tend to develop over time. Initially, these spots don't interfere with vision, but with time, they can expand, fogging your eyesight as though you were looking through a gauze veil. They can even lead to blindness.

What to eat

Your body needs . . .	Some sources include . . .
Vitamin A and beta-carotene	Deep orange fruits, tropical fruits, deep orange winter squash, carrots and carrot juice, broccoli, dark green leafy vegetables, fish-liver oil, liver, fortified reduced-fat and fat-free milk, butter, eggs
Vitamin C	Cantaloupe, strawberries, citrus fruits, citrus fruit juices, cranberry juice, tropical fruits, vegetables, dark green leafy vegetables, cruciferous vegetables
Carotenoids	Cantaloupe, oranges, carrots, tomatoes, sweet potatoes, winter squash, dark green leafy vegetables
Vitamin E	Dark green leafy vegetables; vegetable oils such as cotton seed, peanut, sunflower, and safflower; wheat germ; nuts; seeds; whole grain cereals
Folate	Fruits, dark green leafy vegetables, legumes
Lutein	Dark green leafy vegetables, broccoli, corn, green peas, parsley
Riboflavin	Dark green leafy vegetables, lean meats, fish, chicken, whole grain breads, milk and milk products
Zeaxanthin	Dark green leafy vegetables, broccoli, parsley

What not to eat

Avoid salt and chips. If you do eat chips, look for packages marked "low-sodium," "reduced-sodium," or "no salt added."

Food/medication interactions

To get proper absorption of the vitamin A–rich foods that you're eating, it's important that you get adequate fat, protein, vitamin E, and zinc. Malnutrition or decreased protein intake decreases absorption of vitamin A.

Celiac Disease

Celiac disease is a sensitivity to gluten, a protein found in wheat, barley, oats, and rye. Gluten damages the villi in the intestines and, consequently, many digestive enzymes. The way to help cope with celiac disease is to eliminate gluten from your diet and identify any nutritional deficiencies that may result. Remarkably, many people with celiac disease who eliminate gluten from their diets find that they can digest dairy products without problems. Consult with a registered dietitian to be sure that you're getting all the nutrients you need. Be sure to read food labels since gluten products are added to many foods.

What to eat

Your body needs . . .	Some sources include . . .
Gluten-free flours	Corn, potato, rice, soy, tapioca, arrowroot, milo, and lentil flours
Magnesium	Root vegetables, dark green leafy vegetables, seafood, legumes, whole grains, wheat germ, brown rice, ready-to-eat cereals, nuts, seeds

Colds and Flu

Viruses cause both colds and flu; therefore, antibiotics aren't effective against them. Viruses seem to be passed by hand contact from person to person. Most of the many viruses that cause colds are rhinoviruses. Immunity to a particular rhinovirus lasts only about 2 years, which is why we keep getting colds. Colds are marked by scratchy throat and an initial feeling of malaise followed by runny nose and coughing. Flu, short for influenza, is identified by fever, chills, headache, generalized muscular aches, and loss of appetite. Tea and other hot beverages will help clear congestion. Try chicken soup, horseradish, onions, or lemon for congestion.

What to eat

Your body needs . . .	Some sources include . . .
Allicin	Garlic, onions
Vitamin B$_6$	Bananas, figs, prunes, prune juice, avocado, potatoes, sweet potatoes, cabbage, cauliflower, dark green leafy vegetables, acorn squash, beans, chickpeas, meats, poultry, kidney, pork, fish, eggs, walnuts, wheat bran, whole and enriched grains, fortified cereals
Beta-carotene	Deep orange fruits, tropical fruits, deep orange winter squash, carrots and carrot juice, broccoli, dark green leafy vegetables
Vitamin C	Cantaloupe, strawberries, citrus fruits, citrus fruit juices, cranberry juice, tropical fruits, vegetables, dark green leafy vegetables, cruciferous vegetables
Capsaicin	Chile peppers, including ground red pepper and crushed red-pepper flakes
Vitamin E	Dark green leafy vegetables; vegetable oils such as cotton seed, peanut, sunflower, and safflower; wheat germ; nuts; seeds; whole grain cereals
Glutathione	Fruits, asparagus, winter squash, okra, cauliflower, broccoli, tomatoes, potatoes
Hot beverages	Chicken soup
Sinigrin	Horseradish
Theophylline	Hot tea

| Zinc | Lean meats, liver, seafood, poultry, lentils, whole grains, wheat germ, buckwheat, Brazil nuts |

Herbs to use

Cayenne added to food helps thin phlegm so that it can move out of the lungs and thus help prevent and treat coughs, colds, and bronchitis. Thyme tea is good for sinuses because it's a drying herb. Combine ginger, cinnamon stick, coriander seeds, cloves, a lemon slice, and water to make a tea. Horseradish helps break up congestion, as does wasabi.

Constipation

Constipation is defined as a decrease in your usual number of bowel movements. When they do happen, they can be strained and difficult. To get things moving, add more fiber, both insoluble and soluble, to your diet. Be sure to increase your consumption of water to 8 to 10 glasses per day.

What to eat

Your body needs . . .	Some sources include . . .
Dihydroxyphenyl isatin	Prunes
Fiber (insoluble)	Vegetables, whole grains, legumes
Fiber (soluble)	Apples, citrus fruits, seaweed, legumes, oat bran, barley
Fluids	Water, fruit juices, thin soups
Sorbitol	Prunes

Dental Problems (Gingivitis)

Gingivitis occurs when bacteria cause infection in the gums and other tissue that surround and support the teeth.

What to eat

Your body needs . . .	Some sources include . . .
Vitamin A and beta-carotene	Deep orange fruits, tropical fruits, deep orange winter squash, carrots and carrot juice, broccoli, dark green leafy vegetables, fish-liver oil, liver, fortified reduced-fat and fat-free milk, butter, eggs
Vitamin C	Cantaloupe, strawberries, citrus fruits, citrus fruit juices, cranberry juice, tropical fruits, vegetables, dark green leafy vegetables, cruciferous vegetables
Calcium	Low-fat or fat-free dairy products, broccoli, dark green leafy vegetables, sardines and salmon with bones, calcium-fortified foods
Fiber	Fruits (especially with skin), dried fruits, vegetables, cruciferous vegetables, legumes, whole grains and cereals, oats and oat bran products, brown rice

What not to eat

Avoid low-calorie sweeteners and artificial sweeteners. Avoid sugary and especially sticky foods such as candy and dried fruits. Steer clear of potato chips, as starch sticks to your teeth even longer than simple sugar. The high acid content in diet sodas can erode tooth enamel.

When to eat

Eat a little cheese with dinner to prevent tooth decay. There appear to be compounds in cheese that neutralize tooth-damaging acids.

Depression

Depression can run the gamut from an ordinary feeling of "the blues" to a major depression. Signs include trouble sleeping and feelings of low self-esteem and guilt.

What to eat

Your body needs . . .	Some sources include . . .
Vitamin B$_6$	Bananas, figs, prunes, prune juice, avocado, potatoes, sweet potatoes, cabbage, cauliflower, dark green leafy vegetables, acorn squash, beans, chickpeas, meats, poultry, kidney, pork, fish, eggs, walnuts, wheat bran, whole and enriched grains, fortified cereals
Vitamin B$_{12}$	Any animal product, such as lean meats, liver, poultry, seafood, low-fat dairy products, eggs
Vitamin C	Cantaloupe, strawberries, citrus fruits, citrus fruit juices, cranberry juice, tropical fruits, vegetables, dark green leafy vegetables, cruciferous vegetables
Carbohydrates (unrefined)	All fruits, vegetables, dark green leafy vegetables, legumes, buckwheat, whole grain foods, brown rice, bran
Folate	Fruits, dark green leafy vegetables, legumes
Niacin	Lean meats, fish, canned white tuna, legumes, nuts, fortified white rice, enriched grains, whole grain breads
Omega-3 fatty acids	Fish such as anchovies, bluefish, herring, mackerel, salmon, sardines, trout, canned white tuna (not light tuna), canned albacore tuna; canola oil; flaxseed oil; flaxseed
Riboflavin	Dark green leafy vegetables, lean meats, fish, chicken, whole grain breads, milk and milk products
Selenium	Broccoli, fish, seafood, lean meats, chicken, bulgur, whole grain cereals and breads, barley, Brazil nuts
Thiamin	Corn, lean pork, organ meats, legumes, seeds, unrefined cereals, enriched grains and cereals, rice, wheat germ, fresh pasta

What not to eat

Avoid consuming too much caffeine and sugar.

Food/medication interactions

If you're taking monoamine oxidase inhibitors (MAO inhibitors), restrict your intake of red wines, sherry, and fermented sauces such as soy, tamari, and teriyaki. Also restrict aged cheeses such as American, Camembert, Cheddar, and Gouda. You may eat unfermented cheese such as ricotta and cottage cheese. The list of foods to avoid includes dried, salted, smoked, or pickled fish; sausage; pepperoni; dried meats; fava beans; Italian broad beans; sauerkraut; fermented pickles; olives; cheese-filled breads, crackers, and desserts; and salad dressings with cheese in them.

Diabetes

People with adult onset diabetes, known as type 2 diabetes, either don't produce enough insulin or the insulin they do produce doesn't work efficiently. In either case, glucose in the bloodstream isn't able to get inside the cells.

What to eat

Your body needs . . .	Some sources include . . .
Vitamin C	Cantaloupe, strawberries, citrus fruits, citrus fruit juices, cranberry juice, tropical fruits, vegetables, dark green leafy vegetables, cruciferous vegetables
Carbohydrates (unrefined)	All fruits, vegetables, dark green leafy vegetables, legumes, buckwheat, whole grain foods, brown rice, bran
Chromium	Grapefruit, broccoli, fortified breakfast cereals
Vitamin E	Dark green leafy vegetables; vegetable oils such as cotton seed, peanut, sunflower, and safflower; wheat germ; nuts; seeds; whole grain cereals

Fiber	Fruits (especially with skin), dried fruits, vegetables, cruciferous vegetables, legumes, whole grains and cereals, oats and oat bran products, brown rice
Magnesium	Root vegetables, dark green leafy vegetables, seafood, legumes, whole grains, wheat germ, brown rice, ready-to-eat cereals, nuts, seeds
Monounsaturated fats	Avocados, olives, olive oil, canola oil, nuts
Potassium	Fresh fruit, dried fruit, prune juice, vegetables, lean meats, seafood, legumes, milk

Food/medication interactions

Sugar or sorbitol is added to many liquid drugs to make them palatable, so people with diabetes who have to watch their intake of simple sugars should be aware of the amount of sugar or sorbitol in their medications.

Diarrhea

Diarrhea—loose, watery stools—usually occurs when bacteria or viruses cause inflammation in the intestine.

What to eat

Your body needs...	Some sources include...
Bland foods	Rice, noodles, bananas, applesauce
Minerals	Fruit juice, diluted sports drinks, bananas
Sugars	Fruit juice, flat cola, diluted sports drinks
Zinc	Lean meats, liver, seafood, poultry, lentils, whole grains, wheat germ, buckwheat, Brazil nuts

Herbs to use

Ginger tea eases pain from diarrhea, and cinnamon tea is thought to have an astringent effect.

Diverticulosis

Less fiber in our diets has made it harder for the intestines to pass stool. Straining creates small pouches known as diverticula in the intestine. About one in every six people in Western countries develops diverticulosis after age 45. If the pockets become inflamed or infected, the condition becomes diverticulitis. If the diverticula rupture, a serious, life-threatening situation arises. Keep in mind that during flare-ups of diverticulosis, too much fiber can be irritating to the intestinal tract. If you have a flare-up, check with your doctor.

What to eat

Your body needs . . .	Some sources include . . .
Fiber	Fruits (especially with skin), dried fruits, vegetables, cruciferous vegetables, legumes, whole grains and cereals, oats and oat bran products, brown rice

What not to eat

Reduce the amount of fat in your diet.

Eczema

Eczema is a hypersensitive response in the skin that typically appears as a red, itchy, swollen rash on the neck and face and the folds of the knees and elbows. In some cases, it can also affect the hands and feet, or even the whole body.

What to eat

Your body needs . . .	Some sources include . . .
Biotin	Liver, fish
Omega-3 fatty acids	Fish such as anchovies, bluefish, herring, mackerel, salmon, sardines, trout, canned white tuna (not light tuna), canned albacore tuna; canola oil

What not to eat

Avoid the most common allergy triggers, which are dairy products, eggs, soy, peanuts, wheat, and tree nuts. If you have an allergy to fish or shellfish, do not eat these foods to increase the omega-3 fatty acids in your diet. Shellfish can cause anaphylaxis, so check with your doctor before trying either fish or shellfish.

Fibrocystic Breasts

Fibrocystic tissue occurs when tiny, fluid-filled sacs form in the milk-producing glands of the breasts. For many women, making a few simple changes in their diets can help keep it under control. In fact, by giving up a few foods, you may be able to eliminate any pain associated with fibrocystic breasts entirely.

What to eat

Your body needs . . .	Some sources include . . .
Vitamin E	Dark green leafy vegetables; vegetable oils such as cotton seed, peanut, sunflower, and safflower; wheat germ; nuts; seeds; whole grain cereals
Fiber	Fruits (especially with skin), dried fruits, vegetables, cruciferous vegetables, legumes, whole grains and cereals, oats and oat bran products, brown rice
Less fat	Fruits, vegetables, low-fat or fat-free milk, legumes, whole grains

What not to eat

Avoid products with methylxanthines, such as caffeine, found in foods including coffee, tea, cola, and chocolate. Some women have found that this compound can cause breasts to become inflamed and tender. Don't expect instant results; forgo these beverages for 2 to 3 months to see if it makes a difference. Eat less fat, especially saturated fat, found in foods such as meats and dairy products.

Food Allergies

People may have sensitivities to certain foods, but these are not true allergies. A true food allergy is the adverse reaction by the body to foods that involve an immune response. Food allergies may or may not involve symptoms. To diagnose them, you must be tested for antibodies. About 2 percent of the adult population has true food allergies. If you are food-sensitive, on the other hand, you may be able to decrease your body's reaction to a food by eating the culprit food only once in 4 days.

What not to eat

Avoid foods that trigger your food allergies. The following foods cause about 90 percent of food allergies: cow's milk, eggs, wheat, soy, fish, shellfish, peanuts, and tree nuts. Tomatoes have chemicals called salicylates in them, which are the active ingredients in aspirin. If you're allergic to aspirin, avoid tomatoes unless you have the approval of your doctor. Some people are allergic to corn, and since corn is in so many foods, be sure to read food package labels carefully. Some people, especially babies, are sensitive to the natural acids in citrus fruits.

Gallstones

Gallstones form in the gallbladder, the storage area for bile. Bile is normally in a liquid state, but too much dietary fat and cholesterol can cause gallstones to form. One way to avoid gallstones is to eat more often. This keeps the gallbladder active and moves the debris along. The gallbladder contracts when you eat, so the more contractions, the less chance for stones. Just remember to eat nutritious foods and stay active, because maintaining a healthy body weight also protects your gallbladder.

What to eat

Your body needs . . .	Some sources include . . .
Fluids	Water, fruit juices
Iron	Dried fruit, vegetables, dark green leafy vegetables, lean red meats, poultry, seafood, legumes, eggs, fortified ready-to-eat cereals, cream of wheat
Omega-3 fatty acids	Fish such as anchovies, bluefish, herring, mackerel, salmon, sardines, trout, canned white tuna (not light tuna), canned albacore tuna; canola oil; flaxseed oil; flaxseed

What not to eat

Eat less fat and red meat, but don't cut out red meat altogether, as research shows that low iron may increase risk for gallstones.

When to eat

Eat smaller quantities, and more frequently.

Gas

Gas is often caused by eating foods containing lots of carbohydrates, such as sugars, starches, and fibers. You can test suspect foods by avoiding them for a period of time to see if you get relief. If you're trying to get more fiber in your diet, add it slowly to prevent gas.

What to eat

Your body needs . . .	Some sources include . . .
Capsaicin	Chile peppers, including ground red pepper and crushed red-pepper flakes
Chamomile	Chamomile tea
Fiber	Fruits (especially with skin), dried fruits, vegetables, cruciferous vegetables, legumes, whole grains and cereals, oats and oat bran products, brown rice
Peppermint	Peppermint tea

What not to eat

Avoid artificial sweeteners like sorbitol, zylitol, and mannitol. Fructose can cause gas, so avoid honey (as little as 1½ tablespoons can cause gas in some people), concentrated fruit juices, and soft drinks sweetened with high-fructose corn syrup. Avoiding foods that produce gas—like beans, milk, and cheese—helps, but these are nutritious foods, so eat "anti-gas" foods along with the big offenders. Add cumin to beans, including soybeans, ginger to milk, and cayenne to cheese. Find the quantity that suits you. Adults may have to watch their intake of dairy products or use reduced-lactose milk.

Herbs to use

Cayenne added to food eases gas. Fennel's soothing properties help ease gas and gas pains; ginger also eases the pain. Peppermint may relieve nausea, vomiting, and gas. Don't confuse spearmint with peppermint. Peppermint (*Mentha piperita*) is a digestive aid, but spearmint (*Mentha spicata*) is not.

General Vision Problems

It's a fact of life that sooner or later your vision is probably going to fade a bit. Eating a healthful diet can go a long way toward slowing the process.

What to eat

Your body needs . . .	Some sources include . . .
Vitamin A and beta-carotene	Deep orange fruits, tropical fruits, deep orange winter squash, carrots and carrot juice, broccoli, dark green leafy vegetables, fish-liver oil, liver, fortified reduced-fat and fat-free milk, butter, eggs
Antioxidants	Fruits and juices, including citrus and tropical fruits and juices; vegetables, especially cruciferous vegetables, dark green leafy vegetables, and deep orange vegetables; wheat germ; whole grains; nuts; seeds; cooking oils

Folate	Fruits, dark green leafy vegetables, legumes
Lutein	Dark green leafy vegetables, broccoli, corn, green peas, parsley
Omega-3 fatty acids	Fish such as anchovies, bluefish, herring, mackerel, salmon, sardines, trout, canned white tuna (not light tuna), canned albacore tuna; canola oil; flaxseed oil; flaxseed
Zinc	Lean meats, liver, seafood, poultry, lentils, whole grains, wheat germ, buckwheat, Brazil nuts

Gout

Gout is a form of arthritis where slivers of uric acid build up in the joints. Our bodies make uric acid when they break down protein by-products called purines. Normally, uric acid dissolves in the blood and is moved out of the body through the kidneys and the urine. Not so in people with gout who, perhaps through some metabolic glitch, either produce too much uric acid or have trouble getting rid of it. Over time, the excess acid condenses into the uric acid crystals. Lowering body weight reduces the amount of uric acid in the blood. In a study in Baltimore of 1,200 medical students, researchers found that those who gained the most weight during early adulthood were the ones at highest risk to develop gout later in life. Even a slight weight gain—6 to 10 pounds—between the ages of 25 and 35 has been shown to nearly double a person's risk of developing gout.

While there's no scientific evidence to suggest that cherries may help, some people swear by them to ease gout pain. Black cherry juice reportedly has the same effect. For some people, eating ½ pound of cherries (about 34) daily for a week will help relieve the symptoms. If you don't get relief after a week, discontinue.

What to eat

Your body needs ...	*Some sources include ...*
Fluids	Water, fruit juices

What not to eat

Avoid alcohol, and eliminate foods high in purines, such as organ meats, scallops, crab, lobster, oysters, sardines, mackerel, asparagus, mushrooms, and beans. Cauliflower is high in purines, but try its cruciferous pals such as broccoli, cabbage, and Brussels sprouts, which contain fewer purines.

Hay Fever

The medical term for hay fever is *seasonal allergic rhinitis*. Simply translated, this means that your nose is stuffed up and running, and you're sneezing because of allergens you're breathing in the air. The standard culprits are pollens from ragweed, grasses, and trees. While the usual treatment for hay fever is to stay inside and take antihistamines, there's some evidence that a few foods may make it worse.

What not to eat

Doctors have found that the immune system responds to certain fruits and vegetables. For example, because melons and bananas are related to ragweed, some people may experience hay fever symptoms from them. Similarly, cherries, peaches, carrots, and potatoes are related to tree and grass pollens and may cause symptoms. Red wine contains histamines, so some people may be sensitive to it. And because honey is made from pollen, some people may react if it contains a certain pollen to which they are allergic. Try different brands of honey until you find one that you don't have a reaction to.

Headaches

There are two main types of headaches. Muscle contraction or tension headaches often are caused by tense neck and scalp muscles. Vascular or migraine headaches are caused by expansion and contraction of blood vessels in the head, neck, and face.

What to eat

Your body needs . . .	Some sources include . . .
Vitamin B$_6$	Bananas, figs, prunes, prune juice, avocado, potatoes, sweet potatoes, cabbage, cauliflower, dark green leafy vegetables, acorn squash, beans, chickpeas, meats, poultry, kidney, pork, fish, eggs, walnuts, wheat bran, whole and enriched grains, fortified cereals
Calcium	Low-fat or fat-free dairy products, broccoli, dark green leafy vegetables, sardines and salmon with bones, calcium-fortified foods
Carbohydrates (unrefined)	All fruits, vegetables, dark green leafy vegetables, legumes, buckwheat, whole grain foods, brown rice, bran
Iron	Dried fruit, vegetables, dark green leafy vegetables, lean red meats, poultry, seafood, legumes, eggs, fortified ready-to-eat cereals, cream of wheat
Magnesium	Root vegetables, dark green leafy vegetables, seafood, legumes, whole grains, wheat germ, brown rice, ready-to-eat cereals, nuts, seeds

What not to eat

Common triggers of migraines are chocolate, red wine, and aged cheeses. All these foods contain tyramine, an amino acid that causes the body to release hormones that cause blood vessels to constrict. Nitrites and preservatives such as monosodium glutamate (MSG) may cause vascular headaches.

Herbs to use

Sip rosemary tea for migraines. Or, nibble fresh ginger or add ginger (grate it or use a garlic press instead of chopping or slicing) to your cooking.

Heartburn

Heartburn, also known as acid reflux or gastroesophageal reflux, occurs when acid-laden digestive juices in the stomach surge upward into the esophagus, the tube that connects the mouth with the stomach. Normally, a little muscle at the base of the esophagus (the cardiac, or gastroesophageal, sphincter) prevents juices from escaping. But when the sphincter relaxes at the wrong times, juices splash upward, literally scorching tender tissue in the esophagus. To reduce heartburn, you'll need to minimize consumption of fatty foods and spicy foods, maintain a healthy body weight, and avoid eating late in the evening before sleeping. Another trick is to chew sugarless gum after meals. It stimulates the production of saliva, helping to neutralize acid.

What to eat

Your body needs . . .	Some sources include . . .
Carbohydrates (unrefined)	All fruits, vegetables, dark green leafy vegetables, legumes, buckwheat, whole grain foods, brown rice, bran
Ginger	Ginger tea
Natural "antacid"	Bananas

What not to eat

Cut down on butter, fats, red meats, and fried and fatty foods. Also try to decrease or eliminate spicy foods when you're experiencing a bout of heartburn. Onions may be a culprit (just one slice can cause heartburn in some people). Chocolate and peppermint may cause the cardiac sphincter to relax, causing heartburn.

Herbs to use

Turmeric stimulates digestive juices, moves food along, and prevents acid buildup. Ginger helps the lower esophageal sphincter do its job, so try some ginger tea.

Heart Disease (see also *High Blood Pressure, High Cholesterol, Stroke*)

Heart disease, also known as cardiovascular disease, is a term used to describe all diseases of the blood vessels and the heart. It's the nation's number one cause of death among adults. Narrowing of the arteries, which is often caused by plaque buildup, is the main cause of heart disease. When bloodflow to the heart muscle is interrupted, the result is a myocardial infarction, which is also called a heart attack or a coronary. If bloodflow to the heart muscle is stopped, the muscle is damaged, and if the damage is extensive, heart failure or death can occur.

We can easily delay complications of this problem—such as heart attack or stroke—for a decade or more with good diet, exercise, and lifestyle practices such as avoiding smoking, accompanied by appropriate medications when needed. When heart muscle or brain tissue is deprived of blood—for example, when a blood vessel to the heart or brain is blocked—a heart attack or stroke results. It's the same basic process, and although stroke may be more likely if blood pressure is high and heart attack more likely if cholesterol is high, both risk factors affect both diseases.

Reaching for the right foods is one of the best ways to lower cholesterol and high blood pressure, two of the biggest risk factors for the heart.

What to eat

Your body needs . . .	Some sources include . . .
Anthocyanins	Blackberries, blueberries, strawberries, cherries, grapes
Antioxidants	Fruits and juices, including citrus and tropical fruits and juices; vegetables, especially cruciferous vegetables, dark green leafy vegetables, and deep orange vegetables; wheat germ; whole grains; nuts; seeds; cooking oils

(continued)

What to eat (cont.)

Your body needs . . .	*Some sources include . . .*
Vitamin B$_6$	Bananas, figs, prunes, prune juice, avocado, potatoes, sweet potatoes, cabbage, cauliflower, dark green leafy vegetables, acorn squash, beans, chickpeas, meats, poultry, kidney, pork, fish, eggs, walnuts, wheat bran, whole and enriched grains, fortified cereals
Vitamin B$_{12}$	Any animal product, such as lean meats, liver, poultry, seafood, low-fat dairy products, eggs
Vitamin C	Cantaloupe, strawberries, citrus fruits, citrus fruit juices, cranberry juice, tropical fruits, vegetables, dark green leafy vegetables, cruciferous vegetables
Vitamin E	Dark green leafy vegetables; vegetable oils such as cotton seed, peanut, sunflower, and safflower; wheat germ; nuts; seeds; whole grain cereals
Fiber	Fruits (especially with skin), dried fruits, vegetables, cruciferous vegetables, legumes, whole grains and cereals, oats and oat bran products, brown rice
Flavonoids	Concord grape juice, apples, blueberries, cranberries, olives, oranges, onions, kale, legumes, wine, green and black tea
Folate	Fruits, dark green leafy vegetables, legumes
Lycopene	Tomatoes and tomato products, guavas
Monounsaturated fats	Avocados, olives, olive oil, canola oil, nuts
Omega-3 fatty acids	Fish such as anchovies, bluefish, herring, mackerel, salmon, sardines, trout, canned white tuna (not light tuna), canned albacore tuna; canola oil; flaxseed oil; flaxseed
Phenols	Olives, wine
Phytoestrogens	Flaxseed
Quercetin	Cranberries, onions, kale, buckwheat
Resveratrol	Concord grape juice, red wine, peanuts

| Rutin | Buckwheat |
| Sulfur compounds | Onions, garlic, chives, shallots, leeks |

What not to eat

Avoid saturated fat, found in red meat, fried foods, butter, and high-fat dairy products such as cheese and sour cream. Substitute olive oil or trans-free margarine for butter. Limit the amount of oil you consume in a day to between 5 and 8 teaspoons. Limit meat servings to 3 to 4 ounces a day, use less butter, and avoid high-fat snacks.

Food/medication interactions

When taking aspirin for heart disease, do so when you have food in your stomach. This will reduce nausea and possibly reduce gastric irritation and bleeding. Diuretics (used to treat congestive heart failure and high blood pressure) can speed up the excretion of calcium, potassium, magnesium, and zinc, so be sure to eat foods high in these nutrients.

Hemorrhoids

Hemorrhoids are swollen and stretched-out veins in the anus and rectum, often caused by straining or as a result of constipation or diarrhea. Pregnant women often develop hemorrhoids—both the pressure of the fetus on the abdomen and hormonal changes cause blood vessels around the anus to enlarge.

What to eat

Your body needs . . .	Some sources include . . .
Anthocyanins	Cranberries, grapeseed, blueberries, cocoa, barley
Fiber	Fruits (especially with skin), dried fruits, vegetables, cruciferous vegetables, legumes, whole grains and cereals, oats and oat bran products, brown rice
Fluids	Water, fruit juices

What not to eat

Avoid coffee, alcohol, and spicy foods. They can make the pain of hemorrhoids even worse.

High Blood Pressure
(see also *Heart Disease*)

Blood pressure is the force of the blood on the walls of the blood vessels. High blood pressure is sustained elevated pressure in the arteries, which makes the heart work harder to move the blood. Called the silent killer, high blood pressure contributes to the diseases that kill—stroke, heart attack, and heart failure. It is a clear sign that the cardiovascular system is in trouble. Turn around high blood pressure by eating a diet rich in fruits, vegetables, and starch-based foods.

A large study by the National Institutes of Health found that a diet plan called the DASH diet lowers blood pressure and may help prevent and control high blood pressure. (DASH is short for Dietary Approaches to Stop Hypertension.) Researchers found that with the DASH diet, blood pressure was lowered just as much as with medication. The DASH diet is rich in fruits and vegetables and low in salt and animal and dairy fat. It's high in dietary fiber, potassium, calcium, and magnesium and has a moderate amount of protein. And it's low in saturated and total fat and cholesterol. Some tips for following the DASH diet: Center your meal around complex carbohydrates such as vegetables, whole grains, or fruit; make meat just one part of the meal, not the main event; and snack on fruit.

What to eat

Your body needs...	*Some sources include...*
Allicin	Garlic, onions
Calcium	Low-fat or fat-free dairy products, broccoli, dark green leafy vegetables, sardines and salmon with bones, calcium-fortified foods

Carotenoids	Cantaloupe, oranges, carrots, tomatoes, sweet potatoes, winter squash, dark green leafy vegetables
Fiber	Fruits (especially with skin), dried fruits, vegetables, cruciferous vegetables, legumes, whole grains and cereals, oats and oat bran products, brown rice
Oleic acid	Avocados, olive oil, olives, nuts
Potassium	Fresh fruit, dried fruit, prune juice, vegetables, lean meats, seafood, legumes, milk

What not to eat

Avoid caffeine, high-fat cheeses, fried foods, processed foods, and those containing lots of added fat, such as salad dressings. Read labels to be sure that you are avoiding hydrogenated oil or trans fatty acids often present in cookies, crackers, and chips. Keep your sodium intake below 2,400 milligrams a day, which is the amount of sodium in about 1 teaspoon of salt (you need only 500 milligrams of sodium a day to maintain normal bodily functions).

When to eat

Eat a meatless dinner two times a week.

Food/medication interactions

Diuretics (used to treat congestive heart failure and high blood pressure) can speed up the excretion of calcium, potassium, magnesium, and zinc, so be sure to eat foods high in these nutrients. Avoid excess amounts of grapefruit and its juice if taking calcium-channel blockers, as grapefruit can increase the action of some of these medications.

Herbs to use

Rosemary can ease circulation problems.

High Cholesterol

You can't live without cholesterol. Your body uses cholesterol, which is made in the liver, to make cell membranes, sex hormones, bile acids, and vitamin D. But too much cholesterol in your diet or too much saturated fat can mean excess cholesterol. As LDL cholesterol (the "bad" type) circulates in the bloodstream, it undergoes a process called oxidation. Essentially, this means that it spoils and turns rancid. The immune system cells spot the decaying LDL and gobble up the cholesterol molecules. Once engorged, they stick to the walls of arteries, hardening into a dense, fatty layer called plaque. As more plaque gathers, there's less room for blood to flow. To cut cholesterol intake, use the healthy cooking techniques mentioned on page 23. Reduce the amount of saturated fat in your diet to less than 10 percent of your total calories. Include 1% or fat-free milk instead of whole or 2% in your diet and include lots of fruits and vegetables. A study in Canada found that orange juice increases HDL cholesterol, the "good" kind of cholesterol.

What to eat

Your body needs . . .	Some sources include . . .
Allicin	Garlic, onions
Antioxidants	Fruits and juices, including citrus and tropical fruits and juices; vegetables, especially cruciferous vegetables, dark green leafy vegetables, and deep orange vegetables; wheat germ; whole grains; nuts; seeds; cooking oils
Daidzein	Soy foods
Vitamin E	Dark green leafy vegetables; vegetable oils such as cotton seed, peanut, sunflower, and safflower; wheat germ; nuts; seeds; whole grain cereals
Fiber	Fruits (especially with skin), dried fruits, vegetables, cruciferous vegetables, legumes, whole grains and cereals, oats and oat bran products, brown rice
Flavonoids	Concord grape juice, apples, blueberries, cranberries, olives, oranges, onions, kale, legumes, wine, green and black tea

Folate	Fruits, dark green leafy vegetables, legumes
Genistein	Edamame (green soybeans boiled in their pods) and other soy foods
Hesperidin	Pith and peel of oranges
Monounsaturated fats	Avocados, olives, olive oil, canola oil, nuts
Oleic acid	Avocados, olive oil, olives, nuts
Omega-3 fatty acids	Fish such as anchovies, bluefish, herring, mackerel, salmon, sardines, trout, canned white tuna (not light tuna), canned albacore tuna; canola oil; flaxseed oil; flaxseed
Phytoestrogens	Flaxseed, edamame (green soybeans boiled in their pods) and other soy products
Potassium	Fresh fruit, dried fruit, prune juice, vegetables, lean meats, seafood, legumes, milk

What not to eat

Avoid saturated fat, found in red meat, fried foods, and high-fat dairy products such as cheese and sour cream. Limit the amount of oil you consume in a day to between 5 and 8 teaspoons. Limit meat servings to 3 to 4 ounces a day, use less butter, and avoid high-fat snacks.

Food/medication interactions

If taking nicotinic acid to reduce cholesterol levels, take it with food or milk to decrease gastrointestinal distress.

Immunity Problems

Your immune system gives your body the ability to identify and get rid of foreign invaders. To maintain your immune health or pump it up when it wavers, eat a variety of vegetables, fruits, seafood, whole grains, seeds, and nuts.

What to eat

Your body needs...	Some sources include...
Vitamin A and beta-carotene	Deep orange fruits, tropical fruits, deep orange winter squash, carrots and carrot juice, broccoli, dark green leafy vegetables, fish-liver oil, liver, fortified reduced-fat and fat-free milk, butter, eggs
Antioxidants	Fruits and juices, including citrus and tropical fruits and juices; vegetables, especially cruciferous vegetables, dark green leafy vegetables, and deep orange vegetables; wheat germ; whole grains; nuts; seeds; cooking oils
Vitamin B_6	Bananas, figs, prunes, prune juice, avocado, potatoes, sweet potatoes, cabbage, cauliflower, dark green leafy vegetables, acorn squash, beans, chickpeas, meats, poultry, kidney, pork, fish, eggs, walnuts, wheat bran, whole and enriched grains, fortified cereals
Vitamin C	Cantaloupe, strawberries, citrus fruits, citrus fruit juices, cranberry juice, tropical fruits, vegetables, dark green leafy vegetables, cruciferous vegetables
Vitamin E	Dark green leafy vegetables; vegetable oils such as cotton seed, peanut, sunflower, and safflower; wheat germ; nuts; seeds; whole grain cereals
Omega-3 fatty acids	Fish such as anchovies, bluefish, herring, mackerel, salmon, sardines, trout, canned white tuna (not light tuna), canned albacore tuna; canola oil; flaxseed oil; flaxseed
Zinc	Lean meats, liver, seafood, poultry, lentils, whole grains, wheat germ, buckwheat, Brazil nuts

What not to eat

Reduce the amount of total fat you eat and be sure that you're eating healthy fats instead, such as omega-3's.

Indigestion

When you have indigestion—caused by uneasy, disagreeable, or incomplete digestion—you may experience heartburn, abdominal pain, intestinal gas, belching, nausea, and even vomiting.

What to eat

Your body needs...	Some sources include...
Bromelain	Fresh pineapple, fresh pineapple juice
Gingerols	Ginger tea

Herbs to use

Cayenne stimulates gastric secretions. Added to food, cayenne relieves indigestion. Fennel contains volatile oils, including one called anethole, that helps stimulate appetite and digestion.

Infections

Infections occur when microorganisms invade and multiply in the body. Infections can occur topically, as in wounds, and internally, as in sinus or blood infections.

What to eat

Your body needs...	Some sources include...
Allicin	Garlic, onions
Beta-carotene	Deep orange fruits; tropical fruits; deep orange winter squash; carrots and carrot juice; broccoli; dark green leafy vegetables
Vitamin C	Cantaloupe, strawberries, citrus fruits, citrus fruit juices, cranberry juice, tropical fruits, vegetables, dark green leafy vegetables, cruciferous vegetables
Vitamin E	Dark green leafy vegetables; vegetable oils such as cotton seed, peanut, sunflower, and safflower; wheat germ; nuts; seeds; whole grain cereals

(continued)

What to eat (cont.)

Your body needs ...	Some sources include ...
Flavonoids	Concord grape juice, apples, blueberries, cranberries, olives, oranges, onions, kale, legumes, wine, green and black tea
Protein	Lean meats, poultry, fish, legumes, whole grains
Quercetin	Cranberries, onions, kale, buckwheat
Riboflavin	Dark green leafy vegetables, lean meats, fish, chicken, whole grain breads, milk and milk products
Sulfur compounds	Onions, garlic, chives, shallots, leeks
Zinc	Lean meats, liver, seafood, poultry, lentils, whole grains, wheat germ, buckwheat, Brazil nuts

Food/medication interactions

The antifungal medication griseofulvin is absorbed better if you take it with meals.

Herbs to use

Fennel contains volatile oils, including one called anethole, which helps combat infection.

Insomnia

Often a temporary condition, insomnia is the inability to fall asleep. Some of the more common causes include anxiety, depression, jet lag, and misuse of barbiturates.

What to eat

Your body needs ...	Some sources include ...
Carbohydrates	All fruits, vegetables, dark green leafy vegetables, legumes, buckwheat, whole grain foods, brown rice, bran
Copper	Legumes, lentils, nuts, meat, seafood, whole grain foods

Iron	Dried fruit, vegetables, dark green leafy vegetables, lean red meats, poultry, seafood, legumes, eggs, fortified ready-to-eat cereals, cream of wheat
Magnesium	Root vegetables, dark green leafy vegetables, seafood, legumes, whole grains, wheat germ, brown rice, ready-to-eat cereals, nuts, seeds
Melatonin	Bananas, sweet corn, rice, ginger, barley, oats
Niacin	Lean meats, fish, canned white tuna, legumes, nuts, fortified white rice, enriched grains, whole grain breads
Tryptophan	Turkey, milk, cheese

What not to eat

Avoid caffeine and alcohol and eating a lot of food just before bedtime.

When to eat

Have a small bowl of oatmeal, a small banana, or a glass of milk before bed, but don't eat too much.

Irritable Bowel Syndrome (IBS)

With IBS, your digestive tract rumbles and rolls out gas. You may experience frequent diarrhea, diarrhea alternating with constipation, or just constipation. There's usually abdominal pain as well as flatulence and bloating. For relief, eat more foods high in soluble fiber if you have diarrhea with your IBS, and more foods with insoluble fiber if your symptoms include constipation.

What to eat

Your body needs . . .	Some sources include . . .
Insoluble fiber	Vegetables, including well-cooked asparagus, beets, carrots, mushrooms, potatoes, spinach, sweet potatoes, winter squash, and zucchini; legumes; bran cereals; natural bran

(continued)

What to eat (cont.)

Your body needs . . .	Some sources include . . .
Soluble fiber	Ripe fruit, including baked apples, applesauce, soft bananas, grapefruit, grapefruit juice, kiwifruit, peaches, and pears; oatmeal; rice

What not to eat

Reduce your intake of fatty and fried foods, such as hamburgers, french fries, cheese, and butter. Get 30 percent or even less of your total calories from fat. Avoid caffeine, alcohol, tobacco, and refined sugars. Cut back on dairy foods to see if your symptoms improve.

When to eat

Eat smaller, more frequent meals. The more food you put into your body at one time, the harder the intestines have to work, and that can cause problems for people with IBS. Having several small meals is usually easier for the body to handle than having two or three big meals.

Herbs to use

Peppermint can help soothe symptoms of IBS. Try a cup of hot peppermint tea.

Kidney Stones

Kidney stones are little crystals of salt and minerals that form in the kidneys and can be extremely painful when they finally pass. The stones that respond best to dietary changes are calcium and uric acid stones. Alkaline foods increase the level of a mineral called citrate in the urine, which helps block the formation of stones. To raise your levels of citrate, you need to get more fruits and vegetables into your diet. Many of the foods that are high in citrates, like citrus fruits and vegetables, are also good sources of potassium. A large study found that women with a high intake of dietary calcium, mostly from dairy products, actually decreased their risk of developing stones. Calcium in supplement form, however, was associated with increased incidence of stones. If you're prone to stones, aim for two to three servings of dietary calcium.

What to eat

Your body needs . . .	Some sources include . . .
Calcium	Low-fat or fat-free dairy products, broccoli, dark green leafy vegetables, sardines and salmon with bones, calcium-fortified foods
Fiber	Fruits (especially with skin), dried fruits, vegetables, cruciferous vegetables, legumes, whole grains and cereals, oats and oat bran products, brown rice
Fluids	Water; fruit juices, especially cranberry juice
Magnesium	Root vegetables, dark green leafy vegetables, seafood, legumes, whole grains, wheat germ, brown rice, ready-to-eat cereals, nuts, seeds
Potassium	Fresh fruit, dried fruit, prune juice, vegetables, lean meats, seafood, legumes, milk

What not to eat

Cut back on meat consumption and replace it with plenty of fruits and vegetables. Avoid foods high in oxalates, such as black tea, chocolate, okra, beets, almonds, peanuts, pecans, Swiss chard, raw spinach, raspberries, blueberries, citrus peel, strawberries, and rhubarb.

Food/medication interactions

Diuretics (used to treat kidney disease, congestive heart failure, and high blood pressure) can speed up the excretion of potassium, magnesium, and zinc, so be sure to eat foods high in these nutrients.

Leg Cramps

Leg cramps are painful spasmodic contractions of the leg muscles. They often occur at night or after exercise and may be caused by low blood sugar levels, depleted electrolytes such as magnesium and calcium, or dehydration.

What to eat

Your body needs . . .	Some sources include . . .
Calcium	Low-fat or fat-free dairy products, broccoli, dark green leafy vegetables, sardines and salmon with bones, calcium-fortified foods
Carbohydrates	All fruits, vegetables, dark green leafy vegetables, legumes, buckwheat, whole grain foods, brown rice, bran
Fluids	Water, fruit juices
Magnesium	Root vegetables, dark green leafy vegetables, seafood, legumes, whole grains, wheat germ, brown rice, ready-to-eat cereals, nuts, seeds
Potassium	Fresh fruit, dried fruit, prune juice, vegetables, lean meats, seafood, legumes, milk

What not to eat

Avoid eating foods that are high in sodium, such as canned vegetables and broth and processed foods.

Lupus

Lupus is considered an immune disease. The name *lupus* is short for lupus erythematosus and is a form of arthritis. There is no known cure, but there's increasing evidence that what you eat can give you an edge in battling it. Cutting back on fat intake may help boost your immune system. People with lupus tend to get more heart disease than the general population, so cutting back on fat also will decrease your risk of heart disease. Adding more vegetables to your diet will leave less room for fat-laden foods.

What to eat

Your body needs . . .	Some sources include . . .
Alpha-linolenic acid	Flaxseed oil
Lignans	Flaxseed, flaxseed oil, rye or whole grain crackers such as Wasa or Finn Crisps

What not to eat

Avoid fat, particularly saturated fat from meat and high-fat dairy products. Alfalfa sprouts may make lupus worse. Keep a record of what you eat when the disease is active to see which foods may cause problems.

Macular Degeneration

This eye disease results when the macular area of the eye deteriorates. People with macular degeneration can't see through the center area of the eye. It's age-related and is the leading cause of incurable blindness in people over age 65.

What to eat

Your body needs . . .	Some sources include . . .
Beta-carotene	Deep orange fruits, tropical fruits, deep orange winter squash, carrots and carrot juice, broccoli, dark green leafy vegetables
Vitamin C	Cantaloupe, strawberries, citrus fruits, citrus fruit juices, cranberry juice, tropical fruits, vegetables, dark green leafy vegetables, cruciferous vegetables
Folate	Fruits, dark green leafy vegetables, legumes
Lutein	Dark green leafy vegetables, broccoli, corn, green peas, parsley

(continued)

What to eat (cont.)

Your body needs . . .	Some sources include . . .
Omega-3 fatty acids	Fish such as anchovies, bluefish, herring, mackerel, salmon, sardines, trout, canned white tuna (not light tuna), canned albacore tuna; canola oil; flaxseed oil; flaxseed
Zeaxanthin	Parsley
Zinc	Lean meats, liver, seafood, poultry, lentils, whole grains, wheat germ, buckwheat, Brazil nuts

When to eat
Eat fish twice a week, more if possible.

Herbs to use
Parsley contains lutein, which helps with macular degeneration.

Memory Problems

Sometimes memory problems can be caused by marginal nutritional deficiencies, lack of fluids, or the body's inability to absorb nutrients as one ages. Not all memory problems are caused by diet, so be sure to consult with your doctor for severe memory problems.

What to eat

Your body needs . . .	Some sources include . . .
Anthocyanins	Blackberries, blueberries, strawberries, cherries, grapes
Vitamin B$_6$	Bananas, figs, prunes, prune juice, avocado, potatoes, sweet potatoes, cabbage, cauliflower, dark green leafy vegetables, acorn squash, beans, chickpeas, meats, poultry, kidney, pork, fish, eggs, walnuts, wheat bran, whole and enriched grains, fortified cereals

Vitamin B$_{12}$	Any animal product, such as lean meats, liver, poultry, seafood, low-fat dairy products, eggs
Boron	Pears, raisins, peanut butter, peanuts, parsley
Vitamin C	Cantaloupe, strawberries, citrus fruits, citrus fruit juices, cranberry juice, tropical fruits, vegetables, dark green leafy vegetables, cruciferous vegetables
Vitamin D	Fatty fish, such as herring, salmon, and sardines; fish-liver oil; egg yolks; vitamin D–fortified milk and cereals
Vitamin E	Dark green leafy vegetables; vegetable oils such as cotton seed, peanut, sunflower, and safflower; wheat germ; nuts; seeds; whole grain cereals
Folate	Fruits, dark green leafy vegetables, legumes
Vitamin K	Broccoli, Brussels sprouts, dark green leafy vegetables, liver, legumes, eggs
Niacin	Lean meats, fish, canned white tuna, legumes, nuts, fortified white rice, enriched grains, whole grain breads
Pantothenic acid	Avocados, broccoli, mushrooms, legumes, meats, whole grain cereals
Thiamin	Corn, lean pork, organ meats, legumes, seeds, unrefined cereals, enriched grains and cereals, rice, wheat germ, fresh pasta

What not to eat

Decrease fat and cholesterol consumption and limit alcohol.

Menopausal Problems/Hot Flashes

A woman approaching menopause produces less estrogen. This causes hot flashes, irritability, and mood swings. When estrogen dips, total cholesterol levels rise, and HDL cholesterol (the "good" kind) levels fall, increasing the risk of heart disease. Lower estrogen levels also decrease calcium levels in a woman's bones, increasing her risk for osteoporosis. To help counter the effects of less estrogen on your bones and your heart, it's important to eat more calcium-rich foods and less saturated fat.

What to eat

Your body needs...	Some sources include...
Calcium	Low-fat or fat-free dairy products, broccoli, dark green leafy vegetables, sardines and salmon with bones, calcium-fortified foods
Phytoestrogens	Flaxseed
Riboflavin	Dark green leafy vegetables, lean meats, fish, chicken, whole grain breads, milk and milk products

What not to eat

Reduce your intake of saturated fat.

Herbs to use

Sage tea can help reduce or sometimes eliminate night sweats. Herbalists believe that cinnamon may help regulate the menstrual cycle and lessen excessive bleeding during menopause.

Nausea

Nausea can be caused by eating too much or eating very rich foods. Nausea may also be caused by motion sickness, which is the result of movement during travel, whether by car, train, boat, airplane, or an amusement park ride. It may be caused by sensory receptors in your body getting mixed messages. If nausea is caused by motion sickness, these suggestions may help ease your discomfort, too.

What to eat

Your body needs . . .	Some sources include . . .
Carbohydrates	Bread, crackers
Fluids	Water, ginger tea
Ginger	Ginger tea

What not to eat

High-fat foods weaken the muscle between your esophagus and your stomach temporarily, and digestive juices may back out of your stomach up into your esophagus and cause burning (heartburn) and nausea. Don't eat too much food or too much fat, which can trip a sensor in your brain that triggers nausea. Consume peppermint (*Mentha piperita*), which aids digestion, unlike spearmint (*Mentha spicata*).

Herbs to use

For nausea and vomiting, make a tea with 1 teaspoon grated fresh ginger and 1 cup boiling water. Steep for 10 to 15 minutes. Adding ginger and cayenne to food can help relieve nausea. Peppermint tea may help as a stomach tonic and aid digestion.

Night Blindness

If your vision is worse at night, you probably have what's called night blindness. With night blindness, you have difficulty seeing after flashes of bright light at night or when you're in a dimly lit area. It's an early symptom of vitamin A deficiency.

What to eat

Your body needs . . .	Some sources include . . .
Vitamin A and beta-carotene	Deep orange fruits, tropical fruits, deep orange winter squash, carrots and carrot juice, broccoli, dark green leafy vegetables, fish-liver oil, liver, fortified reduced-fat and fat-free milk, butter, eggs

Osteoarthritis

Osteoarthritis is caused by wear and tear on cartilage, the shock-absorbing material between the joints. When cartilage wears away, bone grates against bone, causing pain and stiffness in the fingers, knees, feet, hips, and back. High intake of vitamin C may help reduce knee pain and disease progression. In those people who get 120 milligrams or more a day, osteoarthritis does not seem to worsen as much as in those who get less vitamin C.

What to eat

Your body needs . . .	Some sources include . . .
Beta-carotene	Deep orange fruits, tropical fruits, deep orange winter squash, carrots and carrot juice, broccoli, dark green leafy vegetables
Vitamin C	Cantaloupe, strawberries, citrus fruits, citrus fruit juices, cranberry juice, tropical fruits, vegetables, dark green leafy vegetables, cruciferous vegetables

Osteoporosis

As people age, their bones become porous and fragile due to a loss of minerals, such as calcium. Known as osteoporosis, this condition can be prevented and treated by getting enough calcium, engaging in weight-bearing activities, and cutting back on or stopping cigarette use. Vitamin D increases calcium absorption, so plan meals to include foods rich in both.

What to eat

Your body needs . . .	Some sources include . . .
Vitamin A and beta-carotene	Deep orange fruits, tropical fruits, deep orange winter squash, carrots and carrot juice, broccoli, dark green leafy vegetables, fish-liver oil, liver, fortified reduced-fat and fat-free milk, butter, eggs
Calcium	Low-fat or fat-free dairy products, broccoli, dark green leafy vegetables, sardines and salmon with bones, calcium-fortified foods

Vitamin D	Fatty fish, such as herring, salmon, and sardines; fish-liver oil; egg yolks; vitamin D–fortified milk and cereals
Vitamin K	Broccoli, Brussels sprouts, dark green leafy vegetables, liver, legumes, eggs
Manganese	Pineapple, sweet potatoes, spinach, chick-peas, whole grains, brown rice, nuts, seeds
Phytoestrogens	Flaxseed, edamame (green soybeans boiled in their pods) and other soy products
Zinc	Lean meats, liver, seafood, poultry, lentils, whole grains, wheat germ, buckwheat, Brazil nuts

What not to eat

Limit alcohol intake to one drink a day or less. Avoid using too much salt, as it may block calcium absorption.

When to eat

Wait 1 to 3 hours after meals before taking calcium carbonate supplements as an antacid; take them with meals as a supplement.

Food/medication interactions

Calcium and vitamin D can be hustled out of the body too quickly by the use of laxatives, such as mineral oil. Tetracycline and calcium bind to each other, so don't take this medication with milk, milk products, or antacids that contain calcium. The calcium will limit your body's absorption of the drug.

Overweight

If you expend less energy than you take in, the result over time will be weight gain. Choose high-satisfaction foods, such as potatoes and whole grains, so that you feel full longer (carbohydrates have a lower energy density; they weigh more than high-fat foods but contain fewer calories). One of the best things you can do is figure out what situations make you eat more than you want to, such as periods of boredom, stress, or worry, and find ways to handle these times without reaching for food. Another tip: Don't eat food in front of the TV.

What to eat

Your body needs . . .	Some sources include . . .
Calcium	Low-fat or fat-free dairy products, broccoli, dark green leafy vegetables, sardines and salmon with bones, calcium-fortified foods
Carbohydrates (unrefined)	All fruits, vegetables, dark green leafy vegetables, legumes, buckwheat, whole grain foods, brown rice, bran
Fiber	Fruits (especially with skin), dried fruits, vegetables, cruciferous vegetables, legumes, whole grains and cereals, oats and oat bran products, brown rice
Fluids	Water, fruit juices
Monounsaturated fats	Avocados, olives, olive oil, canola oil, nuts
Omega-3 fatty acids	Fish such as anchovies, bluefish, herring, mackerel, salmon, sardines, trout, canned white tuna (not light tuna), canned albacore tuna; canola oil; flaxseed oil; flaxseed
Pantothenic acid	Avocados, broccoli, mushrooms, legumes, meats, whole grain cereals
Pectin	Apples, citrus fruits, gooseberries

What not to eat

Avoid fried foods, deep-fried foods, and low-nutrient snacks like potato chips, cookies, candy, and cakes. Instead, reach for nutrient-dense fruits and vegetables.

PMS

Premenstrual syndrome (PMS) affects between one-third and one-half of all American women of childbearing age. Discomfort usually begins 10 to 14 days before menstruation. There are swings in hormones (estrogen and progesterone), blood sugar, and serotonin. In a small study conducted at the Massachusetts Institute of Technology in Cambridge, women with PMS reported that eating a carbohydrate-rich meal lightened their premenstrual depression and tension.

What to eat

Your body needs ...	Some sources include ...
Vitamin B$_6$	Bananas, figs, prunes, prune juice, avocado, potatoes, sweet potatoes, cabbage, cauliflower, dark green leafy vegetables, acorn squash, beans, chickpeas, meats, poultry, kidney, pork, fish, eggs, walnuts, wheat bran, whole and enriched grains, fortified cereals
Calcium	Low-fat or fat-free dairy products, broccoli, dark green leafy vegetables, sardines and salmon with bones, calcium-fortified foods
Carbohydrates	All fruits, vegetables, dark green leafy vegetables, legumes, buckwheat, whole grain foods, brown rice, bran
Vitamin D	Fatty fish, such as herring, salmon, and sardines; fish-liver oil; egg yolks; vitamin D–fortified milk and cereals
Magnesium	Root vegetables, dark green leafy vegetables, seafood, legumes, whole grains, wheat germ, brown rice, ready-to-eat cereals, nuts, seeds
Omega-3 fatty acids	Fish such as anchovies, bluefish, herring, mackerel, salmon, sardines, trout, canned white tuna (not light tuna), canned albacore tuna; canola oil; flaxseed oil; flaxseed
Riboflavin	Dark green leafy vegetables, lean meats, fish, chicken, whole grain breads, milk and milk products

What not to eat

Avoid sugary foods such as candy, cookies, and cake. Stay away from saturated fat, which is found in meats, high-fat dairy foods, and many processed foods. Use olive oil in place of butter, corn oil, and safflower oil. Reduce salt intake, as it can cause bloating and breast tenderness, and avoid caffeine.

Herbs to use

Herbalists claim that cinnamon helps regulate the menstrual cycle. Parsley may be able to help prevent premenstrual bloating.

Prostate Problems

In males, urine moves from the bladder to outside the body via the urethra. The prostate gland encircles the urethra just below the bladder, so when there's trouble with the prostate, urination can be a problem. If you have problems with urination, be sure to see your doctor. All males over age 50 should be tested regularly for prostate cancer.

What to eat

Your body needs . . .	Some sources include . . .
Lycopene	Tomatoes and tomato products, guavas
Phytochemicals	Broccoli, Brussels sprouts, cabbage, cauliflower, soybeans
Phytoestrogens	Flaxseed, edamame (green soybeans boiled in their pods) and other soy products

Psoriasis

With psoriasis, the body makes far too many skin cells, causing the skin to become thick and scaly. It can affect the scalp, elbows, knees, stomach, groin area, or the entire body.

What to eat

Your body needs . . .	Some sources include . . .
Antioxidants	Fruits and juices, including citrus and tropical fruits and juices; vegetables, especially cruciferous vegetables, dark green leafy vegetables, and deep orange vegetables; wheat germ; whole grains; nuts; seeds; cooking oils
Omega-3 fatty acids	Fish such as anchovies, bluefish, herring, mackerel, salmon, sardines, trout, canned white tuna (not light tuna), canned albacore tuna; canola oil; flaxseed oil; flaxseed

Rheumatoid Arthritis

Rheumatoid arthritis occurs when the immune system, instead of protecting the body, begins attacking it. These attacks cause swelling of the membrane that lines the joints, eventually eating away at the joints' cartilage. It is one of the forms of arthritis most affected by diet for some people. Some experts have observed that populations such as the rural Chinese that eat lots of unprocessed fruits, vegetables, and grains don't get a lot of rheumatoid arthritis. In a study of people in Norway with rheumatoid arthritis, those who ate no meat, poultry, or fish had less joint swelling and stronger grips than those who continued with their typical diets. The experimental group also avoided gluten, refined sugar, salt, alcohol, and caffeine.

What to eat

Your body needs . . .	Some sources include . . .
Diet low in fat, especially low in saturated fat, and high in fiber	Vegetables, fruits, whole grains
Vitamin E	Dark green leafy vegetables; vegetable oils such as cotton seed, peanut, sunflower, and safflower; wheat germ; nuts; seeds; whole grain cereals
Omega-3 fatty acids	Fish such as anchovies, bluefish, herring, mackerel, salmon, sardines, trout, canned white tuna (not light tuna), canned albacore tuna; canola oil; flaxseed oil; flaxseed

What not to eat

Avoid meats and other foods high in saturated fat. (Limit fat intake to no more than 25 percent of total calories in a day; limit saturated fat intake to no more than 7 percent.) Avoid processed foods. Some people are sensitive to wheat, gluten, dairy foods, corn, citrus fruits, tomatoes, and eggs—these foods can switch on the body's inflammatory response. Also avoid refined sugar, salt, alcohol, and caffeine.

Food/medication interactions

Methotrexate is used to treat rheumatoid arthritis. It competes with folic acid for specific binding sites within the body because it has a similar structure to folic acid. Doctors may prescribe folic acid supplements to compensate. If you're taking methotrexate, it's also a good idea to try to get plenty of folic acid in your diet.

Stress/Fatigue

Stress and fatigue produce feelings of heightened discomfort and lessened efficiency, often caused by excessive exertion. Fatigue may be caused by dehydration or an iron deficiency. Be sure to drink plenty of water daily and include high-iron foods in your diet.

What to eat

Your body needs . . .	Some sources include . . .
Vitamin B$_6$	Bananas, figs, prunes, prune juice, avocado, potatoes, sweet potatoes, cabbage, cauliflower, dark green leafy vegetables, acorn squash, beans, chickpeas, meats, poultry, kidney, pork, fish, eggs, walnuts, wheat bran, whole and enriched grains, fortified cereals
Biotin	Soybeans, liver, fish, egg yolks, whole grains
Vitamin C	Cantaloupe, strawberries, citrus fruits, citrus fruit juices, cranberry juice, tropical fruits, vegetables, dark green leafy vegetables, cruciferous vegetables
Carbohydrates	All fruits, vegetables, dark green leafy vegetables, legumes, buckwheat, whole grain foods, brown rice, bran
Fluids	Water, fruit juices, herbal tea
Iron	Dried fruit, vegetables, dark green leafy vegetables, lean red meats, poultry, seafood, legumes, eggs, fortified ready-to-eat cereals, cream of wheat

Niacin	Lean meats, fish, canned white tuna, legumes, nuts, fortified white rice, enriched grains, whole grain breads
Pantothenic acid	Avocados, broccoli, mushrooms, legumes, meats, whole grain cereals
Potassium	Fresh fruit, dried fruit, prune juice, vegetables, lean meats, seafood, legumes, milk
Riboflavin	Dark green leafy vegetables, lean meats, fish, chicken, whole grain breads, milk and milk products
Thiamin	Corn, lean pork, organ meats, legumes, seeds, unrefined cereals, enriched grains and cereals, rice, wheat germ, fresh pasta

What not to eat

Avoid caffeine and sugar.

When to eat

Eat every 3 to 4 hours. It's generally better to eat several small meals a day instead of two or three large meals to help keep blood sugar levels stable.

Food/medication interactions

Grapefruit and its juice can increase the effectiveness of triazolam (Halcion), an anti-anxiety drug. One dose may seem like five when taken with grapefruit juice, so avoid grapefruit.

Herbs to use

Cinnamon contains an oily chemical called cinnamaldehyde, which has a calming effect that can lessen anxiety and stress.

Stroke

When brain tissue is deprived of blood—for example, when a blood vessel in the brain is blocked—a stroke results.

What to eat

Your body needs...	Some sources include...
Antioxidants	Dark chocolate; cocoa powder; orange juice; tropical fruits, such as guavas, mangoes, papayas; fruits, especially cranberries; vegetables, especially onions, kale, green beans, carrots, broccoli, celery, endive
Vitamin B_6	Bananas, figs, prunes, prune juice, avocado, potatoes, sweet potatoes, cabbage, cauliflower, dark green leafy vegetables, acorn squash, beans, chickpeas, meats, poultry, kidney, pork, fish, eggs, walnuts, wheat bran, whole and enriched grains, fortified cereals
Vitamin B_{12}	Any animal product, such as lean meats, liver, poultry, seafood, low-fat dairy products, eggs
Fiber	Fruits (especially with skin), dried fruits, vegetables, cruciferous vegetables, legumes, whole grains and cereals, oats and oat bran products, brown rice
Flavonoids	Concord grape juice, apples, blueberries, cranberries, olives, oranges, onions, kale, legumes, wine, green and black tea
Folate	Fruits, dark green leafy vegetables, legumes
Omega-3 fatty acids	Fish such as anchovies, bluefish, herring, mackerel, salmon, sardines, trout, canned white tuna (not light tuna), canned albacore tuna; canola oil; flaxseed oil; flaxseed
Potassium	Fresh fruit, dried fruit, prune juice, vegetables, lean meats, seafood, legumes, milk
Quercetin	Cranberries, onions, kale, buckwheat
Resveratrol	Concord grape juice, red wine, peanuts
Rutin	Buckwheat
Sulfur compounds	Onions, garlic, chives, shallots, leeks

What not to eat

Avoid saturated fat, found in red meat, fried foods, butter, and high-fat dairy products such as cheese and sour cream. Limit the amount of oil you consume in a day to between 5 and 8 teaspoons. Limit meat servings to 3 to 4 ounces a day and avoid high-fat snacks.

Food/medication interactions

Diuretics (used to treat congestive heart failure and high blood pressure) can speed up the excretion of calcium, potassium, magnesium, and zinc, so be sure to eat foods high in these nutrients.

Herbs to use

Flavones in thyme may help prevent blood clotting.

Thyroid Problems

The thyroid gland has a direct effect on your weight, energy levels, and your ability to absorb nutrients from food. When the thyroid produces either too much hormone or too little, it can interfere with all these bodily processes. Thyroid disease is almost always treated with medications, but it can take several months for the medication to start working. During this time, people with underactive thyroid (hypothyroidism) may need only half the calories of other adults. They'll also want to limit their consumption of fatty foods and switch to fat-free milk and low-fat or fat-free cheese and yogurt. And they'll want to eat lots of complex carbohydrates, such as vegetables, fruits, whole grain breads, and cereals, until the medication kicks in. People with overactive thyroid (hyperthyroidism) are advised by their doctors to eat foods high in fat and protein until the medication takes full effect. Meat, fish, poultry, whole milk, cheese, butter, nuts, and seeds are good sources of both fat and protein. With the proper medication, thyroid levels will return to normal.

What to eat

Your body needs . . .	Some sources include . . .
Calcium (this is important for people with overactive thyroid, where the calcium is removed from the blood and excreted in the urine)	Low-fat or fat-free dairy products, broccoli, dark green leafy vegetables, sardines and salmon with bones, calcium-fortified foods
Fiber (helps relieve constipation often caused by an underactive thyroid)	Fruits (especially with skin), dried fruits, vegetables, cruciferous vegetables, legumes, whole grains and cereals, oats and oat bran products, brown rice
Goitrogens (may help naturally slow down overactive thyroid)	Cabbage (raw or in juice form), raw broccoli, Brussels sprouts, spinach, cauliflower, kale, mustard greens, turnips, soybeans, peanuts, millet

What not to eat

If you've just started taking thyroid medication, your physician may suggest that you stay away from iodine-rich foods such as shellfish, spinach, and kelp. Once the medication has fully taken effect, however, you can resume your normal diet.

Ulcers

Most stomach ulcers are caused by the bacteria *Helicobacter pylori* and are treated with antibiotics. When you have an ulcer, a sore forms in the lining of your stomach or duodenum, where acid eats away at the lining. Overall, it's important to eat a healthful diet.

What to eat

Your body needs . . .	Some sources include . . .
Fiber	Fruits (especially with skin), dried fruits, vegetables, cruciferous vegetables, legumes, whole grains and cereals, oats and oat bran products, brown rice

Glutamine	Cabbage
Lactobacillus bulgaricus and *L. acidophilus*	Yogurt with live active cultures
Mucus producers	Plantains, bananas

What not to eat

Avoid milk. While initially milk may have a neutralizing effect on the acid, after 30 minutes or so, there may be a "rebound effect," in which the calcium and protein from the milk actually stimulate acid production. Although caffeine in coffee doesn't cause ulcers, it can make you more susceptible to getting them. Along with cigarettes and alcohol, caffeine also can make existing ulcers worse.

Upset Stomach

Upset stomach can have many causes, including the flu or other viruses, so if it occurs frequently or persists, check with your doctor. Initially, the best thing to do for an upset stomach is to eat nothing for 4 to 6 hours until the feeling passes.

What to eat

Your body needs . . .	*Some sources include . . .*
Bland foods	Plain toast, broth, bland soup, plain pasta, plain bread, ginger tea, cola, water, ice cubes

Urinary Tract Infections (*UTIs*)

UTIs occur when bacteria are in the bladder or urethra. Common signs and symptoms include pain and a burning sensation when urinating, urinating frequently, voiding just a few drops at a time, or passing blood in the urine.

What to eat

Your body needs . . .	Some sources include . . .
Apiol	Parsley
Fluids	Water, fruit juices
Myristicin	Parsley
Tannins	Cranberry juice, blueberry juice, tea

What not to eat

If you have a UTI and you find that certain foods make it more painful to urinate, avoid those foods until the infection clears up. Some foods that might have this effect are citrus fruits, tomatoes, cheese, spicy foods, and coffee.

Herbs to use

Parsley tea is an excellent diuretic.

Wrinkles

As we age and expose our skin to the sun, the layers of our skin get thinner and less resilient. The collagen and elastin fibers in our skin break down, causing wrinkles.

What to eat

Your body needs . . .	Some sources include . . .
Antioxidants	Fruits and juices, including citrus and tropical fruits and juices; vegetables, especially cruciferous vegetables, dark green leafy vegetables, and deep orange vegetables; wheat germ; whole grains; nuts; seeds; cooking oils
Fluid	Water

What not to eat

Avoid high-sugar foods, including soda, baked goods, sweet desserts, ice cream, and frozen yogurt.

Yeast Infections

These bothersome infections are usually caused by the fungus *Candida albicans*, which normally lives in the vagina, mouth, and intestines. But when that ecosystem's balance is thrown off, itching, burning, odor, and unpleasant discharge from the vagina can result. Medication is often needed, but some foods may help limit the infections.

What to eat

Your body needs ...	Some sources include ...
Allicin	Garlic, onions
Beta-carotene	Deep orange fruits, tropical fruits, deep orange winter squash, carrots and carrot juice, broccoli, dark green leafy vegetables
Vitamin C	Cantaloupe, strawberries, citrus fruits, citrus fruit juices, cranberry juice, tropical fruits, vegetables, dark green leafy vegetables, cruciferous vegetables
Vitamin E	Dark green leafy vegetables; vegetable oils such as cotton seed, peanut, sunflower, and safflower; wheat germ; nuts; seeds; whole grain cereals
L. acidophilus	Yogurt with live active cultures

What not to eat

Reduce or eliminate sugary foods. Yeast likes sweets just as much as we do. Research shows that women who eat a lot of honey, sugar, or molasses get more yeast infections than women who eat less of these foods.

cure finder

B

BREAST CANCER

C

CANCER

CATARACTS

COLDS AND FLU

CONSTIPATION

DEPRESSION

DIVERTICULOSIS

H

HEADACHES

HEARTBURN

HEART DISEASE

P

R

S

STRESS/FATIGUE

U

ULCERS

URINARY TRACT INFECTIONS (UTI)

W

WRINKLES

Y

YEAST INFECTIONS

index

Underscored page references indicate boxed text.
Boldface references indicate photographs.

Conversion Chart

These equivalents have been slightly rounded to make measuring easier.

Volume Measurements

U.S.	Imperial	Metric
¼ tsp	–	1 ml
½ tsp	–	2 ml
1 tsp	–	5 ml
1 Tbsp	–	15 ml
2 Tbsp (1 oz)	1 fl oz	30 ml
¼ cup (2 oz)	2 fl oz	60 ml
⅓ cup (3 oz)	3 fl oz	80 ml
½ cup (4 oz)	4 fl oz	120 ml
⅔ cup (5 oz)	5 fl oz	160 ml
¾ cup (6 oz)	6 fl oz	180 ml
1 cup (8 oz)	8 fl oz	240 ml

Weight Measurements

U.S.	Metric
1 oz	30 g
2 oz	60 g
4 oz (¼ lb)	115 g
5 oz (⅓ lb)	145 g
6 oz	170 g
7 oz	200 g
8 oz (½ lb)	230 g
10 oz	285 g
12 oz (¾ lb)	340 g
14 oz	400 g
16 oz (1 lb)	455 g
2.2 lb	1 kg

Length Measurements

U.S.	Metric
¼"	0.6 cm
½"	1.25 cm
1"	2.5 cm
2"	5 cm
4"	11 cm
6"	15 cm
8"	20 cm
10"	25 cm
12" (1')	30 cm

Pan Sizes

U.S.	Metric
8" cake pan	20 × 4 cm sandwich or cake tin
9" cake pan	23 × 3.5 cm sandwich or cake tin
11" × 7" baking pan	28 × 18 cm baking tin
13" × 9" baking pan	32.5 × 23 cm baking tin
15" × 10" baking pan	38 × 25.5 cm baking tin (Swiss roll tin)
1½ qt baking dish	1.5 liter baking dish
2 qt baking dish	2 liter baking dish
2 qt rectangular baking dish	30 × 19 cm baking dish
9" pie plate	22 × 4 or 23 × 4 cm pie plate
7" or 8" springform pan	18 or 20 cm springform or loose-bottom cake tin
9" × 5" loaf pan	23 × 13 cm or 2 lb narrow loaf tin or pâté tin

Temperatures

Fahrenheit	Centigrade	Gas
140°	60°	–
160°	70°	–
180°	80°	–
225°	105°	¼
250°	120°	½
275°	135°	1
300°	150°	2
325°	160°	3
350°	180°	4
375°	190°	5
400°	200°	6
425°	220°	7
450°	230°	8
475°	245°	9
500°	260°	–